OAKWOOD LIBRARY OF RAILWAY HIST

The South Yorkshire Joint Railway and the Coalfield

by

B.J. Elliott Ph. D.

THE OAKWOOD PRESS

First edition published as *The South Yorkshire Joint Railway* in 1971
Second edition published in 2002

British Library Cataloguing in Publication Data
A Record for this book is available from the British Library
ISBN 0 85361 595 0

Typeset by Oakwood Graphics.
Repro by Ford Graphics, Ringwood, Hants.
Printed by Cambrian Printers Ltd, Aberystwyth, Ceredigion.

SYJR bridgeplate No. 38, from the overbridge at Stainton Woodhouse Farm.
Chris Booth

Front cover: Brush type '2' (class '31') No. 5654 still carries its BR green livery as it works a train of empty coal wagons over the SYJR line to either Maltby or Harworth on 27th June, 1973. *Geoff Warnes*
Rear cover: Class '56' No. 56095 *Harworth Colliery* propels its train back to the reception lines at Maltby to form a train for Drax power station, 13th March, 1995. *Chris Booth*

Published by The Oakwood Press (Usk), P.O. Box 13, Usk, Mon., NP15 1YS.
E-mail: oakwood-press@dial.pipex.com
Website: www.oakwood-press.dial.pipex.com

Contents

Acknowledgements

I wish to record my gratitude to the following persons who kindly gave of their time, assistance, sources and in some cases recollections to make this book possible.

In the 1971 edition I had occasion to thank:

Mr E.H. Fowkes, Chief Archivist and his staff at the British Transport Historical Records.
The staff at the Doncaster Divisional HQ of British Rail.
Mr F. Sanderson, Regional PRO of the NCB, Doncaster.
Mr F.J. Collins, Transport Manager of the East Midlands Motor Co.
The Librarians and Staff at the Public Central Libraries of Doncaster, Rotherham, Sheffield and Worksop.
Former railwaymen, W. Calvert, W. Davison, C. England, A. Fisher, W. Haynes, E. Wakefield and E. Wilkinson.

For the 2002 edition, I wish to thank:

The Right Hon., the Earl of Scarbrough.
The Directors and staffs of the British Library, Boston Spa and St Pancras.
The Keeper of Public Records and the staff of the Public Record Office, Kew.
Mr P. Atkins and staff of the Reading Room, National Railway Museum, York.
The Librarian and staff of the University of Sheffield Library.
The Librarians and staffs of the Public Central Libraries and Local Archives of Doncaster, Harrogate, Rotherham and Sheffield.
Ms Jane Sumpter, Bassetlaw Museum, Retford.
The Director of the Yorkshire Air Museum.
The Curator of Cusworth Hall Museum, Doncaster.
Mr John Goodchild of The John Goodchild Collection, Wakefield.
Ms Candice Lo, Reader Services, Guardian Newspapers Limited.
Mr M. Garness, Company Secretary, RJB Mining PLC, Harworth, Doncaster.
Messrs W. Dent, W. Sims and P. Wilkinson of Railtrack (Doncaster and York).
Mr D. Campbell and Mr J. Readshaw of AES-Drax.
The Port Director, ABP, Grimsby and Immingham.
Mr A. Scargill, President of the National Union of Mineworkers, 1981-2002.
Mr P. Wright.
Mr Maurice Clayton, verger of Stainton parish church.

Former and current railwaymen:

Messrs M.G. Atkinson, M. Francis, G. Helmsley, D. Stanyard, P. Stanyard, A. Wyatt and Ray Williams.

I owe a very special debt to Chris Booth for allowing me to use his extensive photographic collection and for his search for further illustrations and relevant anecdotal evidence of the recent history of the SYJR.

I wish also to record my debt to the authors of all the sources cited in the Bibliography for so lightening my task.

Abbreviations and Measurements

To avoid inconsistencies, metrication and post-1971 decimal currency have been used throughout, with some imperial conversions included. By reason of price inflation (but deflation, 1921-1933), pounds of 1913 should be multiplied approximately by 60 to convert to 1999 prices, those of 1930 by 37, those of 1946 by 23 and those of 1970 by 10.

T (t) = ton of 2,240 lb. or tonne of 1,000 kg/2,205 lb.; billion = 1,000 million

AGR	Advanced gas-cooled reactor
ASLEF	Associated Society of Locomotive Engineers and Firemen
BC	British Coal
CCGT	Combined Cycle Gas Turbine
CEGB	Central Electricity Generating Board
DAC	Doncaster Amalgamated Collieries
DVR	Dearne Valley Railway Co.
ECML	East Coast main line
EWS	English, Welsh & Scottish Railways Co.
GCR	Great Central Railway
GER	Great Eastern Railway
GNR	Great Northern Railway
H&BR	Hull & Barnsley Railway
L&YR	Lancashire & Yorkshire Railway
LD&ECR	Lancashire, Derbyshire & East Coast Railway
LMS	London, Midland & Scottish Railway
LNER	London & North Eastern Railway
MFGB	Miners' Federation of Great Britain
MR	Midland Railway
NACODS	National Association of Colliery Overmen, Deputies and Shotfirers
NBR	North British Railway
NCB	National Coal Board
NER	North Eastern Railway
NUM	National Union of Mineworkers
NUR	National Union of Railwaymen (later RMT)
OPEC	Organisation of Petroleum Exporting Countries
PSU	Police Support Unit
RDC	Rural District Council
REC	Railway Executive Committee
RM&LR	Rotherham, Maltby & Laughton Railway
RMT	Rail, Maritime and Transport Union
ROF	Royal Ordnance Factory
SYCOA	South Yorkshire Coal Owners Association
SYJR	South Yorkshire Joint Railway
TGWU	Transport and General Workers Union
TUC	Trades Union Congress
UDC	Urban District Council
UDM	Union of Democratic Mineworkers
YAC	Yorkshire Amalgamated Collieries
YMA	Yorkshire Miners' Association

bn t	billion tons (tonnes)	m t	million tons (tonnes)
ha	hectare (10,000 square metres)	MW	megawatt (one million watts)
Jn	junction	oms	output per man shift
Jt	Joint	opmy	output per man year
k t	1,000 tons (tonnes)	pa	per annum
Km	1,000 metres or 0.62 miles.	pc	per cent
lph	litres per hour	pcm	per calendar month
m	metre or million, as appropriate	pd	per day
m-g-r	merry-go-round (train)	ph	per hour

Preface

My interest in the South Yorkshire Joint Railway (henceforth, the SYJR) and the coalfield it serves, stems from a childhood spent in Doncaster and Rotherham, frequently walking and cycling close to the line and through the villages it served. Later I learnt the original name of the line and some of its ancestry, that it opened as late as 1909, had withdrawn its regular passenger service as early as 1929, several years before I was born, and that it was (is) still a very important mineral line. All this stimulated my interest and led me to write the first history up to 1970. This revised edition brings the story to 2001.

By reason of its unusual constitution, the SYJR kept very detailed operating and financial records, separate from those of its five (later two) parent companies, but regrettably only from 1903-1939. These however enabled the early management committees to keep accurate records of the large profits (coal traffic) and small losses (passenger traffic) of the single branch line, which unlike others (at least until 1940) were not totally submerged within the accounts of a parent company.

Thus it is possible to record in detail the unsuccessful struggle to operate a profitable passenger service, leading to its eventual and early withdrawal. This experience clearly indicates that unprofitable passenger services existed even in the so-called 'golden age' before 1914.

Nevertheless, the losses incurred by the passenger service were far outweighed by the profits of the coal trains, which were the *raison d'etre* of this line. Since the end of the last great coal dispute in 1984-1985, this industry has contracted very considerably, not least in South Yorkshire, the very heart of that struggle.

Of the eight collieries with access to the SYJR in the 1930s, only Maltby, Harworth and Rossington remained open in 2001, but the last has almost ceased to use the line. Nevertheless the prosperity of the SYJR, if not its very survival, is still closely bound up with the first two 'survivors'. By reason of this mutual inter-dependence, both the rail and coal industries have been given virtually equal study and analysis here.

A period postcard, wishing 'Greetings from Dinnington'. *John Goodchild Collection*

Chapter One

The South Yorkshire Coalfield before 1914

Early mining

'The leading peculiarity of South Yorkshire' wrote the Rev. A. Gatty in *South Yorkshire in General*, published in Rotherham in 1876, 'is undoubtedly the richness of its coal bed . . .what unmeasured coal may exist in the lower sweep of the strata can scarcely be calculated. The expense and difficulty of working these . . . will not be encountered as long as the present accessible supply lasts'.

Although at the time Gatty was writing, it would be almost 100 years before a legal political entity of South Yorkshire came into existence, the term has been used since 1876, to describe, using various geographical limits, that area of the larger geological coalfield where the seams became deeper and thicker and it is to this area, including the northern tip of Nottinghamshire, that the title alludes.

The accessible supply in South Yorkshire in 1876 was found at a depth of about 200 m and had been providing for the needs of the area for about 700 years. The first period of expansion came between 1550 and 1650 as supplies of timber fuel became exhausted. By the latter date there were at least 11 coal pits in the Sheffield-Rotherham area and a further five around Barnsley. Each produced between 500 and 2,000 tons/tonnes per annum (henceforth, t pa). In addition there were innumerable open-cast workings, with almost all this production being used locally, much of it in the metallurgical industries.

The Industrial Revolution

Between 1760 and 1914, there took place the second, much greater and more prolonged period of expansion in the South Yorkshire district. The continued evolution of new techniques in mining made this possible. The demands of an industrialising nation and later of export markets encouraged this production. Landowners, dazzled by the prospects of large royalties, were eager to have mines sunk on their properties. The building first of canals and then railways provided the necessary facilities to move out this growing production.

Thus by 1855 there were some 81 coal mines in South Yorkshire concentrated around Barnsley, producing an average of 35,000 t pa, a grand total of 2.8 million tons (henceforth, m t). The even larger West Yorkshire coalfield with 255 mines, but averaging only 19,500 t pa each produced more than 5 m t in total. The whole Yorkshire average output was 23,226 t per colliery. The workforce of about 24,000 men was shared equally between South and West.

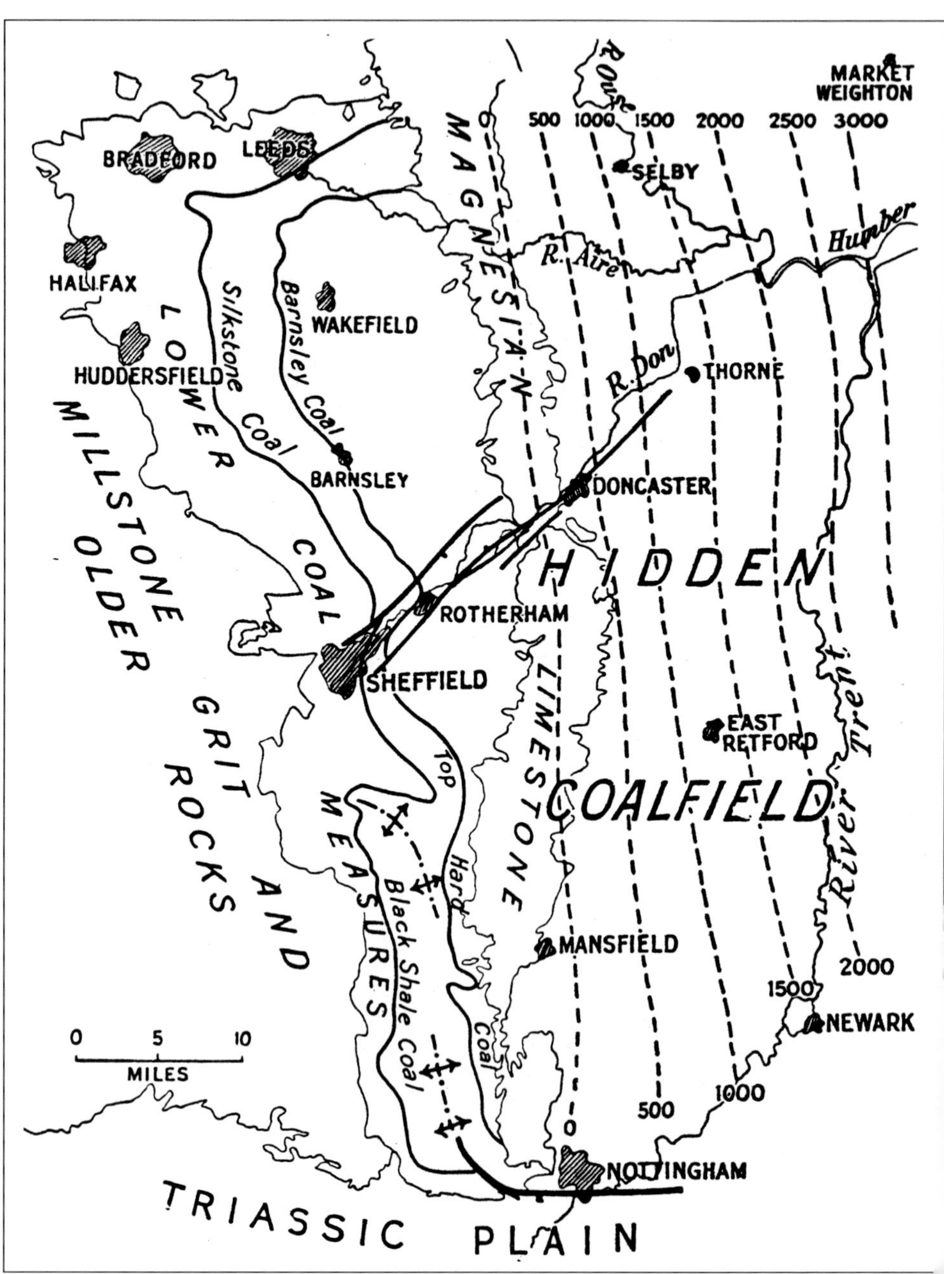

Map of the East Midlands coalfield, 1963. *Stamp & Beaver*

The East Midlands coalfield

The Yorkshire coalfield was thus sub-divided into South and West regions a little to the north of an approximate line Penistone-Barnsley-Doncaster; but the whole is geologically part of the large North Midlands (or East Pennine) coalfield stretching from Nottingham to Leeds and covering an area of 8,000 sq. km. Later it was normally referred to (and henceforth will be, to include all Yorkshire also) as the East Midlands coalfield.

In the west the boundary could be defined easily because the coal was found at the surface. The most westerly seams found along a line from Sheffield to Huddersfield were of *pot clay* (ganister) used primarily in steel-making processes. Some 10 km east of this was the limit of the Silkstone seam and a further 5 km came the much prized Barnsley seam. The last, known in West Yorkshire as Warren House and as Top Hard in Nottinghamshire, was the most valuable and sought-after coal in the East Midlands field. It was suitable for both coking and steam-raising and was found in seams 2-3 m thick. In 1889 a borehole sunk at Haxey, 20 km east of Doncaster and the southern terminal of the Axholme Joint railway, proved the Barnsley seam at a depth of 1,000 m.

The existence of great reserves in the concealed coalfield had been established well before the 1889 Haxey borehole. In 1861 the geologist E. Hull, in *Coalfields of Great Britain*, had estimated the known reserves of the North Midlands field at 8.8 billion tons (henceforth, bn t) and the probable reserves at 12 bn t. In 1870 Walter Rowley MICE, FGS told a Doncaster audience that in their neighbourhood 'are represented all the seams belonging to the Yorkshire coalfield numbering 40, with an aggregate thickness of 90 ft (27 m), of which 30 ft (9 m) will be workable sooner or later'. He expressed his astonishment that the upper seams were not already being worked, since 'Doncaster is unequalled in its geographical position by any colliery district in the Kingdom'. He concluded that he thought it possible that 'enterprising capitalists can be found to develop such vast resources'.

Until the late 19th century almost all coalmining in South Yorkshire took place in this so-called exposed coalfield. This consisted of the 20 or so seams which reached the surface between Penistone and Conisborough, 8 km south-west of Doncaster. Beyond Conisborough lay the concealed coalfield, whose seams dipped gently eastwards at an average gradient of 1 in 18, diminishing in number and thickness as they reached into Lincolnshire, and more free from severe faults than any other field. The eastern boundary could be detected only by boreholes and geophysical prospecting, but as early as 1905 it was known that some seams reached the North Sea. The area of the concealed coalfield was approximately twice that of the exposed field, with the Barnsley bed estimated to cover an area of 1,500 sq. km.

Shireoaks colliery. *Bassetlaw Museum, Retford*

Deep mining

By 1870 the increasing demand for coal began to exhaust the westerly exposed seams, as production increased to 4.4 m t from the 108 mines in South Yorkshire, although West Yorkshire with 308 mines (6.25 m t) still remained larger. New collieries began to be sunk in the concealed areas until by 1914 there were almost 400 in Yorkshire, producing virtually every known category of coal.

In the Don Valley, the most important sinkings were at Denaby Main (1864) and Manvers Main (1870) and, to the south of Rotherham at Treeton (1875). One development in 1859 was the successful sinking and the discovery of the Barnsley seam at 50 m at Shireoaks, near Worksop. This was close to the main line of the Manchester, Sheffield and Lincolnshire Railway Company (MS&LR), later the Great Central Railway (GCR). From 1910 -1920, Shireoaks was also the southern passenger terminal of the SYJR.

The main technical and financial effort in the last quarter of the century was being concentrated further north, between Barnsley and Doncaster. In 1878 the Barnsley seam was reached at a depth of 600 m at South Kirby. In 1894 it was found at Hickleton at 500 m and three years later at Grimethorpe. In 1892, the start of production at 720 m at Cadeby colliery in the Don valley marked the first major exploitation of the concealed coalfield close to Doncaster.

Technical problems

The failure to develop these vast resources until the end of the 19th century can be traced to two major difficulties, technical or geological, and financial. As the seams dipped eastwards, they also contained some 'faults'. This meant that the seams were broken and continued at higher or lower levels. If a colliery was planned near a fault it could lose production or even be abandoned eventually.

As the seams sank deeper, especially between 600-1,000 m, severe problems are caused for miners by the rise in temperature to at least 26°C (80°F) and often much more. This meant very efficient ventilation is needed, which had to be upgraded as galleries lengthened. Explosive firedamp gas is present, especially prevalent around Doncaster. Pressure upon the roofs of underground galleries increases squeezing the workings inward, with coal 'bursting off' the face being one particularly unpleasant danger at great depths.

Even before deep coal could be reached, the engineers sinking the shaft had to penetrate through heavily water-bearing Permian rocks. Water caused serious delays and required and technical innovations and large capital investments, and only the certainty of assured and profitable markets could attract such outlays.

However by the late 19th century world demand for coal was rising by 4 pc pa and whilst Britain was still the world's largest producer and exporter in 1890, it was overtaken in output by the USA by 1900.

10.77 billion tons

In 1901 such was the importance of coal to the economy that the Government appointed a Royal Commission on Coal Supplies, to inquire into 'the extent and available resources of the United Kingdom'. Reporting four years later, the Commission verified the existence of the huge concealed coalfield of the East Midlands, stretching eastwards into Lincolnshire, but at a depth there (1,200 m at the River Trent), beyond the prospect of profitable working.

The proven portion of the greater East Midlands field, by one calculation in 1901, was 26.5 bn t. Of this, the 'South Yorkshire' coalfield had 10.77 bn t, divided amongst five categories of coal : House, 22.75 pc ; Gas, 21.8 pc; Steam 6.5 pc; Manufacturing 31.2 pc ; Coking 17.7 pc. The principal seams were Barnsley, for steam and coking; Parkgate - for gas and steam, Swallow Wood and Haigh Moor - for steam, gas and domestic and Silkstone - for coking and domestic.

At that time, these reserves were considered sufficient for 400 years' consumption. By 1913 reserves to a depth of 1,200 m in the East Midlands were recalculated by the International Geological Congress at 40 bn t, out of a UK total of 135 bn t. There was also within the East Midlands, the possibility of a further 14.8 bn t and, at between 1,200 to 1,800 m, almost 1 bn more, but only 50 pc of this being considered workable.

Yorkshire's collieries alone were already producing more than 28 m t pa in 1900 or 12.5 pc of the UK total. Furthermore after a long period of deflation, prices of all raw materials began to rise from 1898, helped along by the demands of the war (1899-1902) in South Africa. Yorkshire coal in 1900 sold at 50p (10*s.*) per ton (£33 in 1999 prices), although the price fell temporarily by one-third in 1905. The financial incentive to develop the South Yorkshire coalfield therefore existed, as overall profits quadrupled between 1896 and 1904. The second prerequisite, the technical skills to overcome the problems of deep-mining were being developed in the Ruhr in western Germany. The successful operation, 720 m below Cadeby colliery in 1892 was the example to follow, but certainly not that of the 88 men and boys killed there in two terrible explosions in 1912.

Dalton Main Collieries' locomotive in 1909.

Archives and Local Studies, Rotherham Central Library

Bullcroft colliery sinkers, 1912. *Museum of South Yorkshire Life*

East of the Don

In the very first months of the 20th century there began the first sinking of a deep colliery east of the River Don, in the so-called 'Maltby trough'. The site at Silverwood, 5 km north-east of Rotherham, was owned by Dalton Main Collieries, a subsidiary of the famous ship-building and armour-plate manufacturing firm, John Brown & Co. Sinking operations, employing 300 men, lasted more than three years. The main problem occurred beyond 165 m when huge quantities of water were encountered. At the peak some 318,000 litres per hour (henceforth lph) were being pumped out. Once this problem had been solved, progress was relatively smooth, with the Barnsley bed being reached at 720 m in December 1903. The seam was nearly 2 m thick, of which half was excellent quality steam coal. The problems of a deep sinking in a 'trough', clearly contrasted with the more favourable position at the neighbouring Roundwood colliery where the Barnsley seam was found at only 55 m.

Silverwood, like many other collieries in South Yorkshire was eventually equipped with French-designed Simon-Carves coke ovens, 36 initially but later increased to 80, to provide metallurgical fuel. A Baum coal-washer was installed also capable of handling 130 t ph. By 1909, with an all-male workforce of almost 2,600 underground and 635 above, Silverwood had become the largest colliery in Yorkshire. The daily production target of 5,000 t was achieved in 1911, which was equal to several years' output from a 17th century mine and in eight working days it could therefore equal the annual output (40,000 t) of the average South Yorkshire mine in 1875.

North-west of Doncaster

Sinking operations had begun also in the so-called 'Frickley Trough', north-west of Doncaster. The Carlton Main and Grimethorpe colliery group had reached the Barnsley seam at 630 m at Frickley in May 1905, after three years' sinking operations and predicted output of 2,500 t pd. Six km east of Frickley, the Staveley Iron and Coal Co. and the Hickleton Main Colliery Co. had jointly invested almost a third of a million pounds in Brodsworth Main colliery. Beginning work late in 1905, the sinkers expected to go down to 850 m, with the possibility of producing Yorkshire's deepest mine, because of a known fault in the seams of the area. Fortunately, this proved unnecessary when in October 1907 a 3 m seam was reached at 570 m. Forecasts were made of production of between 5,000 and 6,000 t pd, but the latter was not achieved until February 1924.

Operations at Barber Walker's Bentley site, where trial borings had shown evidence of quicksand, and at Bullcroft Main, a few km north of Doncaster did not proceed as smoothly. The former lay alongside the Great Northern Railway's (GNR) East Coast main line, (henceforth, the ECML), which ran from London through Doncaster/Shaftholme Jn where it was linked with the North Eastern Railway (NER) and, which in turn beyond Berwick joined the North British Railway (NBR) to Edinburgh and beyond. Quicksand at Bentley 30 m deep was indeed reached at 15 m, when work on the main shaft began in 1905, but was overcome by the use of wooden piles, fixing tubbing over these and lining the shaft with bricks. In April 1908, the Barnsley seam 3 m thick was reached at 600 m and a further 20 m down, the bonus of a workable seam of Dunsil coal.

At Bullcroft Main where sinking began in June 1908, the problem of water reoccurred when 60,000 lph was encountered after 30 m. This was tubbed back, but at 60 m a virtual underground river was encountered. Powerful centrifugal pumps were installed, drawing off 1.5 million lph at one stage: the shaft began to collapse under the strain and pumping was abandoned. The sinkers then called in the Shaft Freezing Co. led by a German engineer, Emil Dietz. He drilled 26 holes around the shaft to depth of 30 m and into these inserted freezing tubes. An ammonia cooling plant was installed, but this took four months to freeze the area around the shaft. Further complications arose and eventually it was January 1911, more than two years after the start of operations, before the sinkers could pass beyond the frozen belt.

North-east of Doncaster

In ascending order of distance, were three colliery developments north-east of Doncaster. Markham Main at Armthorpe was delayed until after World War I, although the site was to be connected by a temporary line to the new SYJR in 1917. Further from Doncaster were Hatfield Main, and finally Thorne, where borings in 1905-1908 had proved coal at 841 m. Shaft sinking at both sites was started in 1912, with Barnsley coal at the former being reached in May 1916, but water at Thorne proved an ongoing problem and only 143 men were employed there in 1920.

Railways in the coalfield

It was quite clear from the early experiences of sinking new collieries in the concealed coalfield along the Don Valley and north and west of Doncaster that profits were not going to be gained cheaply or easily, at least in the early stages. These districts did however have one advantage, good rail and canal transport links. Silverwood had a private connection to the GCR and Midland Railway (MR) lines between Doncaster and Sheffield. Frickley lay in a triangle bounded by the MR, Hull and Barnsley Railway (H&BR) and GNR lines, but with no access to the last. Brodsworth had connections to the GNR and the South Yorkshire Junction line which connected the GCR at Denaby to the H&BR. Bentley lay alongside the ECML, whilst Bullcroft also stood north-east of Doncaster next to the GNR's, Wakefield to Hatfield line.

A new coalfield

Bounded by the ECML, the GCR's Retford to Sheffield line and the MR's main line through Rotherham, there lay, south of Doncaster, a large triangle of pleasant undulating agricultural land. Within this area, neither railway nor mining engineers had penetrated by 1900, except on exploratory surveys. As early as 1871, the old MS&LR had published plans for a direct line from Doncaster to Worksop. Yet between 1900 and 1914 six major collieries were sunk within this triangle and preliminary borings carried out at two others.

The first of these noted above was at Silverwood. Within a year of Silverwood's success the Barnsley seam was reached at Dinnington, then a small village of 250 persons, 5 km north-west of Shireoaks. The mineral rights at Dinnington, under some 4,000 ha owned by the 10th Duke of Leeds and the 10th Earl of Scarbrough (1857-1943), the latter at that time also holding the office of Lord-Lieutenant of the West Riding of Yorkshire. Their lands had been bought in 1900 by the Sheepbridge Iron and Coal Co. and the Sheffield Coal Co. Sinking at the Dinnington Main colliery site, under the direction of W.H. Dyson (who later became the first colliery manager) began at the No. 1 shaft in September 1902 and at the No. 2 shaft in six months later, with a total of 350 men being employed.

Despite tapping large quantities of water, around 200,000 lph, and having to go to 650 m, or 100 m deeper than expected, operations went smoothly without any loss of life or even a serious accident. The Barnsley bed of 1.3 m below No. 1 shaft was reached in 23 months, believed to be a world record time for such a depth, in August 1904. The No. 2 shaft improved even on this in January 1905, at only 22 months. Each shaft was 5.8 m in diameter and bricked throughout with the exception of 65 m of cast-iron tubbing on each to hold back water.

Around the workings there grew up the usual motley collection of metal huts known locally and typically as 'Tin Town', housing 60 families, but this was mostly demolished in 1911. The permanent housing provided was in traditional terraces rather than in a 'model village' as was built later in nearby Edlington, Maltby and Rossington. Nevertheless Dinnington was an immediate success, producing 250,000 t in 1909, and contributing to Yorkshire's total that year of almost 36 m t, (13.6 pc of UK output), valued at £13.6 m. A Simon-Carves coke oven plant of 80 ovens was erected there, supplying coke for the pig-iron industry. By 1913, Dinnington reached an output 750,000 tons, variously of coking gas, house and steam coal. That year also saw the all-time record for the saleable output of the British coal-mining industry of 287 m t, of which 98 m t went for export and shipping use. However, 1913 does *not* hold the all-time record for the UK consumption of coal.

The Sheepbridge company with 57 per cent of the shares had a controlling interest in another new colliery at Maltby, 6 km north-east of Dinnington. This was situated on 4,000 ha of land leased in 1902 for a 60 year period, from the Sandbeck Park estate of the Earl of Scarbrough. The first rental of almost £2,850 paid in 1907 was equal to £170,000 in 1999 prices. Sinking in Maltby wood, close to the ruins of Roche Abbey, a 13th century Cistercian foundation, began in June 1908, also under the direction of W.H. Dyson. Progress downwards at a cost of £4 per m, was brisk, but also cost nine lives, including three men who fell down the shaft in 1909 and three killed in 1911 by an explosion.

The Barnsley seam was reached at 740 m in June 1910. and the No. 2 shaft arrived seven months later. The results were excellent. Maltby produced not only coke (120 ovens), gas and house coal, but reputedly had the best steam coal

The 10th Earl of Scarbrough (*centre*) with guests at Sandbeck *c*.1912. The presence of the car helps explain why first class passengers began to desert the railways. *Earl of Scarbrough*

Harworth colliery locomotive, 1914. *Worksop Library*

south of Doncaster. With a 2.5 m workable seam, Maltby's fast rising annual output reached 250,000 tons in 1912 and it was still in production in 2001.

The Sheepbridge Co. had begun to develop two other sites in this area. First in co-operation with John Brown and Co., it formed the Rossington Main Colliery Co. in 1911 with a share capital of £500,000 to exploit the Barnsley bed in an area of 3,500 ha south-east of Doncaster close to the ECML, to which it was connected in 1913. Sinking operations began in June 1912 and, despite wartime labour shortages, the Barnsley seam, more than 2.2 m thick was reached at 795 m in May 1915. The first coal shipments started in March 1917 and three years later 1,128 miners were employed there. Rossington was still in production in 2001. By 1914 the Derbyshire-based Sheepbridge Co. had decided to join the South Yorkshire Coal Owners Association (SYCOA), whose membership tended to define the limits of the South Yorkshire coalfield.

Yorkshire Main and Thurcroft

South-west of Doncaster, close to the road to Sheffield and connected to the new Dearne Valley Railway (DVR), the Staveley Co. sank Yorkshire's deepest shaft at Edlington's Yorkshire Main colliery. After encountering huge problems with water, the sinkers reached the Barnsley bed at 825 m in July 1911. Despite the presence also of firedamp, the production of gas, coking, house and steam coals quickly developed towards 4,000 t pd and by 1920 Yorkshire Main was employing 2,694 workers.

Between 1909-1912, another new 750 m shaft was sunk at Thurcroft, just north of Dinnington, unfortunately sited right over an east-west fault with a 140 m 'throw-down', which combined with the outbreak of war to delay operations. Full production commenced only after 1918, but, by reason that the Barnsley seam was around 1.65 m in height enabling miners to extract coal whilst standing, production continued despite further problems with gas and floods. Owned by Rothervale Collieries, a subsidiary of United Steel, Thurcroft was employing 1,462 workers by 1920.

The Yorkshire coalfield 1913

During the early years of the 20th century very large amounts of capital and labour were being employed in the Yorkshire coal industry, especially in the southern area. By 1913 the county had almost 400 collieries, of which 214 were in the West, with an average workforce of 265 miners at each extracting 66,349 t. In the South 184 operations with an average of 524 miners each or 96,500 in total, produced 27.7 m t in 1913. Almost 80 pc of all miners worked underground.

By 1913 the new deep collieries of the Doncaster area had helped to raise Yorkshire's output to 43.7 m t or 15 pc of the UK figure, exceeded only by South Wales at 56.8 m t. Moreover, such was the importance of the British industry in 1913, that the whole East Midlands coalfield (including Yorkshire) produced 74.1 m t or 5.6 pc of the world's total. The UK produced 25 pc of the latter and supplied 55 pc of all coal traded internationally.

Nottinghamshire

At the Sheepbridge Co.'s other site, at Firbeck in Nottinghamshire, 7 km north of Worksop, sinking operations were also delayed for several years by wartime restrictions. This was principally the lack of labour to build a (future SYJR) branch line to the site. Also just over the Nottinghamshire border at Harworth, almost halfway between Rossington and Firbeck, the exploration lease was held by a German combine headed by Hugo Stinnes. A line connecting the site to the ECML at Scrooby was authorised in August 1912 and a temporary line laid for the sinkers, using a German locomotive. Inevitably, with the outbreak of war, all work at Harworth ceased in August 1914.

Wages of death

By reason of falling coal prices, despite general inflation after 1898, average earnings of all mineworkers were falling. They fell from £1.69 (£1 13*s.* 9½*d.*) per week during the Anglo-Boer war (1900) to £1.45 (£1 9*s.*) per week in 1909. By 1914, they were back to £1.70 (£1 14*s.*). This last figure represented 34p (6*s.* 9½*d.*) per daily shift in Yorkshire, the equivalent of £20 in 1999 prices and the highest rate amongst UK coalfields. More seriously, from 1900 onwards more than a thousand UK miners (and more than 1,750 in 1913) were killed annually in accidents, the majority by 'falls of ground' and explosions, but some in colliery yards also. Thousands more were injured.

The prize

By 1914, the Sheepbridge Co. alone had invested almost £38 m (in 1999 prices) in Dinnington, Maltby and Rossington collieries, but surprisingly the UK coal industry remained technologically backward, with only 8 pc (2.8 m tons) being cut mechanically. However, as coal prices generally continued to rise from 1905 until 1920, excluding 1908-1909, the owners could expect even larger profits. Through 1909-1913 for the whole UK industry, these profits averaged a total of almost £13 m pa *net* (equal to more than £775 m in 1999 prices).

These huge coal shipments were also attracting the six railway companies (GCR, GNR, MR, NER, L&YR and H&BR), whose lines all ran past the new coalfields south and east of Doncaster in 1900, but did not then provide the necessary rail facilities for the deep collieries being sunk.

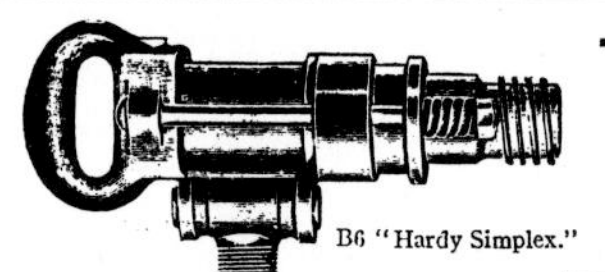

The "HARDY SIMPLEX"
HAMMER DRILL
is the Fastest and Best Drill on the Market.
Driven by Compressed Air or Steam.
"HARDY" ROCK DRILLS & COAL CUTTERS.
SIMPLEST AND BEST MACHINES FOR MINES AND QUARRIES.

Extract from advertisement of Hardy Patent Pick Co. Ltd of Sheffield. *Colliery Yearbook*

Chapter Two

The Building of the SYJR, 1903-1908

Early plans

By 1902, five major railway companies serving Yorkshire had made plans to penetrate the new coalfield, developing south and east of Doncaster, depositing Bills in Parliament to this effect. The GCR and MR Jt Committee had been the first to see the possibilities. In August 1901 they had taken over the powers of the Shireoaks, Laughton and Maltby Co. with plans to build a line connecting the GCR west of Shireoaks (Brantcliffe East Jn, later Brancliffe) through Maltby, north across the ECML and connecting with the GCR's Doncaster to Humberside main line at Kirk Sandall. The NER and L&YR were planning a joint line from east of Doncaster to Ravenfield and Dinnington. The GNR planned a branch from the ECML at Bawtry westwards to Maltby and possibly extending to Rotherham. Another scheme was for an independent 16 km Rotherham to Maltby line to link the Lancashire, Derbyshire & East Coast Railway (LD&ECR) at Treeton Jn with the proposed NER line at Sandbeck near Maltby.

By 1900 Britain already had considerable over-capacity in its railway system. The building of even two competing new lines in the concealed coalfield would have been uneconomic. Three or four new lines would have been utterly nonsensical. The realisation that a single joint line would be ample for the likely traffic and profitable brought the five rival companies together. Once the GCR and MR agreed with the NER and L&YR about the Dinnington to Kirk Sandall route, both the GNR and independent schemes fell.

Spurred by mutual rivalry and jealousy, the five rail companies settled their differences in 1902 and, by February 1903 the first reading of the South Yorkshire Joint Railway Bill was being held in the House of Commons, with Royal Assent given on 14th August. Only the East London Railway with six parent companies had more owners than the SYJR.

The SYJR was the fourth railway to carry the prefix *South Yorkshire*. The original South Yorkshire Railway, Doncaster and Goole Railway Co. from Sheffield to Swinton was incorporated in 1847, opened in 1849 and renamed the South Yorkshire Railway and River Dun Navigation Co. in 1850. It was extended to Thorne in 1855 and became part of the MS&LR in 1874. In 1890 the South Yorkshire Junction Railway was authorised to connect the Denaby-Cadeby mine complex to the H&BR line at Wrangbrook Junction. Opening in 1894, it ran a passenger service only until 1903 and then continued as a freight line.

The South Yorkshire Joint Line Committee

Control of the SYJR was vested in a committee (henceforth the Committee) consisting of two Directors from each of its five parent companies, each member receiving a fee of £25 pa. Three members (i.e. three companies) constituted a

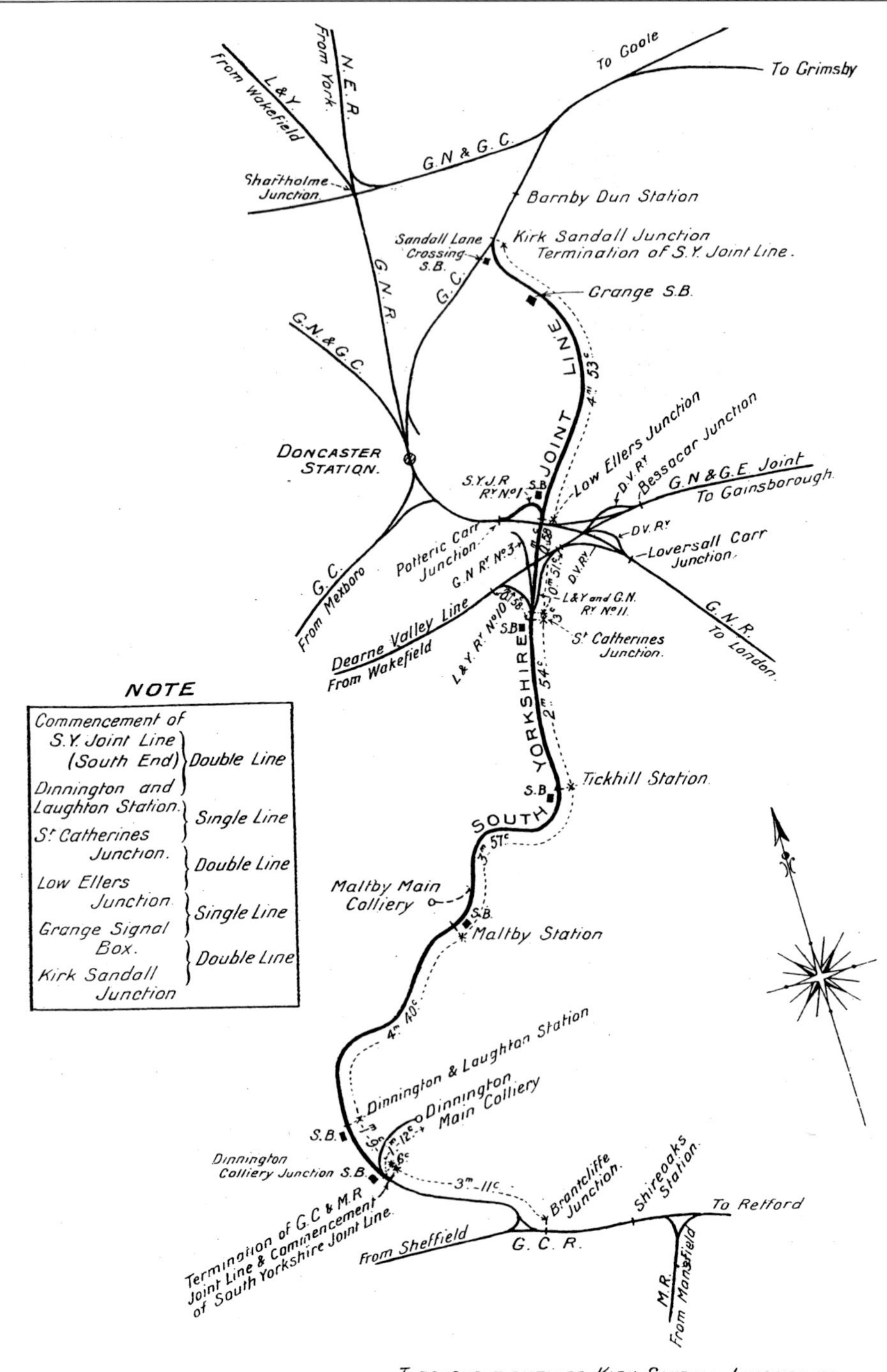

Map of the South Yorkshire Joint Railway and connections in 1908. *Railway Gazette*

quorum with decisions being by majority vote. The first meeting of the Committee was held on 16th February, 1904, chaired by the Rt Hon. Rupert Allerton (GNR) and attended by an impressive list of knights and MPs. W. Marriott of the L&YR was appointed secretary of the Joint Committee, Messrs Butterworths as solicitors for an annual fee of £1,000, Sir Francis Dunnell Bt, KCB as learned counsel and J.D. Wallis as land agent. The committee also appointed Edward Parry of Westminster as consultant engineer on a fee of 3.75 p c of the construction costs, which eventually earned him £11,000 (equal to £660,000 in 1999 prices). By contrast, the Common Seal of the SYJR, designed by Allen Wyon FSA of London, former Chief Engraver of HM's Seals, cost £52.50 (£52 10*s).*

The route and construction

The Act of 1903 gave the Committee powers to construct a railway and other works from an end-on junction with the GCR-MR Jt line at Dinnington.

The latter had been authorised by an Act of July 1902 and built by Mitchell Bros of Glasgow, was opened on 2nd October, 1905. From Dinnington the line was to proceed past Maltby and Tickhill crossing and connecting with the Dearne Valley Railway (DVR) and the ECML to a junction with the GCR's Doncaster-Humberside line at Kirk Sandall, from whence the major ports of Grimsby, Goole, Hull and Immingham - the last built 1906-1912 - could be reached. The new line would be 28 km in length, but only 24.8 km would be required to be built by reason of the already built and operating GCR-MR Jt line at Dinnington, which was vested in the SYJR.

The first major task of the Committee, specifically Edward Parry and his resident engineer Lloyd Roberts, was to find the shortest and cheapest route, which, bearing in mind safety, excluded level crossings and resulted in 43 bridges being built. Parry submitted his estimates to the Committee in November 1904 with the options of single or double track. He believed the total works could be completed, despite some heavy engineering works, at the relatively cheap cost of £12,000 per km or £1.2m per mile in 1999 prices. By avoiding built-up areas, no large compensation payments were necessary.

Engineer's Estimate

Laughton Junction - Kirk Sandall via Black Carr	
(Double tracks)	
Earthworks	
Rock removal 542,571 cu m at 15p (3*s.)*	
Soft soil removal 307,045 cu m at 8.45p (1*s.* 8*d.)*	
Roads 15,155 cu m at 16.25p (3*s.* 3*d.)*	
Total.	£108,933
Embankments 851,522 cu m	38,150
Accommodation bridges and works	20,000
Viaducts	15,000
Tunnels	Nil
Culverts and drains	8,000
Metalling of roads	1,760
House	500
Fencing off track at 3,350 per km	87,412
Sidings	7,500
Stations	20,000
sub-total 1	£307,815

A contractor's locomotive and tipper wagons near Malby during the construction of the SYJR.
Earl of Scarbrough

A steam navvy at work near Maltby. *Earl of Scarbrough*

Allow 10 pc for emergencies	30,781
sub-total 2	£338,596
Purchase of land	23,041
Estimate 1	£361,637
If single track, deduct	50,000
Estimate 2	£311,637

The Committee decided that sufficient land should be purchased to provide for a double track and that bridges and culverts should also be built as for double track. However, by reason of the expense of digging cuttings and raising embankments these should carry single track only. Initially therefore, the SYJR was a single track line, with heavy type 95 lb. (43 kg) rails, on 2.7 m sleepers set 0.8 m apart. Bottom ballast was broken stone 0.2 m deep covered with a top layer of local limestone. There was double track and passing points at the three stations and also on the sections between the northern exit and Grange signal box, between the southern exit and Dinnington station and between St Catherines and Low Ellers where the line crosses the DVR and ECML, but the line never needed to be double-tracked throughout.

In conformity with engineering practice, the contract to build the line was put out to tender. Twenty-four civil engineering firms put in bids and John Scott of Darlington at £221,429.65 (£221,429 13*s.*) was accepted and approved by Edward Parry. To safeguard against bankruptcy, the committee specified that Scott's should deposit sureties - monies which would be forfeit if they failed to complete the job. Scott's refused and the tender therefore passed to Whitaker Bros of Horsforth, Leeds who had bid £238,180.62½ (£238,180 12*s.* 6*d.* or more than £14m in 1999 prices). Four (male) members of the Whitaker family were involved in the planning and construction of the line.

Construction of the SYJR began at Rotherham road, Dinnington in November 1905, a month after the opening of the erstwhile GCR-MR Jt line into Dinnington Main colliery, whose sidings had also been built by Mitchell Bros for £13,778. The first station master at Dinnington's substantial red brick station, was 30-year-old Henry Hall, on a weekly salary of £1.25 (£1 5*s.*), plus a rent allowance of 30p (6*s.*), until his house was built. He was assisted by a junior clerk, W.O. Cranidge, on £30 pa. Staff at Dinnington wore GCR uniforms lettered with the initials SYJR. To cope with the increasing coal traffic a signal box was installed at Dinnington Jn in July 1906 at a cost of £560.

The passenger question

The expansion of Dinnington colliery led to the recruitment of miners from neighbouring towns and villages, for whom the colliery company sought rail transport via the SYJR from Worksop to replace the tarpaulincovered horse-drawn waggons. As early as March 1906 the clerk to Worksop Urban District Council (henceforth UDC) also unsuccessfully requested a regular passenger service from Worksop to Laughton East Jn. The Committee rejected this request and two further ones in 1907. Amongst the 3,000 people who lived in the Anston, Dinnington and Laughton area, the Committee believed that only

Mitchell Brothers' locomotive No. 3 is seen near Lindrick in 1905. *Chris Booth*

Mitchell Brothers' locomotive No. 8 at Anston Stones Wood in 1905. *Chris Booth*

about 20 per day would wish to use such a service, with possibly 200 on Saturdays.

The Committee had to prepare for the eventual running of passenger trains on the SYJR, because, at the insistence of the Earl of Scarbrough, in return for selling 13 ha of his lands to the SYJR both the 1902 NER Act and Section 56 of the GNR Act of 1906 stated that a station at Maltby had to be built, maintained and kept open for passengers and goods at a point where the line crossed the (now A 634) road to Blyth. Thus Dinnington station also was provided with waiting rooms, including one reserved for ladies and a booking office.

The Navvies

Meanwhile progress on the line was continuing, 'like an enormous serpent stretching its sinuous length across one of the earth's most pleasant Edens' commented the *Doncaster Gazette*. The navvies, paid one pound or so per week, worked between 6.00 am and 5.00 pm and lived either in camps or in lodgings in the villages. Few brought any family with them and unlike some of their mid-19th century predecessors appear to have been relatively well-behaved during leisure hours, apart from some drunkenness. This may have been partly a result of visits by the Navvies' Mission to which the Committee made occasional contributions of £50. Another regular visitor was a Doncaster tailor who measured his clients on the spot for new work clothes. Only one fatal accident occurred during construction, when three navvies were killed by a mishap with explosives.

By 1905 pick and shovel work was passing away amongst railway navvies much more quickly than amongst coal miners. On the SYJR, 15 steam 'navvies' or excavators - invented by Whitaker's - were used, each capable of moving from cuttings up to 1,000 tons of rock and soil daily. Behind these, temporary rails were laid, for the use of 400 tip waggons hauled by 14 locomotives, which removed this debris for use on new embankments.

'The cutting we were in was very deep', wrote Fred Kitchen, in his 1940 autobiography, *Brother to the Ox* (Dent), describing his work as a boy labourer on the SYJR, 'More than a mile in length . . . littered with rails, sleepers, spraggs, broken tip-waggons, and spare parts of machinery . . . I stuck to the steam navvy all summer. And a blazing hot summer it was, with stifling heat in the deep cutting, made much more oppressive with the stink of blastings, tubs of waggon fat and lack of conveniences for the workmen . . . getting fourteen shillings (70p or £45 in 1999 prices) pretty regularly each week'.

Brookhouse viaduct

From Dinnington to Black Carr Jn near Doncaster the line descends steadily, and it was on the southern and central parts that the heaviest engineering work was required. From Dinnington the line was driven through a long cutting to Brookhouse. There the land drops steeply into a river valley, over which the line

Steam navvy at work near Lindrick during construction of the SYJR in 1905. *Chris Booth*

Making the cutting at Wadworth, *c.*1908. *NCB*

Brookhouse viaduct, view looking east. *Author*

was led by a 1.25 km embankment onto the Brookhouse viaduct. Built of 1.5 million bricks and 300 tons of steel, the Brookhouse viaduct has five spans of 16 m each and one of 35 m above the road and river, which it crosses at 13 m at an acute angle.

From Brookhouse the line continues via Slade Hooton along another 1.25 km embankment into two cuttings, the first 1.2 km long at a depth of 10 m. The second close to Roche Abbey was driven for 0.8 km to a maximum depth of 18 m through magnesium limestone, which was later reduced to track ballast by crushing machines. This cutting passed under the road from Maltby to Blyth (now A634) and also cut through a local occupation road. Maltby Parish Council insisted that to preserve this ancient right of way and save locals from a 200 m detour, it should have its own bridge. This added £2,500 to the construction bill. To preserve the rural character of the area Lord Scarbrough, through whose Sandbeck Park estate, as noted, the line ran, stipulated that this bridge should always be painted green. Furthermore he insisted that along a 4 km stretch the line should be enclosed by dry stone walls instead of the usual (16 km) post and railwork.

Maltby and Tickhill stations

Beyond the two bridges, the line runs through another limestone cutting into Maltby Wood, where the new colliery was being sunk and where Fred Kitchen got a labourer's job in 1912, at 22.5p (4*s*. 6*d*.) for an 11 hour shift. Beside the road to

Two views of the station at Tickhill under construction. *(Both) Norman Ellis Collection*

Bawtry (now A631), the red-brick Maltby station was also constructed, with, on the west side a booking office, waiting rooms and a porters' room and a general waiting room on the east, the two 140 m platforms connected by a footbridge.

Maltby also had 450 m of double-tracking to provide a recognised passing place. A goods yard to hold 20 wagons was also provided. The contract for both Maltby and the new station at Tickhill was awarded to F.J. Salmon & Co. of Cudworth for a total of £4,378. Of the three stations on the line, Maltby was the most important, carrying a salary of £80 pa and a free house for the station master, a post to which J.C. Hyde was appointed in January 1908.

From Maltby the line winds through S-bend embankments through the tiny village of Stainton and on to the site of the future Firbeck junctions, one km west of Tickhill. From there to Kirk Sandall junction the remaining 14 km followed a route almost due north. Built on a similar pattern to Maltby, the planned location of Tickhill station was changed following local pressure. The new site 2.5 km up the Doncaster road (now A60) was halfway between the Tickhill and Wadworth, after both of which the station was renamed in 1911. Travellers to either place therefore faced a further journey upon leaving the train. The station master at Tickhill received a smaller salary of £65 pa, because it did not serve a colliery and the first holder of the post, also appointed in 1908, was 23-year-old Wilbert Briggs, a L&YR man.

Obstacles

Between Tickhill and Kirk Sandall, the builders faced two further obstacles. The first was the DVR, itself under construction and, more formidably, the ECML. These were overcome simultaneously by the construction of 4 km of embankments with a gentle gradient, using materials from the Tickhill cuttings, leading to a long low viaduct over the two lines. The DVR was crossed by three spans of 10 m each and the ECML by 12 spans of 9 m each and one of 20 m.

The junctions of the SYJR, the DVR, the GNR and the GNR/GER joint line from Lincoln, all converged on Black Carr and therefore necessitated an elaborate system of fly-overs and bridges at this point.

The SYJR gained access at St Catherine's Jn to the DVR to the east (GNR & L&YR Jt) and west (L&YR) through curves completed in May 1909 and to Doncaster over the ECML at Low Ellers Jn, whilst the 'main' mineral branch continued northwards, past Doncaster's future (1930s) airport and under the Great North Road (later A1, now A638). Here it ran immediately east of the famous race-course, which attracted large numbers of visitors, particularly during the St Leger week. As early as October 1904, the Committee considered tapping this traffic by establishing a race-course station. Edward Parry raised this subject again in 1905 and suggested calling the station Cantley after the nearby village. However it was opposed by the GNR, which regarded the suggestion as an insult to its efficiency in dealing with race traffic, although it had no wish either to share the race-goers' revenue with the three other companies (the GCR already did cater for this traffic). The idea was abandoned permanently in April 1907.

The south end of the viaduct which carried the SYJR over the DVR and the East Coast main line.
Author

Letter heading from Whitaker Brothers Ltd, the principal contractor for the building of the SYJR.
Earl of Scarbrough

Patentees & Sole Makers of Whitakers Steam Crane Navvies, & Steam Hammer Pile Drivers.

From Whitaker Brothers, Limited.
Contractors & Engineers,
Horsforth,
Near Leeds.

National Telephone: 23.
Do. Works: 23a.

Telephone 21, Horsforth. Leeds Division. Telegraphic Address, Quarries, Leeds.

Code 5th Edition A.B.C.

One problem which could not be shelved was that the proposed new line would run behind the butts of Doncaster's rifle range. In September 1904, the SYJR agreed to rebuild the butts so that the line of fire would not cross the railway, and in addition to pay £5,000 in compensation. Further north beyond the race-course, the line passes through Sandall Beat wood, across the Doncaster-Thorne road (now A18) and joined the GCR line close to the River Don navigation.

25 million pounds

The cost of construction, mainly by reason of the rising cost of materials exceeded Parry's original estimate. A request by Whitaker Bros for an extra £5,114 for the steel - 2,300 tons were used in all - was rejected in April 1909. By the time the Board of Trade's officer inspected the completed line in September 1908, land purchases totalling 100 ha had, despite the depressed state of agriculture during the previous 30 years, cost more than 230 per cent above Parry's estimate, with some costing as little as £100 but other areas amounted to £800 per ha. The land for Maltby station and goods yard cost £7,700. A grand total expenditure of £55,011 had been made on land.

On 31st December, 1908, the very eve of the official opening of the line, the capital account, into which each company had paid £87,500, stood at £410,871. Thus in 1999 prices, they had invested a total of about £25 million or £833,000 per km.

As was customary the contractors were responsible for track maintenance for one year after the opening date. For the succeeding five years it was agreed that the GCR would undertake this work. Maintenance staff operated from 18 cabins erected along the line at a cost of £13 each. Some weeks before the opening date, the installation of signal boxes, signals and other equipment was completed.

In addition to the Dinnington box already controlling traffic onto and off the colliery siding, additional boxes, all GCR types, were erected at Dinnington, Maltby and Tickhill stations, St Catherine's (known as Potteric Carr until December 1907), Low Ellers, Grange and Kirk Sandall. St Catherine's was the largest having a frame of 50 levers. The GCR was responsible for the boxes at the extremities of the line, Dinnington and Kirk Sandall, whilst the GNR controlled the Black Carr interchange. Elsewhere the Committee had control.

Both the Tyer's No. 6 electric key token and the electric tablet with block telegraph systems were installed by the Railway Signalling Co. of Fazakerly near Liverpool. Key tokens were used on eight single stretches of line between Kirk Sandall and Dinnington (N), Maltby and Tickhill. Otherwise the porters at each station had this responsibility until after World War II.

For a weekly wage of £1.05 (£1 1*s*.) each signalman worked - and moving the levers was hard work - a 12 hr day for six days per week, with no meal breaks, whilst other SYJR employees worked a seven day week with shifts of 10 hours, which included meal breaks. By comparison, (underground) coal miners had secured an eight hour day in 1909, spending about 6 hrs and 40 mins actually working at the face, although their work was much more dangerous.

A Great Central Railway 0-6-0 and its crew at Anston Junction *c.*1914. *Chris Booth Collection*

NOT TO SCALE

Sandall Lane Crossing
GOOLE
DONCASTER
Kirk Sandall Jc.
Grange S.B.
Potteric Carr Jc.
DONCASTER
Low Ellers Jc.
Childers Drain S.B.
Black Carr Jc.
Black Carr Sidings W. S.B.
Black Carr Sidings E. S.B.
Bessecar S.B.
WAKEFIELD
GAINSBOROUGH
St. Catherine's Jc.
Loversall S.B.
SHIREOAKS
RETFORD

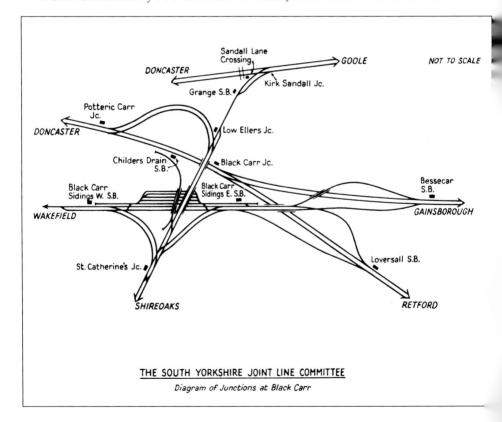

THE SOUTH YORKSHIRE JOINT LINE COMMITTEE

Diagram of Junctions at Black Carr

Chapter Three

The First Years of the SYJR, 1909-1913

First revenues and court battles

When the SYJR opened officially for freight traffic on 1st January, 1909, only Dinnington, amongst the collieries ultimately to be connected to, or able to access the line, was producing coal, its branch line having opened on 20th February, 1905. By reason that the short southern stretches of line around there built by the GCR and MR had been vested in the SYJR by the 1903 Act, including a goods station at Anston, opened in August 1906, revenues had begun to accrue to all five companies as early as 1907. During the last six months of that year, freight trains ran for a total of 2,500 km along the southern-most part of the line, earning £3,958 in gross revenue, of which £501 dividend was paid to each of the five companies. The total revenue had reached £12,838 by the opening day of the full SYJR.

The spirit of co-operation amongst the five soon proved fragile. Following the satisfactory inspection by the Board of Trade in September 1908, the L&YR announced its intention of introducing immediately freight trains from Dinnington northwards and onto the DVR. Simultaneously it informed the GCR that the latter could no longer move coal wagons from Dinnington over L&YR rails between Ancoats Jn (Manchester) and Liverpool, a service begun in February 1907 at a rate of 19p (3*s.* 9½*d.*) p t, because the L&YR could move Dinnington coal there itself. The GCR challenged this decision in the Chancery division of the High Court, but lost the case in November 1908.

A later problem, which had to be arbitrated by the Railways and Canal Commission in 1913, was congestion caused by coal trains leaving the DVR onto the SYJR at St Catherine's and then proceeding through Doncaster *en route* to Grimsby. Presumably, by way of revenge the GCR was refusing to allow the L&YR to use its new (1910) Doncaster avoiding line to by-pass the SYJR.

Freight growth

Coal traffic built up rapidly on the SYJR in 1909-1913, with output at Dinnington almost tripling and Maltby coming onto full, but not maximum, production in 1911-1912. To cope with this extra output a second connecting line and two signal boxes were built for Maltby colliery sidings in June 1911.

Coal Tonnage Moved

	Tickhill	*Maltby*	*Dinnington*	*Total*
1909	3,100	11,995	230,868	245,963
1910	3,251	21,470	348,142	372,863
1911	3,340	29,060	361,422	393,822
1912	2,822	209,038	469,348	681,208
1913	2,721	355,083	648,415	1,006,219

Tickhill figures are for coal received.

Exports and profits

Much of this output went in exports. In 1913, as noted, Britain's collieries produced an all-time record of 287 m t, valued at £145m or £8.7 bn in 1999 prices. South Yorkshire's contribution was 27.7 m t and some 98 m t (34 pc) were exported or used by shipping. To reach these diverse markets in 1913, almost 18.8 m t pcm was carried on UK rails at a total charge of £1.89 m (£113 m in 1999).

Whilst the GNR and MR took the SYJR's southbound coal trade, export, shipping and coastwise traffic along the SYJR went mostly via the Humber ports of Hull (NER), Immingham and Grimsby (GCR) and Goole (L&YR). In 1913 whilst Maltby sent almost 138,000 t through Hull, Dinnington sent 168,000 t, but eventually the latter also exported through 16 other ports.

Total Humber coal shipments more than doubled from 4 m t in 1900 to a record of 8.8 m t in 1913, for which the rail transport cost (pt) was around 12½p (2*s*. 6*d*.), but to which had to be added wagon hire (4p - 9½*d*.) and wharfage and tipping (1p - 2½*d*.). These rail freight charges were fixed several months before the construction of the SYJR and remained unaltered before 1914 despite inflation.

The rapid growth of coal traffic meant that the general profitability of the SYJR increased yearly. Gross receipts, of which 90 per cent came from coal traffic, rose from £13,770 in 1909 to £21,588 in 1911 and £33,840 in 1913, with the last two figures including passenger train receipts. Expenses in 1913, principally in the form of track maintenance and traffic working expenses rose also, slightly exceeding £9,500, of which £2,878 was salaries and wages. From a total of £3,362 in 1907, the net revenue shared by the five companies rose steadily to £16,365 in 1913.

The first brief national strike amongst railwaymen in August 1911 did not affect this upward trend. More seriously, a successful national strike by miners for a minimum wage began on 1st March, 1912 and lasted six weeks. Of the 99,632 members of the Yorkshire Miners Association and part of the Mining Federation of Great Britain (henceforth, YMA and MFGB), 63,700 voted for the strike (85.9 pc of those who actually voted) and 10,477 against.

Capital and revenue

On 31st December, 1913, the SYJR capital account stood at £437,500, of which £395,708 had been spent on construction works, including extra tracks in colliery yards installed after opening day. This brought its total length, expressed as single track, to 55.5 km. A further £5,659 had been spent on non-railway land and more than £36,000 was held in reserve. Thus the net revenue of £16,365 represented a 3.74 pc return in 1913, better than many rail stocks but not exceptional and below the then Bank Rate of 5 pc. This return on capital did not begin to show an improvement until the 1920s when the inflationary effect of World War I sent up both revenue and expenditure, whilst capital investment was not written up, although new construction increased it to more than £710,000 by 1929.

Company operations

By 1913, all five companies were handling traffic on the line. The GCR operated three trains daily, one from Dinnington colliery and two from Maltby entering and leaving the SYJR via Brancliffe Junction. By reason that all companies' trains arriving at a second colliery sometimes halted for up to 30 minutes, it is probable that they took on extra loaded wagons there. The MR also operated three trains through Brancliffe, two from Dinnington and one from Maltby. The three remaining companies used only the northern exits. The NER had four trains leaving through Kirk Sandall Jn, three from Dinnington and one from Maltby, whilst the L&YR had one from each colliery leaving via the DVR at St Catherines. The GNR by contrast had only one train from Dinnington, running onto the ECML. However, it did have the extra responsibility of dealing with all breakdowns on the line (*see timetable page 50*).

A little ironically, by reason of the problems which an excess had posed for the mine-sinkers, the provision of water for these numerous steam-hauled trains was an early problem for the Committee. The suggestion of a well at Sandall Beat wood was rejected by reason that there were no signals to protect halted trains. Initially the L&YR agreed to supply water from its own well at Black Carr. In 1908, a contract was signed with Doncaster corporation to supply 127,000 lpd at a cost of 4p (9½*d.*) per 1,000 litres. A water stack capable of holding 27,000 l was installed at Cantley Bridge close to the Great North Rd. Dinnington colliery was the other major source of water supply for both the SYJR and domestic purposes. Maltby colliery also made supplies available but these proved insufficient. By 1913, water was costing £87.50 (£87 10*s.*) pa (equal to £5,250 in 1999 prices) for the passenger trains alone.

Locomotives

Each of the five railway companies supplied its own locomotives and rolling stock, but also used the wagons of shipping companies and those shipping lines which exported coal. The SYJR owned none of its own. The blue and white wagons of the Wilson line were seen frequently carrying exports from Dinnington to Hull, drawn by the eight-wheeled-coupled (0-8-0) locomotives of the NER. The latter came into service in 1901 and was then much the most powerful locomotive built for the NER. Initially it was hoped it would haul 60 loaded coal wagons and a brake van totalling 985 tons on the steep curved gradients between Stella Gill and Tyne Docks. The 0-8-0 had no difficulty with this load which was steadily increased during 1901 until it reached 81 wagons and the van, a grand total of 1,326 tons. Even though a signal check required the driver to shut off steam on the steepest incline, this journey was completed without wheel slip and at one time a speed of 45 kph was reached. The locomotive weighed 58 t fully loaded and the tender 38.5 t. The cylinders were fitted with piston valves and Stephenson's link motion was used for the valve gear. The boiler 4.65 m (15 ft 3 in.) long and 1.46 m (4 ft 9 in.) in diameter was of steel with copper tube plate. There were 193 steel tubes with an outside diameter of 5 cms (2 in.). Each driving wheel was 1.41 m (4 ft 7¼ in.) in diameter.

An official photograph of Wilson Wordsell's NER class 'T' 0-8-0. No. 2116 was the first example of the class to be built and it remained in service until 1948. These locomotives were reclassified by the LNER as the 'Q5' class.

GNR 'K1' class 0-8-0 No. 446 at Hornsey in North London in 1920. This class was reclassified as 'Q1' by the LNER. *W.J. Reynolds*

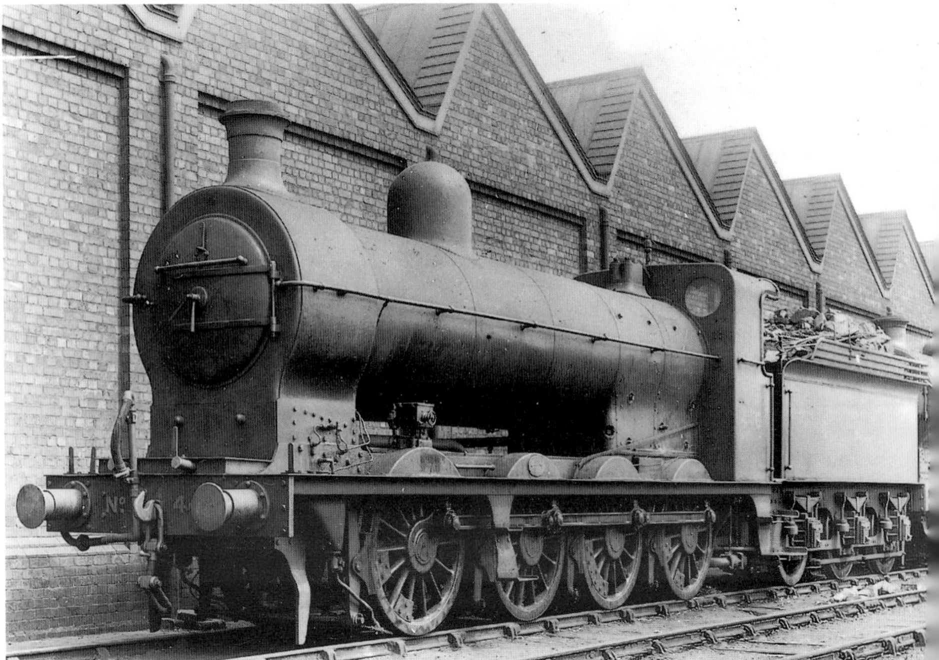

Both the GNR and the L&YR introduced 0-8-0s onto their lines in 1901 in an endeavour to handle more efficiently the growing volume of coal production. The GNR locomotives, designed by H.A. Ivatt and built at the Doncaster works (the Plant) were used on the ECML. Each did a round trip to London on weekdays, reaching a maximum speed of 50 kph and consuming a ton of coal every 45 km. The engine and tender weighed 95 t, carrying 5 t tons of coal and 16,500 litres of water. The working load was 51 wagons of 14 t each, fully laden and a 20 t brake waggon bringing the complete train weight to 843 tons. On the return trip 60 empties could be handled but the limiting factor, in the interests of safety, was the length rather then the weight of the train.

By 1909 the 0-8-0 type had proved itself throughly and was therefore brought onto the SYJR by the three above companies to haul coal trains. The GCR and MR were slower to produce this type, but the efforts of the former proved particularly successful for hauling heavy coal trains in South Yorkshire.

J.G. Robinson, the chief mechanical engineer of the GCR produced initially (1910-1912) some 20 locomotives of the 2-8-0 type, known as the 'Consolidated'.

The 2-8-0 Consolidated was virtually the same as the GCR of 1902, but was fitted with an 'Atlantic' boiler and superheater. The cylinders were 53 cm (21 in.) in diameter by 56 cm (22 in.) stroke having 25 cm (10 in.) inside admission valves between the frames, the steam chests of the two cylinders being carried across the engine and bolted together forming a very rigid front end connection between the frames. By reason of the extra weight at the front end due to the larger boiler barrel, larger cylinders and superheater, it was necessary to provide a leading pony truck to ease some of the load off the leading and intermediate coupled wheels. With the exception of the framing, wheels, axleboxes, hornblocks, spring gear and brake, the working parts were identical with those of the eight-wheeled coupled. The boiler was 4.65 m (15 ft 3 in.) long and 1.5 m (5 ft) in diameter and the firebox 2.55 m (8 ft 4 in.) long. There was a superheater of 18 elements on 12.5 cm (5 in.) tubes and 144 tubes of 5 cm (2 in.) outside diameter. The tube heating surface was 156 sq. m (1,680 sq. ft), larger than that of the NER's 0-8-0, whilst the wheels were 2 cm (0.8 in.)larger. The locomotive was fitted with two 10 mm (0.4 in.) hot water injectors on the back of the firebox and also with a combination automatic steam brake on the coupled wheels as well as on the wheels of the tender. The valve for operating this was controlled by the vacuum in the train pipe, but could also be worked by hand when the locomotive was not hauling vacuum-fitted stock. The superheater damper in the smoke box was controlled by the pressure in the steam pipe, so as to be closed when no steam was passing through the cylinders. The tender was of the GCR's standard six-wheeled type with a capacity of 18,000 l of water and five tons of coal and was fitted with water pick-up gear. The maximum drawbar pull of the engine on the level was 12.5 t which could be maintained up to 16 kph. The weight of the 2-8-0 in working order was 72.5 t and of the tender was 44 t.

J.G. Robinson's 2-8-0, which was built at Gorton, not only worked successfully on the SYJR until 1963, but was chosen as the standard freight locomotive for British Forces overseas during 1914-1918. Most were used in France following modification for continental rolling stock. Westinghouse pumps and piping were

Ex-L&Y 0-8-0 'Q4' class No. 12965 in LMS days. This class was first introduced in 1912.

Ex-GCR Robinson 2-8-0 No. 63693 passes through Doncaster with an up coal train in April 1960.
J.C. Baker

fitted, as were steel fire-boxes on the 521 locomotives built during the war. At the end of hostilities they were sold off at around £2,000 each, many to UK rail operators, but some going as far as Australia and China. The majority returned to the GCR, soon to be part of the London and North Eastern Railway (LNER), where it remained the favourite freight locomotive of the company by reason of its cheap running costs. In World War II it was again chosen for general overseas use and 92 were specially reconditioned with new boilers for this purpose.

The MR was the only one of the five companies which did not develop an eight-wheeled coupled locomotive for hauling coal on the SYJR and other coal lines. In 1910 however, Henry Fowler designed an 0-6-0, fitted with Schmidt's super-heater to its Belpaire-type boiler. The superheater dampers were operated by a small steam cylinder arranged on the side of the smoke box. The valve controlling the supply of steam to this cylinder was patented by Fowler and his colleague J.E. Anderson at Derby. It enabled the superheater to be used fully, whether the train was a fast express or a slow stopping one, by reason that when the control valve was set to 'fast working', the superheater dampers were automatically opened and closed by the opening or closing of the main boiler regulator valve. When the engine had to make frequent short stops, this arrangement would have produced a noticeable loss of superheat. If the stoppages were short, there were moments when the superheater tubes were empty of steam, but there was little chance of any serious harm being done by keeping the apparatus in action. Therefore on a stopping run the control valve handle was turned through 45 degrees, which kept the dampers permanently open irrespective of the regulator position. If the train stopped and the blower were applied while the control valve was in the stopping position, there was a risk that the superheater tubes would be burned by the abnormal draughts passing through the boiler tubes. The control valves were therefore arranged, so that, in the stopping position, the dampers would be closed if the blower exceeded a pre-determined amount. The engine cylinders of the Fowler 0-6-0 were provided with piston guides, giving inside admission. The valve motion was of the standard Stephenson pattern with addition of rocking shaft. An automatically controlled by-pass connected the forward with the back-end of each cylinder to relieve the compression and suction, which would otherwise take place when the locomotive was running with the steam shut off.

The arrangement of steam and water valves was unusual in that both were placed in the cab connected to their respective cylinders by pipes providing direct communication. Steam braking was provided on both the engine and tender to work in co-operation with the vacuum brake on the train. The 0-6-0 locomotive in working order weighed 49 t and the tender, which had a tank capacity of 13,500 l and could carry 4 t of coal, weighed 39 t.

Until their substitution by diesel haulage in the mid-1960s, the foregoing locomotives were those most frequently employed to haul the heavy coal trains on the SYJR. In addition before Nationalisation the LNER 2-8-0s were joined by the LMS's 2-8-0, which Sir William Stanier had built from 1935. The latter were particularly powerful, with a boiler pressure 40 per cent higher than the Midland 0-6-0. Thus a larger capacity water tender of 22,500 l was required.

Despite employing such powerful locomotives on the SYJR, it was unusual for a loaded coal train to exceed 40 wagons, whilst an empty would draw about 60.

An official photograph of LMS Fowler 0-6-0 '4F' class No. 4562

Ex-LMS Stanier '8F' class 2-8-0 No. 48075 at Wakefield on 21st July, 1963. *R.A. Panting*

With a maximum gradient of 1 in 113, the SYJR compared favourably with say several stretches of 1 in 100 on the slightly older LD&ECR, which lay some 13 km south of Brancliffe Junction. Nevertheless the stretch between Dinnington and Tickhill, which had presented problems to the constructors, also provided different ones to the footplate men. On the downwards (northwards) section the guard normally put his brakes on to keep the train 'stretched'. In very poor weather conditions, such as heavy snow, trains travelling southwards up the main gradients, were occasionally stranded and had to call up a second locomotive. Normally loads were reduced in such conditions. This problem was not resolved until the introduction of the new dual auto air braking system on wagons in 1965.

SYJR Staff

By the middle of 1909 16 staff, excluding track maintenance workers had been appointed to the SYJR. This number, including the latter, would rise to 55 by July 1914.

	Dinnington	*Maltby*	*Tickhill*
Station master*	£105 pa	£105 pa	£90 pa
Clerk	£60 pa	-	-
Porter†	85p pw	90p pw	90p pw
Signalmen†	85p pw	90p pw	90p pw
Lad/porter†	-	40p pw	40p pw
Goods shunter†	£1.05 pw	-	-

Signalmen at St Catherine's, Low Ellers and Grange boxes: £1.05 pw each.

Station masters were granted 10 days holiday a year, clerks 6-8, signalmen, four and other employees three. Travel concessions were slightly more generous. Presumably anticipating the inevitable introduction of a passenger service, each employee was to receive annually three free rail passes on the SYJR and on two of these he could take his wife and two children under 15. One free journey could be overseas and an additional journey could be made along the routes of any of the five parent companies. However, by reason of the brief holiday allowance and very low rates of pay, it is not clear when these could be used; (one pound in 1910, as noted, would buy as much as about £60 in 1999, although neither tax, pension contributions nor national insurance were deducted from such pay in 1910). Staff, but not manual workers, were granted one month's sick leave for each 12 months' service. Free uniforms were provided every two or three years but station masters received a new cap each year.

In June 1908 A.J. Constable of the MR and formerly of Central South African Railways was appointed traffic inspector of the SYJR at a salary of £200 pa and initially based at Dinnington, because it had the only operating colliery on the line at the time. However with new shaft sinkings taking place all around Doncaster, it was obvious that, despite the claims of Rotherham, the former would eventually replace Barnsley as the centre of the South Yorkshire

* Each then paid £15.60 (£15 12*s*.) pa rent for a station house.

† 85p = 17*s*., 90p = 18*s*., 40p = 8*s*., £1.05 = £1 1*s*.

coalfield. Accordingly it was logical that the important new line should have its offices there and accordingly, in December 1908 the Committee took a lease from the York City and County Banking Co. on offices at 8 & 9 Bank Chambers, High St, Doncaster.

In April 1909 a new traffic inspector, clearly a high flyer at only 24 years, Wilbert Briggs the station master at Tickhill was appointed to succeed A.J. Constable at a salary of £150 pa. By reason of his association with the line which would last more than 40 years, the SYJR soon became known locally as 'Briggs' railway'. Wilbert Briggs was a large powerful man, a renowned sprinter, rugby player and swimmer in his younger days. Later he became an AAA official handicapper and officiated at the 1934 Empire Games in London. One of his favourite exercises was to do a standing two-footed jump from the permanent way onto the platform, presumably when no trains were timetabled.

Briggs also quickly acquired a reputation for bluntness, firmness, even severity, never hesitating to sack a worker he considered inefficient and he examined signalmen for confirmation of competence. Generally, he was regarded as fair, although his efforts to reduce overtime working were not popular. Highly efficient himself, he reputedly kept a set of unofficial duplicate records of the working of the SYJR, which unfortunately were destroyed deliberately after his death. However his zeal for checking the financial accounts of individual stations brought him a rap across the knuckles from the district auditors.

In return for his long and loyal service, Briggs was given a pass to travel free over all the routes of the (original) five SYJR companies. When ill-health (bronchitis) began to affect him in later years, he received full sick pay until his retirement in 1950, but died of heart failure at Doncaster in March 1956, aged 71 years.

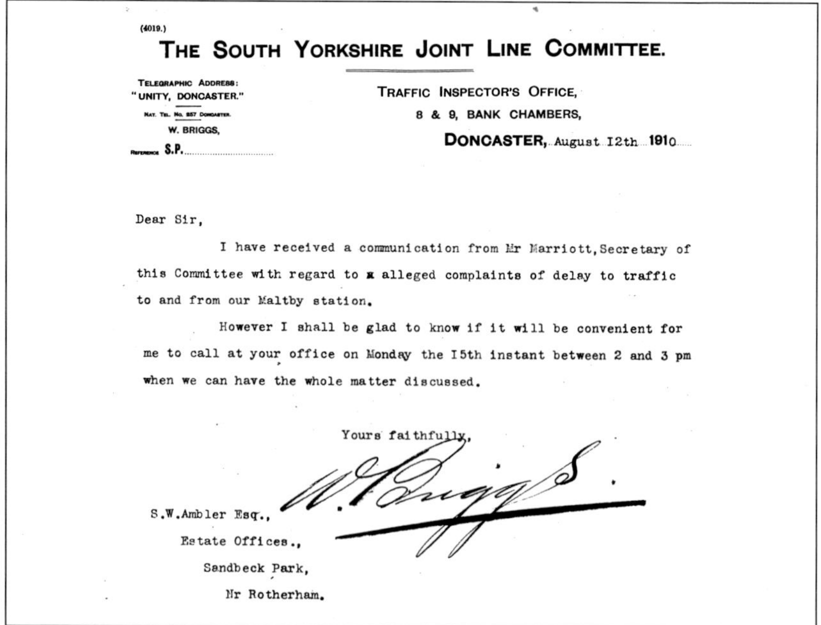

(4019.)

THE SOUTH YORKSHIRE JOINT LINE COMMITTEE.

TELEGRAPHIC ADDRESS:
"UNITY, DONCASTER."
NAT. TEL. No. 857 DONCASTER.
W. BRIGGS,
REFERENCE S.P.

TRAFFIC INSPECTOR'S OFFICE,
8 & 9, BANK CHAMBERS,
DONCASTER, August 12th 1910

Dear Sir,

I have received a communication from Mr Marriott, Secretary of this Committee with regard to x alleged complaints of delay to traffic to and from our Maltby station.

However I shall be glad to know if it will be convenient for me to call at your office on Monday the 15th instant between 2 and 3 pm when we can have the whole matter discussed.

Yours faithfully,

W. Briggs.

S.W.Ambler Esq.,
Estate Offices.,
Sandbeck Park,
Nr Rotherham.

An SYJR letter signed by Wilbert Briggs. *Earl of Scarbrough*

Chapter Four

The First Passenger Services, 1910-1913

Planning for passengers

One of the first duties of Wilbert Briggs, upon taking office, was to prepare for the first passenger services on the SYJR. Following the completion of all engineering work and the installation of signalling equipment at the end of 1908, A.J. Constable's committee had looked forward to the possibility of introducing passenger trains in May 1909. The Committee decided in February that although certain influential individuals, such as (later Sir) Charles N. Nicholson, Liberal MP for Doncaster (1906-1918) and a barrister, had made such requests, there was no mass demand for such a service and accordingly postponed a decision. The persistent clerk of Worksop UDC wrote again calling for a passenger service and was supported by Mr Constable.

In April 1909 the Traffic Officer's committee decided to begin planning for such a service. A.J. Constable had thought that four daily trains in each direction would suffice, provided that signal boxes did not remain open longer than 12 hours, the length of one shift. The suggestion that a one-class motor railcar would suffice was turned down because it was felt that 'it would be desirable to provide first class accommodation for the local gentry using the line'. Instead, first and third class accommodation would be provided in composite coaches, with extra third class seating being provided on Thursdays and Saturdays, the local market days.

Even at this planning stage the Committee promised no late trains and moreover reserved the right to reduce the service if it failed to be profitable. The GCR and GNR companies agreed to work the passenger trains at a rate of 2.5 p per km (9½*d.* per mile) plus an extra 5 pc if a guard was provided. Carriages were to be provided at Clearing House rates. The SYJR would in effect hire the trains and crews and in return issue the tickets and retain the fares.

A provisional timetable was prepared for a 54 minute service between Doncaster and Worksop with stops at Tickhill, Maltby, Dinnington and Shireoaks. Departures from Doncaster were timed for 9.00, 11.46 am, 2.20 and 5.30 pm. Trains from Worksop would leave at 8.20, 11.20 am, 2.40 and 5.25 pm. However, the possibility of these plans becoming a reality in 1909 was discounted in September when the Committee resolved that 'the time for a passenger service is not yet opportune'. Admittedly the national economy was in recession in 1908-1909 with heavy unemployment, but the effect on the South Yorkshire coalfield was slight and it did not delay work on opening new collieries.

By January 1910, with Wilbert Briggs fully installed as traffic superintendent, the situation looked more hopeful, particularly following a Board of Trade inspection which had pronounced the line adequate for passenger services. At the end of March 1910, the General Managers' conference of the five companies agreed that passenger services between Doncaster and Worksop could not long be delayed. Later a contract was signed with W.H. Smith & Son, giving the firm sole rights to run bookstalls at the SYJR stations in return for a 5 per cent share of the gross receipts and 60 per cent of advertising revenue.

Two views of the first inspection train at Tickhill on 16th September, 1908.
Norman Ellis Collection/David Joy Collection

First passengers

Finally on 20th June, 1910 the first passenger trains, albeit two excursions, travelled along the SYJR. Paying a return fare of 15p (3*s*.), 47 miners from Dinnington travelled to Doncaster for the Yorkshire Miners rally. On the same day 300 adults and 200 children from the Dinnington Wesleyan Sunday School steamed southwards out of the village for a day's excursion via the GCR line to Cleethorpes. For the round trip of 160 km, discounted fares of 14p (2*s*. 10*d*.) for adults and 7½p (1*s*. 6*d*.) for children were charged, a total cost of £56. Sixteen days later, amidst heavy rain, 142 adults and 122 children from Tickhill's Wesleyan congregation paid a total of £28 for a similar trip. Like many of the locomotives which ran on the SYJR, the GCR No. 693 which hauled the Tickhill excursionists came from the Mexborough sheds, crewed by driver Turpin and guard Kirk.

Perhaps the first taste of train travel through excursions by people living along the line, and the evidence of a healthy demand persuaded the Committee to proceed with the introduction of a regular passenger service. During the second half of 1910, a steady stream of letters urging this service was received. From the RDCs of Doncaster, Rotherham and Kiveton, the Parish Councils of Dinnington, Maltby and Laughton, the UDC and the Traders' Association of Worksop and from the Earl of Scarbrough, Sir Charles Nicholson and numerous other persons living close to the line. Dinnington Colliery Co. also wrote to the Committee.

Another factor which may have influenced the Committee was the introduction in August 1910 of a 40 minute charabanc service four times daily between Maltby and Rotherham at a return fare of 7p (£4.20 in 1999 prices). If a quick decision had not been made this service would have threatened to divert Maltby residents into the orbit of Rotherham for leisure and shopping, rather than Doncaster.

Establishing the service

Under these pressures the Committee finally took a firm decision and four years after the first request had been received, the first regular passenger service was scheduled to begin on 1st December, 1910. Contrary to previous plans it was decided to operate the service between Doncaster and Shireoaks only, presumably to avoid competition with GCR trains on the 3 km stretch between the latter and Worksop. The GCR and GNR agreed to run two trains each on weekdays to be known as SYJL trains, for which they would be paid 4p per km (1*s*. 3*d*. per mile) for the hire of trains and crews, a 40 per cent increase on the figure mooted in 1909. In addition, the Committee agreed to pay a rent of £250 pa to the GNR for the use of Doncaster station and £100 to the GCR for Shireoaks.

The 1909 suggestion for the use of composite first and third class coaches was accepted, but no extra trains were planned for Thursday or Saturday markets.

The Committee also approved an application from J. Saxton of Tickhill to operate a horse-drawn carriage from that station(1*d*. for the trip). The cheapest SYJR fare was a 3½p (9*d*.) market day return from Tickhill to Doncaster. To Shireoaks a first class return was 27p (5*s*. 5*d*.) from Doncaster (£16.20 in 1999).

The goods station at Anston between Dinnington and Shireoaks was opened for passengers on 20th May, 1912. From here it was possible to buy a market day return to Doncaster for 9p (1s. 10*d*.), and in September 1912 all market day returns on the SYJR were increased by 1*d*.

Timetable problems

As a result of the decision of the Committee not to keep signal boxes open for more than 12 hours daily, passenger services operated only between the hours of 8.30 am and 6.50 pm. This made travel difficult both for potential commuters to Doncaster and for children wishing to go to schools in the town because the first train didn't arrive there until 9.15. Following requests from parents during the early months of 1911, the 8.25 am from Shireoaks was retimed to leave at 7.47, arriving in Doncaster at 8.37 am. Local farmers also complained that the 11.20 from Shireoaks left too late for them to attend Doncaster market, whilst the 2.17 pm returned too early. The farmers asked for the former to depart at 10.20 and for the latter to depart at 2.52 pm. This time the Committee refused because the GNR said that there was no connection from Retford to feed extra passengers onto a 10.20 service. The afternoon train was retimed to leave an hour earlier leaving the farmers to wait for the 5.27 pm! The GNR also opposed a suggestion that an extra train should be run on Saturdays at 10.20. The Committee also received many letters requesting a later evening train from Doncaster. This was tried briefly in the Spring of 1911, but it was found that the extra traffic did not warrant the cost of relief signalmen and the service was withdrawn.

DONCASTER and SHIREOAKS.—South Yorkshire Joint.

Miles		Week Days only. mrn	aft	aft	aft
–	Doncaster .... dep.	9 7	1225	2 17	5 27
–	Tickhill .... "	9 23	1240	2 32	5 42
–	Maltby .... "	9 33	1250	2 42	5 52
–	Dinnington & Laughton "	9 45	1 2	2 58	6 4
–	Shireoaks 649, 654 ... arr.	9 57	1 14	3 6	6 16

Miles		Week Days only. mrn	mrn	aft	aft
–	Shireoaks .... dep.	8 25	1120	1 58	6 5
–	Dinnington & Laughton "	8 37	1132	2 10	6 17
–	Maltby .... "	8 49	1144	2 22	6 29
–	Tickhill .... "	8 59	1154	2 33	6 39
–	Doncaster 343, 348, 648 arr.	9 15	1210	2 50	6 55

Extract from Bradshaw's guide December 1910.

DONCASTER and SHIREOAKS.—South Yorkshire Joint.

Miles		Week Days only. mrn	aft	aft (Except Sats.)	aft (Sats. only)	aft
	Doncaster .... dep.	9 7	1225	2 17	2 52	5 27
6	Tickhill	9 23	1240	2 32	3 7	5 42
9¾	Maltby	9 33	1250	2 42	3 17	5 52
14½	Dinnington and Laughton.	9 45	1 2	2 54	3 29	6 4
19½	Shireoaks 661, 666 ... arr.	9 57	1 14	3 6	3 41	6 16

Miles		Week Days only. mrn (Except Sats.)	mrn (Sats. only)	mrn	aft	aft
	Shireoaks .... dep.	8 0	8 25	1120	1 58	[illegible]
5¼	Dinnington and Laughton.	8 13	8 37	1132	2 10	[illegible]
9½	Maltby	8 25	8 49	1144	2 2[illegible]	[illegible]
13¾	Tickhill	8 36	8 59	1154	[illegible]	[illegible]
19½	Doncaster 353, 358, 660 arr	8 52	9 15	1210	2 50	[illegible]

Extract from Bradshaw's guide July 1911.

DONCASTER and SHIREOAKS.—South Yorkshire Joint.

Miles		Week Days only. mrn	aft	aft
	Doncaster .... dep.	9 7	1 23	5 27
6	Tickhill	9 22	1 38	5 42
9¾	Maltby	9 33	1 48	5 53
14¼	Dinnington and Laughton.	9 45	2 0	6 5
19½	Shireoaks 661, 666 ... arr.	9 57	2 12	6 16

Miles		Week Days only. mrn	mrn	aft
	Shireoaks .... dep.	7 47	1120	3 43
5¼	Dinnington and Laughton.	8 0	1133	3 56
9¾	Maltby	8 12	1145	4 8
13¾	Tickhill	8 23	1156	4 19
19½	Doncaster 353, 358, 660 arr	8 37	1210	4 33

Extract from Bradshaw's guide October 1911.

Reducing the service

During the three months from March-May 1911, a total of 11,585 passengers used the SYJR and 113 were carried on an excursion train, producing a total revenue of £551. This was an average of 145 passengers per day or 18 per train, many of whom bought cheap day returns. Only one or two first class passengers travelled the line each day. It was quickly apparent to the Committee that the passenger service was losing money. On 10th August, 1911, a few days before the first national rail strike closed down the line completely for a few days, it was decided to reduce the service to three trains per day in each direction.

The GCR agreed to supply a single train and crew which would work a shuttle service commencing on 2nd October. Thereafter passenger services were worked solely by locomotives Nos. 688 and 577, four-coupled side-tank engines (4-4-2Ts) of the GCR. These very powerful and reliable locomotives were designed by J.G. Robinson at Gorton and built by the Vulcan foundry at Newton-Le-Willows. The total weight of a 4-4-2T was 67.75 tons, with a water tank capacity of 6,525 l. The five carriages, lacking both corridors and toilets but provided with heating, were built at Dukinfield especially for the SYJR. On Mondays to Fridays, three coaches were ample, with the extra two being kept in reserve for Saturdays and bank holidays.

The reduction of the service to three trains daily saved 64 train km or £2.50 (£2 10*s*.) per day. Additionally the hire charge payable to the GCR was reduced slightly, whilst the station rentals at Doncaster and Shireoaks were also reduced to £200 and £80 respectively. By the end of 1911 the year's receipts from 277 first class ticket sales totalled less than £34 and from 53,252 third class fares almost £1,700. Season tickets and parcels contributed almost another £250.

The actual effect upon passengers was that the two early afternoon trains from Doncaster were replaced by one in between, whilst the early afternoon and evening trains from Shireoaks, were replaced by one at tea-time. Naturally there were complaints about the cut-backs.

> The population of Dinnington and district have had their hopes thwarted by the curtailment of train services [noted the *Doncaster Gazette*]. It has been generally supposed that it would be extended as the service as at first instituted was of little use to the travelling public. Therefore it was no test of the business it would bring in. Most unfortunate is the lack of a late train to Doncaster once or twice a week, yet there are 7,000 persons living within half a mile of the station. Most therefore pay 9*d*. (4p) to go by open carriage to Kiveton Park (station) or to be hurled about in a motor bus on Saturdays and Mondays to Rotherham. The alternative is to walk 12 or 13 miles or sit at home praying for the nationalisation of the railways.

During 1912 the number of passengers fell 5,000 below the 1911 figure. The reduced service was obviously one factor as also was the new form of competition offered by the Rotherham to Maltby trolleybus service, which ran a vehicle every 30 minutes from 6.45 am to 10.45 pm! The main reason was undoubtedly the six week national coal strike from February to April 1912, which resulted in a complete closure of the line for more than a month angering

A locomotive type used on SYJR passenger workings, the ex-GCR 2-4-2T. *R.W. Kidner*

The SYJR passenger service's deadly rival. This view shows the first trolleybus from Rotherham to Maltby. *Archives and Local Studies, Rotherham Central Library*

The South Yorkshire Joint Line Committee.

COAL STRIKE.

In consequence of the strike of Colliers, which has now commenced, the South Yorkshire Joint Line Committee hereby give notice that their service of Passenger Trains will be entirely withdrawn as from MONDAY NEXT, the 4th March, 1912, until further notice.

BY ORDER.

8 & 9, Bank Chambers,
Doncaster,
February 28th, 1912.

The coal strike of 1912 closed the passenger service temporarily. *Earl of Scarbrough*

Station or Junction	G.C. a.m.	Mid. a.m.	L.&Y. a.m.	N.E. a.m.	S.Y.J. (Passr.) a.m.	G.C. a.m.	N.E. a.m.	Mid. p.m.	S.Y.J. (passr.) p.m.	G.N. p.m.	L.& Y. p.m.	N.E. p.m.	G.C. p.m.	S.Y.J. (passr.) p.m.	Mid. p.m.	N.E. p.m.
Kirk Sandall Junction.............pass	...	...	...	6.53	...	...	10.21	...	...	...	...	2.52	...	...	...	5.53
Bawtry Road W.C...................arr.	...	...	...	...	...	...	...	...	...	...	...	...	...	...	...	...
" " " ....dep.	...	...	...	...	...	...	...	...	...	...	...	...	...	...	...	...
Potteric Carr Junction............pass	...	...	...	...	9.11	...	...	...	1.27	1.30	...	...	...	5.22	...	...
Low Ellers Junction............... "	...	...	7.0	...	...	...	...	...	...	...	...	...	...	...	...	...
St. Catherine's Junction.......... "	...	...	...	7.8	9.16	...	10.36	...	1.32	1.40	2.0	3.7	...	5.27	...	6.8
Tickhill and Wadworth Station.....arr.	...	...	...	...	9.21	...	...	...	1.37	1.53	2.9	...	...	5.32	...	...
" " " .....dep.	...	...	...	7.17	9.22	...	10.45	1.15	1.38	2.3	2.19	3.16	4.32	5.33	...	6.17
Maltby Colliery...................arr.	...	...	...	7.35	...	...	11.3	1.28	...	2.16	2.32	3.39	4.43	...	...	...
" " ....dep.	...	...	...	8.5	...	10.0	...	1.58	...	2.30	3.0	4.10	5.15	...	...	...
Maltby Station....................arr.	...	...	...	8.10	9.30	...	...	2.3	1.46	2.35	3.5	...	...	5.41	...	6.40
" " ....dep.	...	...	...	8.20	9.31	10.5	...	2.8	1.47	2.45	3.15	...	5.20	5.42	...	7.12
Dinnington and Laughton Station...arr.	...	...	...	...	9.41	10.25	...	2.28	1.57	3.0	3.30	...	5.40	5.52	...	...
" " " ...dep.	...	...	...	...	9.42	...	...	2.38	1.58	3.10	3.40	4.30	6.0	5.53	...	7.32
Dinnington Colliery Junction......arr.	...	...	8.0	8.45	...	10.30	...	2.43	...	3.15	3.45	4.35	6.5	...	...	7.37
" " " ......dep.	5.50	8.0	...	...	...	11.0	...	3.13	...	...	...	...	6.30	...	4.30	...

DOWN TRAINS.

Station or Junction	G.C. a.m.	Mid. a.m.	L.& Y. a.m.	S.Y.J. (Passr.) a.m.	G.C. a.m.	N.E. a.m.	S.Y.J. (Passr.) a.m.	Mid. a.m.	N.E. p.m.	G.C. p.m.	S.Y.J. (Passr.) p.m.	G.N. p.m.	L.& Y. p.m.	N.E. p.m.	Mid. p.m.	N.E. p.m.
Dinnington Colliery Junction......arr.	4.50	7.0	...	...	...	...	...	10.45	...	2.30	...	...	...	...	3.30	...
" " " ......dep.	...	...	9.0	...	...	10.45	...	11.15	...	2.55	...	4.15	4.30	6.35	...	9.50
Dinnington and Laughton Station...arr.	...	...	...	8.1	8.25	...	11.34	11.20	...	3.0	3.57	4.20	4.35	...	...	...
" " " ...dep.	...	...	...	8.2	8.35	10.57	11.35	11.50	...	3.5	3.58	4.31	5.0	6.47	...	10.2
	...		...					p.m.								
Maltby Station....................arr.	...	...	...	8.12	8.50	...	11.45	12.5	...	3.20	4.8	4.46	5.20	...	...	...
" " ....dep.	...	...	...	8.13	9.0	11.20	11.46	12.15	...	3.30	4.9	4.56	5.25	7.10	...	10.25
Maltby Colliery...................arr.	...	...	...	...	9.5	11.25	...	12.20	...	3.35	...	5.0	5.30	...	...	...
" " ....dep.	...	...	...	...	10.0	p.m. 12.5	...	12.40	1.0	3.55	...	5.19	6.0	...	...	...
Tickhill and Wadworth Station.....arr.	...	...	...	8.22	...	...	11.55	12.53	...	4.8	4.18	5.32	6.13	...	...	...
" " " .....dep.	...	...	...	8.23	...	12.18	11.56	...	1.13	...	4.19	5.42	6.23	7.23	...	10.38
St. Catherine's Junction..........pass	...	...	10.0	8.28	...	12.27	p.m. 12.1	...	1.22	...	4.24	5.50	6.32	7.32	...	10.47
Low Ellers Junction............... "	...	...	...	...	...	...	...	...	...	...	...	...	...	...	...	...
Potteric Carr Junction............ "	...	...	...	8.33	...	...	12.6	...	...	...	4.29	6.0	...	...	...	...
Bawtry Road W.C...................arr.	...	...	...	...	...	12.34	...	...	1.29	...	...	...	...	7.39	...	10.54
" " " ....dep.	...	...	...	...	...	12.39	...	...	2.10	...	...	...	...	7.44	...	10.59
Kirk Sandall Junction.............pass	...	...	...	...	...	12.54	...	...	2.25	...	...	...	...	7.49	...	11.15

SYJR working timetable 1913.

local passenger and traders. Unsurprisingly, the revenue from coal traffic during the first six months of 1912 was the lowest during any comparable period between the beginning of 1911 and the end of June 1917.

1913, boom year

The situation improved dramatically during the record coal production year of 1913, by which date the industry employed 1.128 million workers. The development of the new collieries in South Yorkshire, including Maltby and Dinnington, was particularly rapid. A 'paddy mail' service for miners was introduced between Maltby and Doncaster. A locomotive and two coaches made the round trip four times daily, leaving Doncaster at 5.00 am, 12.00 noon, 5.00 and 9.00 pm and Maltby one hour later in each case.

Total earnings from SYJR freight trains in 1913 amounted to £33,839, (or about £2m in 1999 prices), of which coal and coke amounted to £26,113. Merchandise receipts were £3,108 net and other minerals £1,499, whilst livestock fares amounted to a little over £5. In addition, as the number of coal trains had increased, the original 12 hour limit on the opening of signal boxes had to be abandoned and the line was open for 20 hours daily. The SYJR's offices proved too small and the administration moved, but not until 1915 from Nos. 7 & 8 Bank Chambers into a larger suite at Nos. 2, 3 & 4, leased from the London Joint Stock Bank.

The general boom conditions in coal mining in 1913 was reflected in the growth of passenger traffic, with a record 60,220 passengers (approximately 200 per day) booked at SYJR stations, an increase of 42 per cent over the 1912 figure. In addition 21,676 parcels were carried. Total coaching receipts were £3,046 (equivalent to almost £200,000 in 1999 prices), of which £2,697 was from passenger fares, but to which first class passengers contributed only £17.42½ (£17 8*s*. 6*d*.) The accounts noted also the receipt of £1,763 (equal to about £105,800 in 1999 prices) for 'season tickets' - the fares charged for the use of the 'paddy mails'. Overall, the SYJR's 1913 receipts were not exceeded until 1920-1922, the result of wartime inflation and not in the value and expansion of traffic.

To the casual observer of an SYJR passenger train in 1913, particularly on a Saturday, it might have appeared that the decision to introduce passenger services had at last been justified. The accounts clerks would have seen it differently, if parcels traffic were excluded. Although the deficit was declining the passenger service was still losing money.

SYJR Passenger & Parcels Traffic

	Expenditure	*Receipts*	*Deficit*
1911	£3,948	£1,972	£1,976
1912	£2,840	£1,774	£1,066
1913	£3,912	£3,046*	£866

* Excluding 'paddy mail' receipts of £1,763.

Committee concerns

Although these deficits appear considerable, particularly in view of the 60-fold fall in the value of money between 1913 and 1999, and with the reduced 1913 loss being equivalent to 30 per cent of total SYJR staff wages (£2,878), it still averaged only 37½p (*7s. 6d.*) per passenger train operated. The Committee expressed frequent concern about these losses and particularly about the small number of first class passengers, some 200 per annum, who used the service. This was a telling point, for had only two more first class tickets (20p/4*s*. return) been sold daily between say, Doncaster and Dinnington, the service would have shown a comfortable profit.

However, with agriculture still recovering from recession, neither farmers, nor indeed coalminers would travel first class, certainly not 600 per year on the SYJR. Amongst the gentry, the use of the private motor-car, at least for short journeys, was becoming established, with the number licensed in Britain almost doubling to 105,000 between 1910 and 1913.

One suggestion made in the Committee was that the normal locomotive and three coaches should be replaced by a motor railcar and trailer, but whilst this would have sufficed from Monday to Fridays, a full five-coach train would have had to be kept on standby for Saturdays, an even more uneconomic prospect. Unsurprisingly the Committee rejected a request in March 1913 from Worksop UDC to extend the passenger service there, instead of terminating at Shireoaks.

Another factor worrying the Committee was the delays to the highly profitable coal trains caused partly by the introduction of passenger trains onto the single track. This had been noted as early as March 1911 and, following a special survey between May and November 1912, it was computed that 755 hours of delays had been incurred or approximately 4 hours per day. Passenger trains were not wholly to blame and the emphasis on safety must have prevented any accidents more serious than the killing of two sheep by the 9.07 am from Doncaster one Autumn morning in 1911.

The SYJR did however have its own little omen of the imminent conflagration in Europe when the station buildings at Dinnington were seriously damaged by fire on 18th July, 1914. Rebuilding cost £125 and the five railwaymen who put in six hours' overtime during the fire and clearing up afterwards, were awarded 25p (5*s*.) each, or £15 in 1999 prices, by the grateful Committee.

Chapter Five

The Connecting Lines

Hull & Barnsley Railway

The SYJR proved to be the most important and profitable amongst the new lines and spurs which were built around Doncaster between 1906-1916, mostly to serve new colliery developments. The GCR was the company most involved in these projects which, above all, sought to avoid the centre of Doncaster and the increasing congestion there, particularly where the GCR's Sheffield to Humberside line crossed the ECML. By reason that the SYJR ran through the middle of the new South Yorkshire coalfield it was inevitable that it should link physically with some of these other new projects in the area. Not surprisingly, these new projects were almost all joint lines.

Physically closest to the SYJR and opened only nine months later (October 1910) was the GCR, MR and H&BR joint line. This 8 km stretch formed end-on junctions with the GCR-MR line at Braithwell near Silverwood colliery and the GCR-MR at Anston Junction south of Dinnington, originally and until July 1906 part of the Rotherham, Maltby and Laughton Railway (RM&LR). Its purpose was to provide a southward route for Silverwood coal, both north and south routes for Thurcroft's production and, following the opening of the SYJR spur between Laughton East and West Junctions in January 1911, yet another exit, if needed, northwards for Dinnington coal.

The H&BR company, which had felt itself almost completely excluded from the rich and growing coal traffic south-east of the River Don, sought to make an entry to this market by an Act of 1909, in partnership with the GCR, which provided the extra financial support needed. This gave them powers to build a 33 km line from Braithwell Jn, entering Edlington (Yorkshire Main colliery) by a spur and then by-passing west of Doncaster. Passing over the flat country north of the town and gaining access through more spurs to the new collieries at Bullcroft and Bentley, it formed the Aire Jn with the H&BR main line at Gowdall, west of Snaith. It thus became generally known as the Gowdall and Braithwell Railway. By early 1911 the contract was signed with Logan and Hemingway to build the first 20 km from Braithwell to Thorpe-in-Balne, including the three colliery sidings above and a total of 40 bridges. A new goods terminal, York Rd station, was also provided at Doncaster, as were a number of intermediate passenger halts up to Gowdall, but these latter facilities remained unused throughout the life of the line. Completion of the first section of the line was planned for the summer of 1914. The contract for the remaining 13 km to Gowdall, which included an 800 ton steel opening bridge, which was never to be opened, across the Aire and Calder canal, was also awarded to Logan's in October 1911.

During the first year or so work proceeded, with about 1,000 men being employed at the southern end, where deep cuttings were required at Conisborough and Warmsworth and where the line joined the GCR's Sheffield -Humberside tracks.

A contractor's train on the RM&LR. *Archives and Local Studies, Rotherham Central Library*

The Doncaster avoiding line, west exit (*left*). The Gowdall-Braithwell (GCR &HBR Jt) line ran underneath this junction. *Author*

It is very difficult now to see the need for this new route. Both the GCR and the H&BR already had ample capacity from South Yorkshire to Humberside. It can only be assumed that they saw an almost infinite expansion of coal traffic from the new coalfield including new collieries north of Doncaster, which would eventually result in congestion on their existing lines. Meanwhile shortage of labour and raw materials , exacerbated by the outbreak of World War I, delayed the opening of this line throughout until 1st May, 1916. Although it was then asserted that 'the GCR would make good use of this line', its active life was barely 25 years and no through traffic, other than on the southern end, used it after 1950.

Doncaster avoiding line

The GCR showed considerably more wisdom in its plans for the construction of an east-west Doncaster avoiding line which opened in July 1910. This was an integral part of the GCR's plans for moving coal from its new (1907) mineral concentration yards at Wath-on-Dearne for export via its new (1912) docks at Immingham, near Grimsby. Between Wath and Immingham lay the serious obstacle of the ECML, which all GCR trains had to pass via a complicated system of signals. As the GNR had 700 trains per day passing through Doncaster every 24 hours, there were frequent delays to GCR trains.

The 6 km Doncaster avoiding line ran from Warmsworth to a point 1.5 km east of Bentley. Designed by the GCR's Chief Engineer, C.A. Rowlandson and also built by Logan and Hemingway, whose telegraphic address was 'Avoiding, Doncaster', it removed at one swoop the ECML bottleneck. Despite its brevity, it required six bridges to cross the River Don, two railways, two main roads and a flood plain. The first across the Don was a four-span lattice girder bridge with a 50 m central span. Most of the line had to be carried on an embankment about 15 m high. Even this new facility was insufficient within a year or two to cope with the increasing volume of traffic, which included also, at Kirk Sandall, SYJR traffic moving to Humberside. In 1912 the GCR sought powers to widen its line between Wath and Thorne to four sets of tracks and this was largely completed by March 1916, thus also speeding up the coal trains leaving the SYJR.

Dearne Valley Railway

The final major project involving only one of the five companies, and completed before the SYJR, was the DVR. This line was built by the L&YR, linking Black Carr Junction, where the SYJR crossed the ECML, with Crofton Junction near Wakefield and passing through, and connecting with, the new collieries at Edlington, Cadeby and Grimethorpe. By September 1906, the DVR had opened as far as Cadeby colliery and the final section (10.65 km) to Black Carr was completed on 7th October, 1908. The latter created the greatest engineering difficulties. To cross the Don at Conisborough, an imposing 21-arch

Yorkshire Main colliery, 1930, with, in the far distance, the GCR/HBR Joint line and its spur over the Dearne Valley Railway in the middle distance. *John Goodchild Collection*

A view of the trackbed, after removal of track, of the ex-GCR/MR Joint line south of Thurcroft, looking south on 6th September, 2001. *Author*

viaduct, almost 500 m long and 35 m high and using 12 million bricks and 3,000 tons of cement, was built between the steel sections of the structure. Having bridged the river, the engineers then had to blast out magnesium limestone cuttings, before levelling and finally carrying the DVR via bridges to integrate into the complicated junction system at Black Carr and beyond. This connected it to the SYJR, the ECML, the GNR and GER Jt into Lincolnshire and into Rossington colliery and the opening date for these connections was 17th May, 1909. Thus L&YR coal trains from Dinnington, Maltby and eventually Rossington collieries were able to begin running onto the DVR to head for Manchester and Liverpool. During 1913 a total of 1.99 m t of coal from its several collieries was shipped out along the DVR.

Although the L&YR had no intention, at least initially, of operating a passenger service on the DVR, it did provide several 'halts' along the line and a more substantial station at Edlington. On 1st July, 1912 it inaugurated a shuttle passenger service, of four trains per day and an additional later service on Saturdays between the latter and Wakefield (17½p - 3*s*. 6*d*. return). For this service a 47.5 ton steam railmotor, powered by an 0-4-0 side tank engine was employed until 1933, one of 18 built between 1906-1911 by the L&YR. The coach unit seating 56 passengers was secured to the locomotive by an extended girder and locked in place by a large steel bolt. This passenger service lasted 22 years longer than that on the SYJR, being discontinued in September 1951, with full line closure to Edlington following in July 1966.

Ex-Dearne Valley Railway trackbed 3 km west of the junction with the SYJR, view to the west on 6th September, 2001. *Author*

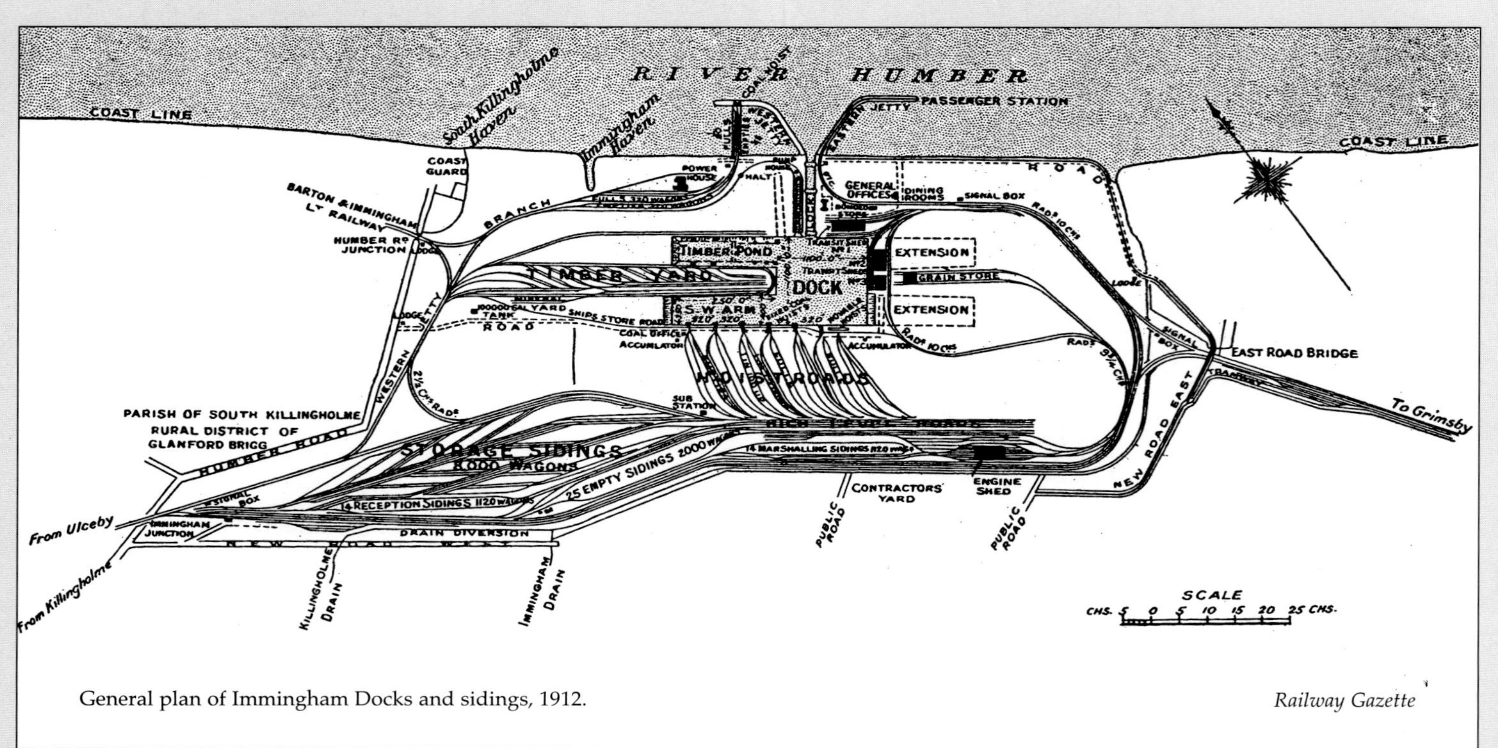

General plan of Immingham Docks and sidings, 1912.

Railway Gazette

Chapter Six

The SYJR at War I: 1914-1918

Coal traffic decline

On 4th August, 1914 the SYJR was, like almost every other UK railway, taken over by the government's Railway Executive Committee (REC). Despite the vital importance of coal to the war effort, particularly to the steel industry and therefore munitions, the outbreak of war brought to an end the expansion of the concealed coalfield. Other factors combined to reduce by almost 20 per cent UK coal production by 1918 from the record levels of 1913. The decline at the two main operating 'SYJR' mines was around 19 per cent at Maltby and 27 per cent at Dinnington, although the figures below from SYJR records exclude coal consumed locally.

Coal tonnages moved on the SYJR

	Markham Main	*Tickhill*	*Maltby*	*Dinnington*	*Total*
1913	-	2,721	355,083	648,415	1,006,219
1914	-	3,157	345,327	600,651	949,135
1915	-	2,527	344,609	546,857	893,993
1916	-	2,319	304,587	576,873	883,779
1917	-	2,991	330,694	566,707	900,392
1918	386	1,794	287,322	474,657	764,159
1919	406	1,666	292,136	399,152	693,360

Markham Main and Tickhill figures are for coal received.

Interestingly, the *Railway Year Book* for 1919 asserted that total SYJR coal tonnages moved in 1915-17 were higher than those above - at 918,000, 943,000 and 912,000 t, respectively. Probably Yorkshire Main output sent along the SYJR and Rossington's coming into production in 1917 would have accounted for these increased totals.

Enlistment of miners

Most serious for UK coal production was the loss of coalminers into the army, from late 1914 onwards, ironically men more suited than most for life in the trenches. The Sheepbridge Co., which had large interests in Maltby and Dinnington, lost a total 1,200 men from these and its several Derbyshire collieries during the first six weeks of the war. By autumn 1915 more than 250,000 UK miners had enlisted, of whom about 2,350 were from the Sheepbridge group and Maltby in particular was suffering from an acute labour shortage. This could not have been helped by the withdrawal of the 'paddy mail' service between Doncaster and Maltby early in the war, a short-sighted act, although planning for a model village of 800 houses by 1917, the Sheepbridge Co. perhaps hoped that there would be enough local labour.

A general view of Anston station *c*.1914. *Chris Booth*

Anston station staff *c*.1914. *Chris Booth*

The loss of skilled men and the difficulties of increasing production by further mechanisation led to a serious fall in productivity. In 1914 each Sheepbridge coalface worker produced 755 tons. By 1919 this had fallen to 668 tons and to 561 in 1920. A serious shortage of wagons due to cut-backs in maintenance also developed by 1918 and reduced coal movements. Aware of the growing shortage of coal the Government had in July 1915 frozen coal prices to 20p (4s.) pt above the level of one year previously, a move which seemed more likely to restrict output.

Coal Controller

On 1st March, 1917, under the Defence of the Realm Act the Government took over the output and distribution of coal. In July the new Coal Controller, Sir Guy Calthrop, made a Coal Transport Order dividing the UK into 20 areas (Yorkshire was No. 5) to reduce inefficiency and waste in train operations. An example of the latter was the widespread dispatch of coal by Yorkshire collieries to nine of these other areas and the purchase of coal within the county from 10 areas. Under the new regulations, unless they obtained special permission, Yorkshire consumers were compelled to use only Yorkshire coal and sales of this outside the county had to be to neighbouring areas. South Yorkshire shipments to the Humber for coast-wise shipment and exports were rapidly reduced (the former eliminated completely) because of the threat of U-boats and the GCR new port of Immingham was taken over by the Admiralty for mine-laying and submarine supply and repair duties. Moreover, SYJR coal was much in demand locally as always.

Government guarantees

The Government take-over of coal mines guaranteed the UK coal owners' profits, which rose from £21 m to £45 m during the war years, roughly in line with inflation. This mirrored the terms of wartime 'nationalisation' of the railways by which each company was guaranteed a fixed return based on 1913 profits. Thus the SYJR should not have suffered financially, despite its coal movements falling by more than 30 per cent between 1913 and 1919, a decline exacerbated in the latter year by a national rail strike from 26th September until 5th October.

Accordingly, during 1915-1919 each SYJR company shared £16,455 pa compared with £16,635 profit in 1913, representing an annual dividend of 3.73 per cent. However these payments did not keep up with inflation, because the cost-of-living index rose by well over 200 per cent during the war. In total, therefore, the underpayment by the Government to the UK's railway companies during the war was about £17 m pa (or one billion pounds in 1999 prices).

Maltby station *c.*1914 with an inspection saloon in the platform. The locomotive appears to be numbered 1000. *Chris Booth Collection*

Rail workers at War

Like collieries, the railways suffered labour shortages during the war. More than 184,000 railwaymen (including almost 40 pc of total H&BR staff!) enlisted during the war of whom more than 21,500 were killed in action or died of disease or wounds. By 1914 the SYJR staff had risen to 55 and five of these men immediately enlisted. Another six followed and by 1918 a total of 17 SYJR employees had enlisted. Fortunately only one was killed, but four were wounded and 10 were back on duty by 1919. Closer to home, no air-raids took place nearer to the SYJR than a very minor bombing incident of a GCR storeyard at Sheffield. Other bombs dropped 'locally' by Zeppelins fell on Hull, Immingham, Derby and Nottingham.

As with other industries, except in underground coal mining, male workers on active service were replaced by women. From a 1914 total of more than 13,000 in all capacities, the number of women employed on UK railways rose through 34,000 - in 135 distinct jobs - at the end of 1916, to a maximum of 68,800 on 30th September, 1918. By the following July, however, this last figure had fallen by almost exactly half.

Many women were employed as munitions workers at the locomotive works, the Doncaster 'Plant', which employed 6,000 workers before hostilities. During the war, some 4.4 million cartridge cases were renovated there and 124,000 six inch shells machined, whilst 50 pedestals and mountings for 18 pounder guns were rapidly produced to arm merchantmen (ships).

On the SYJR in 1914 a Ms F. Cawkwell was employed (as were most other women) in clerical work in the offices at a wage of 75p (15*s*.) per week and a 10p (2*s*.) bonus. Operational duties by women particularly in signal boxes - even on branch lines - were opposed by UK signalmen who said they 'could not accept the responsibility'. Nevertheless, Grange signal box had a woman on duty and her work was judged, presumably by Wilbert Briggs, as 'very satisfactory'.

It had also become necessary to replace Henry Hall as station master at Dinnington when £9 of SYJR funds 'went missing' and in September 1915 T.C. Bottom took over. By 1916 a change of station master had also taken place at Maltby, where Herbert Wharfe had replaced A. Robinson.

Inflation resulted in the first UK railway pay increases (termed a war bonus) of 15p (3*s*.) pw early in 1915. The station masters at Maltby and Dinnington had their annual pay increased to £115 and their house rentals were reduced to 22.5p (4*s*. 6*d*.) per week and their wives were given free passes to travel to Doncaster markets on Saturdays. As the cost of living continued to rise, so did the war bonus to 75p (15*s*.) pw for men and 37.5p (7*s*. 6*d*.) for boys by March 1917. The NUR demanded this should be incorporated into the wages structure and by November 1917, average wages were one pound pw (50p - 10*s*. for boys) higher than in 1914. This rose eventually to £1.90 (£1 18*s*.) pw by October 1919, eight months after railwaymen had secured an eight-hour day. Overall the average wages of railwaymen rose from £1.35 (£1 7*s*.) pw in 1914 to £2.30 (£2 6*s*.) in 1921.

Passenger service cuts

To compensate for the shortage of both labour and materials, the duties of SYJR workers became lighter. The reduction in coal traffic enabled the line to return to a 12 hour day from the 20 hrs of 1913. Overall, most other UK railways suffered congestion as military 'specials' transporting both soldiers and munitions increased. Although SYJR coaching receipts held up quite well in 1914, falling by only £250 from the previous year, inevitably the Committee looked again at the passenger service, especially when passenger numbers continued to decline.

On 23rd February, 1915 the REC demanded various measures to restrict passenger travel, including higher fares and more mixed trains. From 1st April, 1915, the Committee accordingly reduced the service to two trains daily in each direction from Monday to Friday, by making the 11.20 am from Shireoaks and the 1.23 pm from Doncaster a Saturdays-only service. Unsurprisingly, during 1915 the total number of passengers booked from SYJR stations was only 78.5 pc of the 1913 total. Although in 1916 passenger numbers actually rose to 83 pc of the 1913 total, coaching receipts were less than 70 pc.

On 1st January, 1917 the REC brought in new restrictions, with further cuts and decelerations of trains and an increase in ordinary fares of 50 pc, but no increase in those for workmen. Acting in the interests of the wartime economy, the Committee decided that from 1st June the SYJR would operate a Saturdays-only service, with one result being that total sales of first class tickets for that year amounted to only £4.54 (£4 10*s*. 9*d*.). No alternative transport provision was provided by the Committee and no doubt many passengers found their own and said goodbye to the SYJR passenger trains for ever. On the national network restrictions failed to reduce passenger numbers and by Easter 1918 numbers were equalling those of Easter 1913.

Passenger traffic on the SYJR

	No. booked at SYJR stations	*Total coaching receipts*
1913	60,220	£3,046 *
1914	56,669	£3,709
1915	47,297	£2,801
1916	50,267	£2,702
1917	28,309	£1,920
1918	26,790	£1,565
1919	28,061	£1,714

The most interesting observation from the above figures is that, if the two totally peaceful years, 1913 and 1919 are compared, then during the latter, with a Saturdays-only service in operation, almost half (46 pc) as many passengers were carried as in 1913 with a six-day service. It appears therefore that the SYJR carried about four times as many passengers on Saturdays as it did on other days.

* Excludes £1,703 for the year's 'paddy mail service'.

Chapter Seven

The SYJR and the Extension of the Coalfield 1919-1926

Sankey Commission

At the end of 1918 wartime restrictions on new colliery developments were ended. There was a general belief that the coal industry would soon return to the boom conditions of five years previously and the increasing world and UK demand would continue. By early 1919 provisional plans had been announced to sink eight new collieries, all in the 5,000 tons per day class, to the south and east of Doncaster and the Committee indicated a willingness to build 'authorised branches' to Rossington (already producing), Harworth and Firbeck by displaying these on the map in its annual financial report.

Although some routine work was being carried out at the new pit heads, such as at Markham Main at the north end of the SYJR, there was no rush to carry out any new sinking, despite coal prices reaching £1.72½ (£1 14*s*. 6*d*.) per ton in 1920, or more than triple the 1913 price. This was because since March 1917 the coal industry as noted had also been under government control. Furthermore, in March 1919 the Government established a Royal Commission under Mr Justice Sankey to examine the whole future of the coal industry. The powerful MFGB, numbering more than one million members, was demanding both the nationalisation of most of the UK's 3,045 coal mines and large pay increases on top of the average of 94p (18*s*. 10*d*.) per shift/day, (equal to £25 in 1999 prices) which they were earning in 1920. Clearly no private coal-producing company, of which there were 1,673 in the UK, was going to invest in an industry which might soon become state-owned, permanently. To sink shafts and then produce one million tons a year from a deep colliery required an investment of between £1.5 and £2 m (equal to £37-50 m in 1999 prices).

To 'encourage' the Government, Yorkshire miners struck over wages and hours, for a month on 17th July, 1919, pushing down even further the year's production figures and the SYJR's originating freight totals. However ignoring Sankey's recommendation to nationalise, the coalition Government dominated by Conservatives decided in August that the coal industry would be a liability rather than an asset and that it would return the mines to their private owners.

National coal dispute

This hand-over did not take place until 1st April, 1921, upon which more than 1.1 million miners, including 170,000 in Yorkshire went on strike or were locked out over the new lower pay scales offered by the owners. The strikers also included most safety men, of whom about 250 were needed to maintain one deep mine.

The MFGB expected, but did not get, the support of railway and other unions. Without support, the miners held out for three months, reducing UK coal production from 229 m tons in 1920 to 163 m in 1921, but eventually they returned to work for pay reduced comparatively to below 1914 levels.

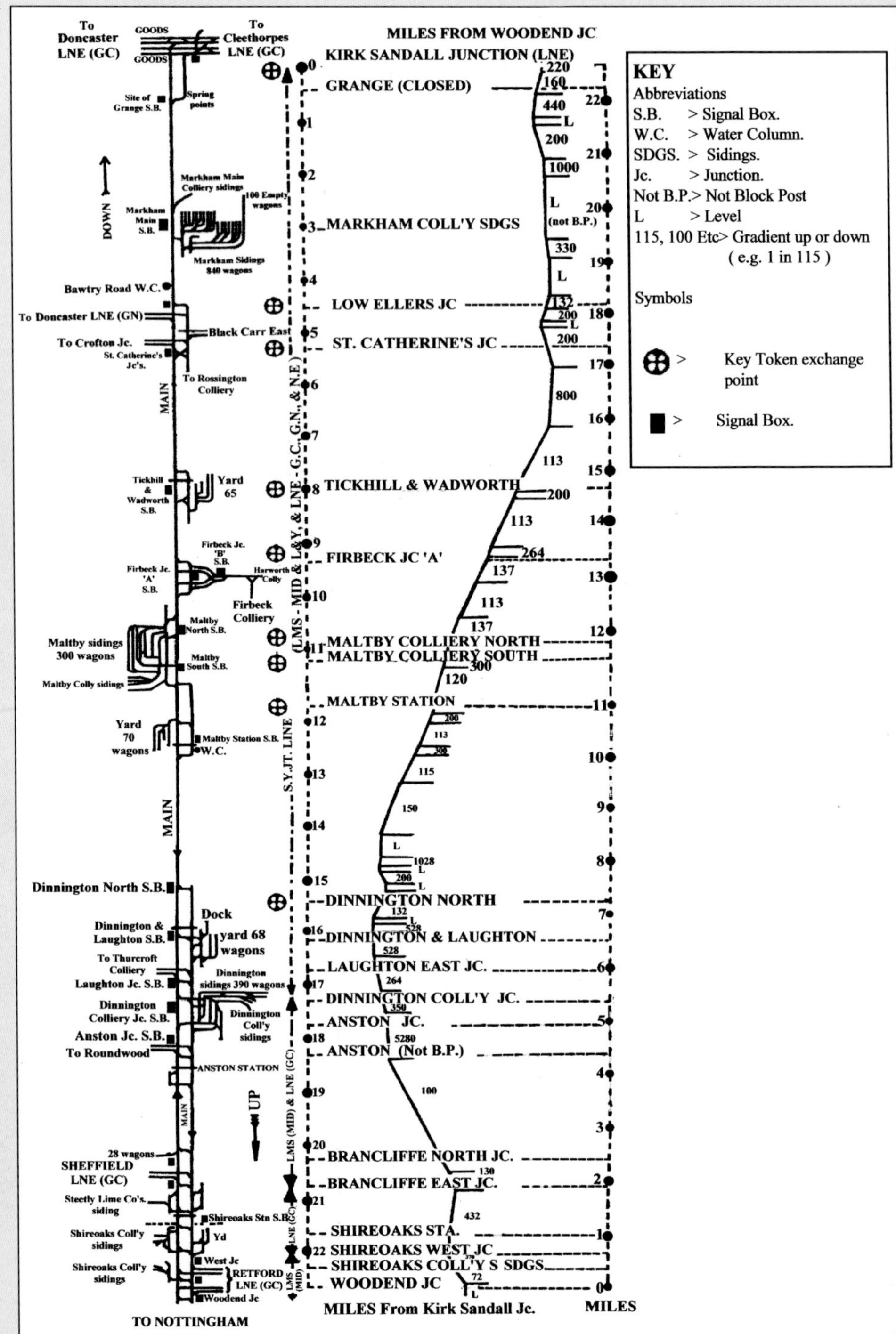

Linear map of the route in 1927 from Woodend Junction to Kirk Sandall Junction.

Chris Booth

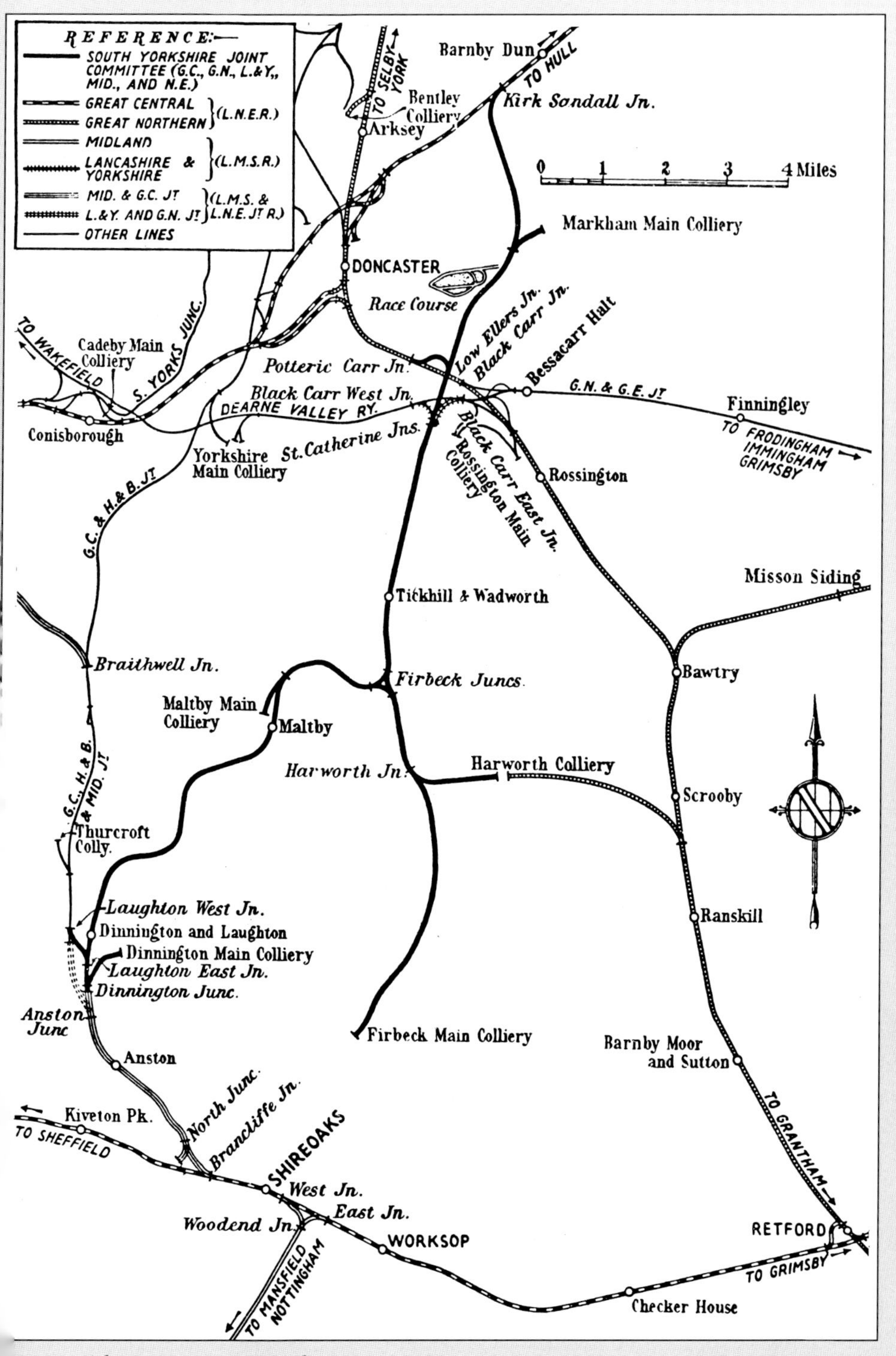

Map of the SYJR route in 1938 showing extensions and connections. *Railway Magazine*

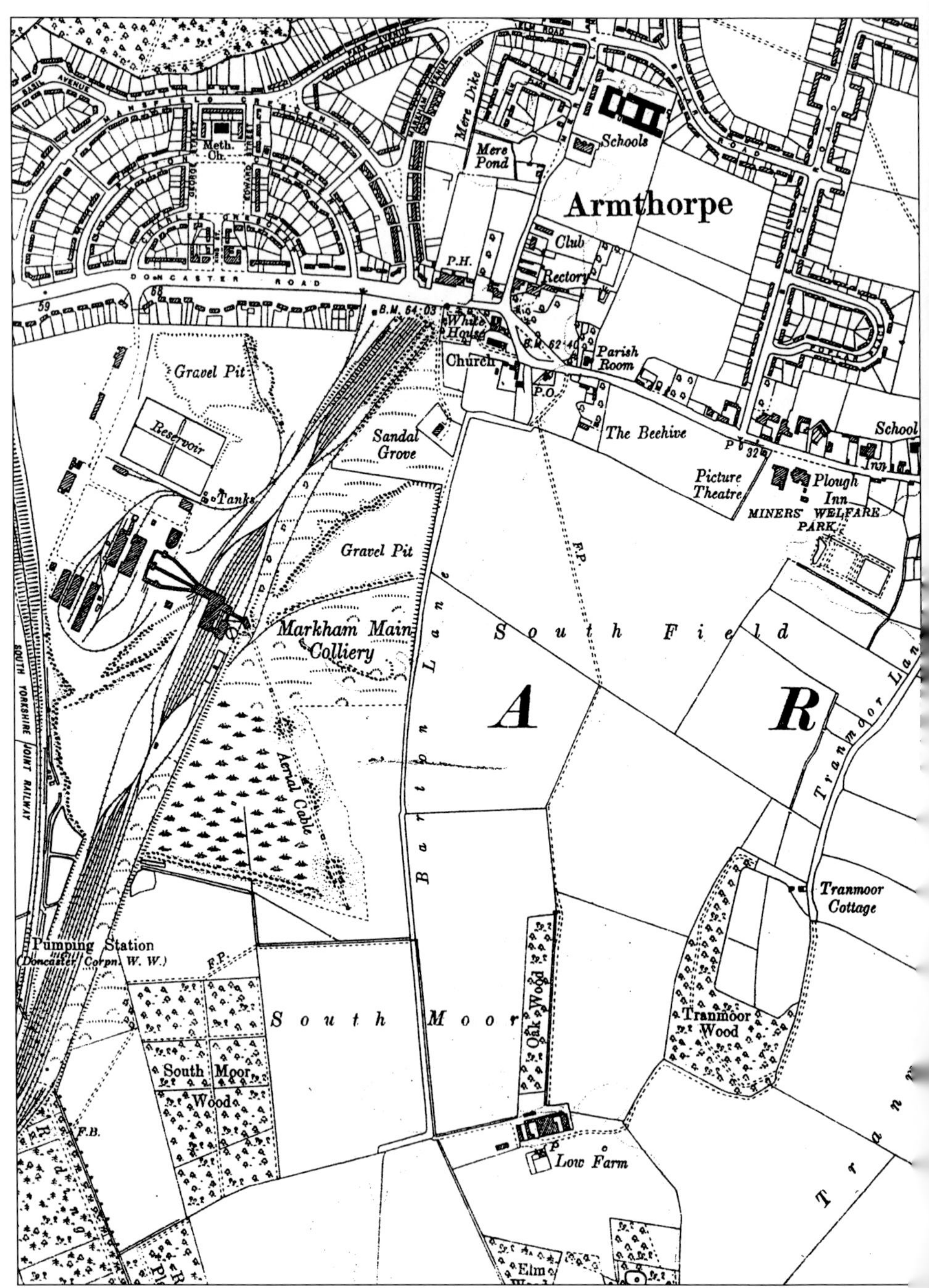

Markham Main colliery. *Reproduced from the 6", 1931 Ordnance Survey Map*

The SYJR closed down completely during this 1921 three-month coal dispute and the profits shared out by the five rail companies fell to £14,732 each, the lowest figure since 1912, but worth much less due to wartime inflation. However, following the settlement of the 1921 dispute, the coal industry had three relatively prosperous years. The basic problem for the coal industry was world over-capacity, brought about by improvements in fuel efficiency and especially the substitution of oil for coal by the world's navies and merchant ships. This caused a decline in the UK's export markets from 73 m t to 39 m t between 1913 and 1932, whilst home demand was maintained.

1922-1923 boom years

The UK industry was boosted by long coal strikes in the USA in 1922 and in Germany in 1923, the latter during the French occupation of the Ruhr. In 1923 British coal companies, employing more than 1.2 million workers, were able to increase production to 276 m t, of which 79 m t were exported or used by shipping, totals almost equalling the 1913 records. Thus for Doncaster, 1922-1923 were boom years, with the lowest unemployment (one pc) in northern England. This led to high immigration into the local coalfield, including many unemployed miners from the North-East, Lancashire, Scotland and Wales. With a defeated and lower paid work force, sales were generally buoyant between 1922 and 1925 and Bentley colliery produced 1.2 m t in 1923-24. Encouraged by one estimate that the Doncaster coalfield would yield more than one billion tons in the next 100 years, the time seemed ripe to resume sinkings held up by the war or to commence new ones. By 1924 as it was well known that deep collieries here had lower costs, higher output per man shift (oms) and were then (from below 550 m) producing 40 pc of South Yorkshire's output, there was no shortage of capital for this work.

New mines

Almost 18 km north-east of Doncaster and close by the GCR main line to Humberside, a borehole at Thorne had proved the Barnsley bed at 840 m with a thickness of 2.75 m in 1908, which led to a production forecast of 1.5 m t pa . Shaft sinking, repeatedly delayed by first water and then by war, was resumed in 1919 with 140 workers on site. The No. 1 shaft finally reached the Barnsley bed after 16 years work in 1924 at a depth of 840 m and the No. 2 shaft in 1926. Production began early in 1925, rising to one million tons pa by 1940.

A promising 3 m wide Barnsley bed at 780 m had been reached also in 1916 at Hatfield Main, almost mid-way between Thorne and Doncaster and alongside the GCR main line and 750 men were employed there in 1920.

Even closer to Doncaster and on the SYJR, between Black Carr and Kirk Sandall Jns at Armthorpe, Markham Main colliery was being sunk. Prospecting rights under 7,000 ha owned by Earl Fitzwilliam and Doncaster Corporation had been obtained in 1910 and sinking by German engineers had been planned to begin in the late summer of 1914, but this was delayed by the war. A temporary connection and a goods depot were eventually installed by January 1918, at a cost of £2,533, close to where sinking began in July 1922. In that year the colliery first appeared on the SYJR map included with each year's financial report.

After meeting the usual difficulties with water, dealt with by cementation, the Barnsley bed 1.8 m thick was reached at 644 m in May 1924. Very optimistic predictions of production of 2 million tons per year were made and accordingly the sidings were extended considerably in 1925-6 at a cost of £24,000, whilst a connecting line to the SYJR costing £3,635 was also installed. The Westinghouse Brake and Saxby Signal Co. installed the signalling there in the GCR's Grange box at a cost of £1,980, of which the colliery company paid £500. This box had about 30 levers and controlled the line as far as Kirk Sandall Jn, whose (battery) power points leading onto the SYJR it could lock.

Three Tyer's-type key tokens were used, one (3 km) to Low Ellers box and two (3.6 km) to Kirk Sandall, the second of the latter being a short section instrument, used when traffic was heavy. This permitted one train to proceed to Kirk Sandall with the normal token and a second to proceed one km towards the same, where it was then stopped by a signal until the first train had cleared the junction. The Markham signalman then operated a special instrument which released a token to the second waiting driver enabling him to proceed to Kirk Sandall. A similar operation worked in reverse, allowing four trains to be waiting to use the line whilst one was moving in the 3.6 km section. The key-token system was used right down the line to Maltby South including on the two new branches to Harworth and Firbeck. From Maltby to Dinnington, the electric tablet method was in operation.

Rossington unconnected

Six km south of Markham Main lay Rossington colliery which, as noted, was sunk successfully in May 1915, when the Barnsley bed was reached at a depth of 800 m. Production began in 1917 and by 1920 some 1,128 miners were employed there. Lying within an apex formed by the ECML, the DVR and the SYJR at Black Carr, Rossington colliery was connected only to the first two (ECML, 1918 and later, the DVR) and, through shunting, to the GNR & GER Jt line.

The SYJR had hoped to reach Rossington directly through the 1913 NER Act and had even costed this 'authorised' 2.37 km line at £35,000. From 1913-1930, leaving the main line south of St Catherine's, this spur appeared on the maps published with each year's SYJR financial report. Since this spur was never built, the L&YR and GNR spur remained the only available link between the SYJR and Rossington colliery and even this was abandoned early. Unfortunately, the main soil there was peat and the spur embankments were frequently smouldering, requiring huge deposits of sand to try to extinguish them. Had Rossington (by the 1913 Act), been linked directly and solely to the SYJR, it would have added even more to the line's exceptional profitability becoming like Dinnington and Maltby eventually a 20,000 tons a week colliery. However apart from periods of unusual congestion and disruption, most of its coal trains during the last century would have departed by the other routes above.

A commercial postcard view of the colliery yard at Rossington.

John Goodchild Collection

Harworth sinking

Further south, in Nottinghamshire, two major sinkings were resumed. Work at Harworth, begun by Germans ceased in 1914 and the operation was sequestered by the Board of Trade. Messrs Barber, Walker & Co. bought Harworth in 1917 for £80,100, carrying out preliminary work in 1919 and becoming fully legal owners in 1921, as part of the War Reparations scheme. They began sinking a shaft in September 1921 and overcame the water problem with injections of liquid cement to form a solid barrier. In October 1923, the Barnsley bed was reached at 848 m, making it the deepest colliery in the area.

Early in 1924 a 4.3 km single line was opened between the Harworth and the ECML, south of Scrooby, authorised by the GNR Acts of 1911 and 1922. With a maximum gradient of 1 in 68, it required a six-span viaduct over the River Ryton and two road bridges, including one over the then A1 (now A638). The ECML, as part of the LNER, was so seriously congested that a lengthy and expensive north-south Doncaster avoiding line was being seriously considered. However, coal represented two-thirds of LNER freight tonnage and this declined from the 1923 levels (86.6 m t) first by more than 50 pc in 1926 as a result of the coal dispute and then, after the temporary recovery in 1929, by up to 25 pc until the mid-1930s. LNER passenger traffic also declined considerably between 1923-1933 so this huge avoiding line expenditure was never taken beyond discussions.

A large shunting engine at Harworth colliery in 1914. *Worksop Library*

Harworth sinkers, 1924. *Worksop Library*

Harworth colliery in 1930. *Worksop Library*

SYJR extensions planned

Nevertheless, with forecasts of production at Harworth reaching 5,000 tons per day, congestion could only increase. In 1923, therefore, the new owners of the SYJR , the LNER and LMS companies, agreed to utilise the powers of the 1914 NER Act to connect both Harworth and Firbeck collieries to the SYJR. Indeed the first appearance of the 'authorised' Harworth branch had been on the 1915 map in the SYJR's annual financial report, and the Firbeck branch followed in 1919.

In September 1923, 23 firms quoted for the contract, which went to James Mitchell & Co. of London for £106,506.60 (£106,506 12*s*. or about £3.5m in 1999 prices). It was planned that the new Harworth branch should make a junction near Styrrup with the second new SYJR branch from Langold, where sinking of the new Firbeck colliery had started in July 1923. To assist these sinking operations at Firbeck, a temporary line was opened 11 months later at a cost of £29,000.

Like Harworth, Firbeck colliery had also originated before the war. In 1911 the Wallingwells Boring Co., a subsidiary of the Sheepbridge Co. had begun work near Langold Lake. The Barnsley bed had been proved and the GCR even surveyed a route there from Shireoaks. By 1914 the Sheepbridge Co. had resolved to exploit the 3,000 ha which it had leased but, without a rail link to the site, no work could proceed. It decided to apply for an Act to build a light railway from the GCR at Worksop through Langold and Harworth to the GNR at Bawtry. This was blocked by the Board of Trade in January 1916 and withdrawn when the Committee promised to build the necessary (SYJR) link 'as soon as possible'.

Shunting locomotive at Firbeck colliery. *Langold Library*

Firbeck sinking

By the time sinking operations at the proposed Firbeck colliery resumed in 1923, the Staveley Iron and Coal Co. had acquired a 50 pc interest in the planned £800,000 capital expenditure. The sinking went much more smoothly than at many other mines in the area. No water problem was encountered until 400 m and less seriously than expected. Unfortunately when the Barnsley seam was reached at 744 m in 1925, it proved disappointingly to be only 1.3 m thick and serious geological faults were present. The original production forecasts of 30,000 tons per week were obviously very over-optimistic, capital was unavailable for further development and Firbeck's financial viability came into immediate question.

Nevertheless, by March 1924 the colliery engine house and pit-head gear had been erected and six months later James Mitchell, who bid £149,545 (or almost £5m in 1999 prices), was also awarded the contract to build the Firbeck colliery branch of the SYJR, conditional on completion within 20 months.

Disaster at Maltby

The growing success of the extended concealed coalfield was seriously retarded at Maltby in 1923. For some time, work at the colliery had been interrupted by 'gob' fires, which were created by the ignition of pockets of gas. At 9.15 am on 23rd July, 1923 when 120 men were working underground trying to extinguish some of these 'gob' fires, an usually large pocket exploded causing a cave-in along one gallery and crushing and burying 27 miners. Fifty-seven children lost their fathers, 22 women were widowed and 3,000 miners were thrown out of work by the temporary closure of the colliery.

Almost a month after the explosion, gas was still being pumped out of the colliery at the rate of 500 cu m. per hour and only one of the 27 bodies had been recovered. Production at Maltby fell steeply as a result of this tragedy and even limited working could not begin for two months. This was serious because before the explosion, production was only 2,800 tons per day or 30 per cent below 'break-even'. By June 1924 it had recovered to only 1,800 tons per day providing work for only 1,850 men, compared with 3,000 before the explosion. Some 860 men found work at Rossington, Dinnington, which also had 93 coke ovens and Thurcroft, which had 60 ovens. Many of these men moved permanently.

As a result of the disaster Maltby lost £63,000 in 1923-4 and £41,000 in 1924-5. However in 1925-6 a recovery was underway, but in 1926-7 as a result of the long coal dispute, Maltby lost a further £45,000 and the Sheepbridge Co. sold its interest into Denaby and Cadeby Amalgamated Collieries, a holding company on which Sheepbridge had five Directors.

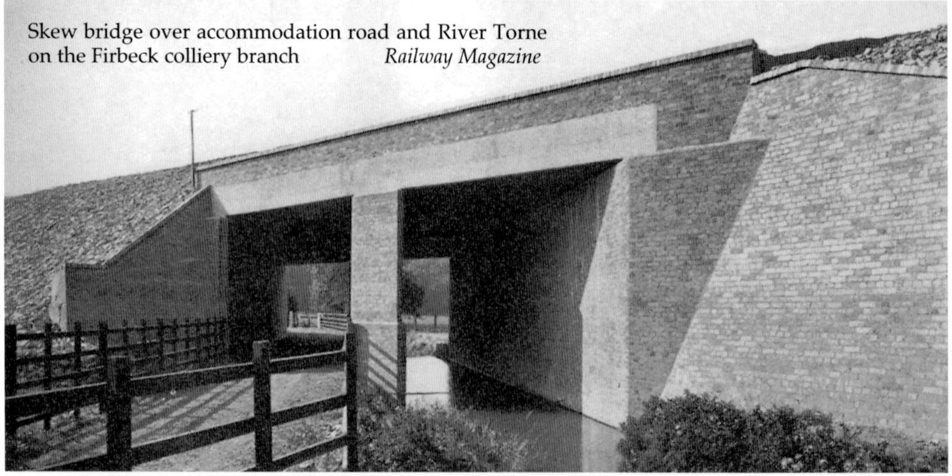

Skew bridge over accommodation road and River Torne on the Firbeck colliery branch *Railway Magazine*

Viaduct on the Firbeck colliery branch near the junction with the main line. *Railway Magazine*

The western junction of the Firbeck and Harworth collieries branch (*right*) with the SYJR. *Railway Magazine*

SYJR extended

Work on the Harworth branch was delayed by legal difficulties because the Committee had agreed with the Northern Union syndicate before the war not to build a line east of the River Torne, the Yorks-Notts boundary. Barber, Walker & Co. were opposed to the building of an SYJR branch to Harworth if it meant that coal trains would pass by the colliery precincts *en route* to the ECML at Scrooby. Negotiations between the Committee and Barber, Walker, eventually resolved successfully, lasted from 1923 to 1925.

By the latter year work was progressing steadily on the 8 km single-track Firbeck branch, from which both north and south access to the main SYJR line could be achieved. This created what became known as known as the Firbeck triangle which enabled locomotives to turn round there because two signal boxes, Firbeck A and B were also constructed here.

Mitchell's employed 250 workers using pneumatic drills to bore holes for explosive charges which loosened up the earth and rock. Three large steam navvies, built at a cost of £12,000 each by the Ruston company, were employed removing some 450,000 cu m. of limestone rock. The steam navvies then moved in after the explosions, filling open freight wagons with two 'bites'. The major engineering feature of the line was a single-span bridge, 15 m above the Tickhill-Maltby road (now A631). Some 4.4 ha from Lord Scarbrough's estate was purchased for almost £1,800 for these extensions.

At a total cost of £229,600, plus an extra £6,032 for signalling equipment, which was operated by the key-token system, the Firbeck branch was opened on 1st October, 1926. This date virtually coincided with the ending of the long and bitter dispute between the miners and the coal-owners, which had also sparked off the short-lived General Strike the previous May. The Harworth branch was completed in 1928 at a cost of £55,700, plus £3,468 for signalling installed by the British Power Signal Co., but did not open until April 1929, by which date the total route length of the SYJR had grown to more than 47.4 km (29.85 miles) or 87 km (54.73 miles) as single track.

SYJR Track Statistics 1929

Road length			
Length of road	29 miles	69 chains	47.4 kms
second track	6	15	13.1
third track	-	8	0.16
Total as single track	38	12	60.6
Sidings	16	47	26.5
Grand total	54 miles	59 chains	87.1 kms

Later, in April 1930 it was agreed to put in, at a cost of £14,500, a connecting curve to Harworth, thus linking Firbeck to Scrooby on the ECML, but a year later with the signal box at Harworth Jn ceasing to be used, the curve was clearly seen to be redundant and it was dismantled in 1938.

Maintenance on the SYJR

Routine maintenance work on the extended SYJR was now carried out by teams based at Brancliffe, Thurcroft, Maltby, Tickhill and Markham Main, with each covering about 6 km daily on foot or by bicycle. In 1933 this work became easier with the provision of a small petrol-driven railcar and trailer, costing £1,069, but saving £1,254 in maintenance costs in its first year. Ballast workings on the SYJR were carried out on Sundays by two consecutive crews from Sheffield (Darnall depot) using ballast wagons from Beighton sidings, each covering a few hundred metres, helped by local platelayers, on the two 6 hr trips.

Maintenance Materials, 1929

Ballast	1,315 cu. metres
Rails	13 tons
Sleepers	2,518
Total cost (including labour)	£19,549

Annual track relaying, including re-sleepering, re-chairing and re-plating covered between two and three kilometres. In 1937 about £11,000 was spent, and £7,000 in 1938, but only £2,120 in 1939. However a new telephone circuit was installed along the full length of the line in the last year for £308.

In March 1936, the two parent companies agreed at a cost of £4,096 to remove that section of the former RM&LR between Anston Jn and Laughton (W) Jn which duplicated the SYJR through Laughton (E) Jn. Recovery of materials (£3,299) and savings (£1,288), it was estimated, would produce a credit of £491 and traffic would be diverted along the parallel, southernmost part of the original SYJR. About four years later another closure, this time of the ex-L&YR and GNR spur at Black Carr East, connecting the DVR to the SYJR severed Rossington colliery's direct access to the latter.

SYJR Harworth branch, showing the viaduct over the A631 road, looking west. *Author*

Chapter Eight

The Closure of the Passenger Service, 1919-1929

Railway Grouping

On 1st January, 1923, SYJR like the vast majority of Britain's railways, was 'grouped' into one or two of four major companies. Although retaining its formal identity, the SYJR was shared between the LNER, which was capitalised at £350 million and took a 60 pc holding and the even-larger LMS (£399m) with 40 pc. This division was reflected in the SYJR freight movements, with nine LNER trains daily and four LMS, although it was reported that at other collieries in South Yorkshire, served by both the Big Two, managers would haggle charges over which company would move particular consignments. The Committee paid the working expenses of the trains (it cost 27.5p (5*s.* 6*d.*), plus 6p (1*s.* 2*d.*) wagon hire to send each ton of coal to the Humber in 1927) and received 25 pc of the gross receipts of the coal freight charges and 33.3 pc of other freight charges.

Managers from the LMS (Euston) controlled accounting on the SYJR and from the LNER, Liverpool St, its engineering work. The LNER was responsible for providing the passenger service and in April 1926 the two parent companies agreed that the LNER's Rules and Regulations would apply on the line. The company received from the Committee station rentals of £280 per annum and 7p per km (2*s.* 3*d.* per mile) for each train run, which co-incidentally was the exact (1929) LNER-computed running cost per km of a steam locomotive over 50,000 km pa.

Despite the prospects of greatly increased mineral revenues and profits accruing to the SYJR through the anticipated opening of Markham Main, Firbeck and Harworth collieries, the Committee was clearly unhappy about subsidising even the small but continual losses of the passenger service and as early as October 1921 began openly discussing the complete and permanent withdrawal of the service. No doubt the Committee was also conscious that such a withdrawal would also help to reduce any delays to the highly profitable coal trains.

Temporary reprieve

Pressure to restore a full passenger service (reduced to Saturdays only in 1917) had begun early in 1919. The Committee accepted that apart from the 54,000 inhabitants of Doncaster, the line passed reasonably close to towns and villages with a total population of 28,000. Nevertheless according to an estimate by Wilbert Briggs, a thrice-daily service with an extra late train on Saturdays would incur an annual loss of £5,200 (more than £170,000 in 1999 prices). Of this, the late Saturday train alone would be responsible for £1,900, by reason of the late manning of signal boxes. Whilst coal prices had less than doubled between 1913-

1922, rail freight charges and passenger fares were subject to government control, the former being much too high in the opinion of the coal owners, whilst wartime inflation had more than doubled wages. This had increased the SYJR's annual wages bill in 1924 for 43 employees to almost £6,400, or about £210,000 in 1999 prices, an average of less than £5,000 per worker.

SYJR Staff in 1924

Doncaster	*Annual Pay* £	*Total* £
Traffic inspector	500 *	
Five clerks (£148)	740	
Signalman	156	1,396
Dinnington		
Station master	230	
Two clerks (£105)	210	
Six signalmen (£136)	816	
Two porters (£119.50)	239	
Two number takers (£135)	270	
Two shunters (£156)	312	2,077
Maltby		
Station master	230	
Two clerks (£120)	240	
Five signalmen (£136)	680	
Two porters (£119.50)	239	
One number taker	91	
Two shunters (£143)	286	1,766
Tickhill		
Station master	220	
One clerk	105	
Four signalmen (£135)	540	
Two porters (£119.50)	239	1,104
Final Total		£6,343

By contrast the average weekly earnings for all LNER locomotive drivers in 1923 were £5.05 (£5 1*s*.) per week or, assuming a 50-week year, £250 pa, of which about 17 pc was overtime. This figure remained virtually unchanged until World War II. Between 1923-1938, LNER signalmen averaged overall around £3.45 (£3 9*s*.) pw or (£172 pa), which was more than the average (£3.16 - £3 3*s*. 2½*d*.) for all adult male railwaymen in 1939, but SYJR signalmen were paid less than these averages.

Near the top of the earnings ladder, in 1930, the locomotive manager at the Doncaster 'Plant' which maintained 1,300 locomotives, earned £900 pa (or £33,000 in 1999 prices). This was the LNER's third largest works, employing 3,560 people in 1923 and, amongst other jobs, built Pacific-type locomotives at £7,844 each. In 1940, the yard manager at the LNER's South Yorkshire Mineral Concentration Yards at Wath (ex-GCR) earned £425 pa.

* Later increased to £525, and to £550 w/e/f 1st October, 1937.

A country station

In June 1920, Charles England was appointed station master at Tickhill and Wadworth station. His salary of £220 pa was an increase of less than 2.5 times the 1909 pay rate whereas since 1914 alone the cost of living had risen by this multiple. His duties began at 8.15 am when the first train for Doncaster arrived. About 20 girls from neighbouring villages and farms travelled this way to Doncaster High School, which had opened in 1911. They were unable to return until the evening train arriving at 6.07 pm. Until his retirement in 1950, Mr England lived in the station house, for which he initially paid a rental of 40p (8*s*.) per week.

As Tickhill did not serve a colliery, it received domestic consignments of coal rather than dispatching it by the train load. Cattle and sheep and agricultural freight to and from local farms were Tickhill's major consignments. Farmers themselves had begun to turn to road transport for both themselves and their produce by the mid-1920s so this was a declining trade. With the departure of the 6.07 pm train to Maltby and Worksop, Charles England's formal duties were finished, although he did find increasing bureaucracy on the line, especially form-filling, after 1923.

Whilst the white collar staff remained relatively stable, with some men like Wilbert Briggs and Charles England spending much of their working lives on the line, the turnover amongst signalmen was particularly rapid. With its infrequent and fairly slow service, the SYJR was considered an ideal training ground for new entrants. From all over the LNER and LMS systems, these trainee signalmen spent a few months on the SYJR, before moving to more complicated stretches of line, which probably explains their lower than average earnings, above.

Terminus, Worksop

From 1st April, 1920, both new and experienced signalmen on the SYJR, excepting of course those on its most northerly stretch, had to deal with the extra complications of a 'full' weekday passenger service. Despite the gloomy forecasts of heavy losses, the Committee felt obliged to end the wartime emergency service and fulfil its moral and legal obligation to the Earl of Scarbrough by restoring a full passenger service to Maltby.

In the hope of attracting more passengers it was decided that, rather than terminate at Shireoaks, trains would run to Worksop, theoretically adding an extra 23,000 persons to the 82,000 already living within the ambit of the line. Accordingly the first train was timed to leave even earlier, arriving at Doncaster at 8.30 am. It returned from Doncaster at 9.07, the only unchanged departure time during the whole period of this service. Apart from the Saturday 'market special', there were no further services until late afternoon with an-out-and-back from Worksop, which terminated there at 6.46 pm. The SYJR therefore offered a virtual but only very limited commuter service to and from Doncaster.

However, 1920 was a relatively prosperous year for British industry, including coal, whose price reached £1.72½ (£1 14*s*. 6*d*.) per ton (50p - 10*s*. in 1914), as the country switched back to peace-time production, whilst European competition was devastated by the war. Optimistically the Committee decided that there might be a

A passenger train from Lincoln to Sheffield at Worksop *c*.1908, with GCR 4-4-0 No. 437.
R.W. Kidner Collection

Ex-GNR 4-4-2 condensing tank No. 4541 on an SYJR train at Shireoaks. *R.W. Kidner Collection*

demand for a late Saturday train. This was duly introduced in October, but the Committee soon came to regret it when they were told that the loss for the first year of restored passenger service was forecast at £3,800. Unfortunately, the three month coal dispute in 1921 also resulted in the complete closure of the line and after it ended the Committee began again to discuss a complete passenger closure. As this was not legally possible, the Committee considered the late Saturday train. Each cost £4.25 (£4 5s.) (£140 in 1999 prices) more to run than it took in fares, because of the need to keep the signal boxes open for an extra six hours.

Withdrawal of the late train would save £900 pa and accordingly, this was done from 1st March, 1922. In 1922 passenger services had operating costs of £5,648 against receipts of £3,807, whilst by 1923 expenditure had fallen to £4,500 whilst revenue fell only slightly to £3,769. This resulted in a reduction of the deficit from £1,841 to £731. In 1999 prices, the latter equalled a loss of only about £24,000, whilst the equivalent 1923 profit (also in 1999 prices) from the coal trains was well over £3 million. However it should be remembered that 1922-1923 and 1929 were unusual in being the coal industry's best 'inter-war' years.

DONCASTER, MALTBY, SHIREOAKS, and WORKSOP.—South Yorkshire Joint.

Miles.	Week Days only.	mrn	aft (Sats.)	aft
	Doncaster............dep.	9 7	1 55	5 52
6	Tickhill and Wadworth....	9 22	2 10	6 7
9¾	Maltby....................	9 31	2 19	6 16
14¾	Dinnington and Laughton.	9 42	2 30	6 27
16¾	Anston....................	9 46	2 34	6 31
19¾	Shireoaks 595, 600.......	9 56	2 44	6 41
21¾	**Worksop 533**.........arr.	10 0	2 48	6 46

Miles.	Week Days only.	mrn	mrn (Sats.)	aft
	Worksop..............dep.	7 35	1120	3 47
1¼	Shireoaks..................	7 40	1125	3 52
4½	Anston.....................	7 50	1135	4 2
7	Dinnington and Laughton	7 55	1140	4 7
11¾	Maltby.....................	8 6	1151	4 18
15¾	Tickhill and Wadworth...	8 16	12 1	4 28
21¾	**Doncaster 307, 312, 594** arr	8 30	1215	4 42

Extract from Bradshaw's guide May 1922.

DONCASTER, MALTBY, SHIREOAKS, and WORKSOP.—South Yorkshire Joint.

Miles.	Week Days only.	mrn	aft
	Doncaster (Central) ...dep.	9 7	1 30
6	Tickhill and Wadworth....	9 22	1 45
9¾	Maltby....................	9 31	1 54
14¾	Dinnington and Laughton.	9 42	2 5
16¾	Anston....................	9 46	2 9
19¾	Shireoaks 910............	9 56	2 19
21¾	**Worksop 692, 905**... arr.	10 0	2 23

Miles.	Week Days only.	mrn	aft
	Worksop..............dep.	1117	3 40
1¾	**Shireoaks**..............	1122	3 45
4½	**Anston**.................	1132	3 55
7	**Dinnington and Laughton** .	1137	4 0
11¾	**Maltby**.................	1148	4 11
15¾	**Tickhill and Wadworth** [904	1158	4 21
21¾	**Doncaster (C.) 811, 817**, arr	1212	4 35

☞ **For OTHER TRAINS between Shireoaks and Worksop, see page 905.**

Extract from Bradshaw's guide November 1927.

MALTBY, SHIREOAKS, and WORKSOP.—South Yorkshire Joint.

Miles.	Week Days only.	aft
	Maltby...............dep.	1240
4½	Dinnington and Laughton.	1251
7	Anston....................	1255
9¾	Shireoaks 910............	1 5
11¾	**Worksop 692, 905**... arr.	1 10

Miles.	Week Days only.	non
	Worksop..............dep.	12 0
1¾	**Shireoaks**..............	12 5
4½	**Anston**.................	1215
7	**Dinnington and Laughton** .	1220
11¾	**Maltby**............arr.	1230

☞ **For OTHER TRAINS between Shireoaks and Worksop, see page 905.**

Extract from Bradshaw's guide November 1929.

East Midland Motor services Leyland Tiger No. 102, registration No. HD 5917, with Yorkshire (WD) chassis and a Willowbrook body. Local bus services killed off passenger services on the SYJR. *Chris Booth Collection*

The 1931 Morris tourer which cost £100. *Morris Register*

Road competition

Like most of Britain's minor lines and many main ones, the SYJR was suffering a fall in the number of passengers. This situation is most evident from a comparison of the total passenger bookings made at SYJR stations in the 'boom' of 1923, but which were only 71 per cent of the 1913 record number. The reasons for this decline in passenger bookings are not hard to find. As Wilbert Briggs noted in a minute of 14th February, 1923, it was the competition from road vehicles.

Overall the number of first class tickets sold by the LNER fell by half between 1923-1933 and a steady desertion from this category on the SYJR, apart from an unusual surge in 1929, was also apparent in favour of the private motor-car. Indeed, the total number of cars registered in Britain had risen from 132,000 in 1914 to almost 580,000 in 1925 and was approaching one million by 1929. The latter year was on the eve of the £100 new motor-car, fuelled by petrol costing 1.6p (nearly 4*d*.) per litre. Resigned to this situation, the LNER was by 1931 providing car-parking facilities at 283 of its stations.

Passengers booked at SYJR Stations

	1st Class	*3rd Class*	*Total Coaching Receipts (£)*
1913	394	60,220	3,046
1920	163	35,818	5,586
1921	91	25,542	4,924
1922	147	44,018	4,522
1923	125	42,839	3,876
1924	99	39,468	2,251*
1925	66	32,581	1,659*
1926	34	7,830	431
1927	3	2,952	169
1928	35	8,829	189
1929	272	8,557	291

Third class passengers, if not amongst the growing army of unemployed, found the new bus services cheaper and more convenient. Bus and particularly trolleybus competition from Maltby to Rotherham before the war has been noted. Even earlier in 1909, a bus service from Tickhill to Rotherham and Doncaster was reported on Tuesdays, Thursdays and Saturdays. By 1917 an omnibus to Rotherham and Sheffield left Tickhill at 9.00 am on Tuesdays and Saturdays and another to Doncaster at 9.30, with an extra service on Thursdays. In 1922 W.T. Underwood, who had started operations in the Dinnington area in 1920, began to work the Harworth-Tickhill-Doncaster route, but failed to get a licence to duplicate the whole SYJR route. As early as 1924, Harworth - which never offered passenger trains - was being served by five daily buses to Doncaster, picking up at Tickhill, and by a service every 30 minutes on Saturdays. The 1927 return fare from the latter was equal to the SYJR's market day return in 1910.

By 1925, a year in which the improved quality and comfort of buses in Britain was being particularly noted, Dinnington was being served not only by Underwood, but also by Sheffield and Rotherham Corporation services and by

* Excluding parcels.

Cuthbert Wigmore's 'charabancs'. By the time Firbeck colliery was fully opened in 1927, its parent village of Langold was on the route of the through services from Worksop to Doncaster run by the East Midland Co., which had also bought out Underwood the same year. In summary, between 1920-1929, the number of miles travelled by UK bus and coach passengers more than tripled, whilst the number by rail fell very slightly.

Against this kind of local competition, the roundabout and more expensive route of the SYJR with only a twice-daily service, simply could not compete. The location of the stations, 2-3 km outside the villages, increased the disadvantages of the SYJR, whereas the new bus services went through the village centres and close to housing areas. Charles England called the stations 'a big mistake', for whilst Joseph Saxton still ran his waggonette between the centre of Tickhill and its station, this merely added to the cost of the journey. Probably the limited number of people catching main-line connections at Doncaster or Worksop found the SYJR stations more convenient but, with luggage, a taxi-fare to the latter would also have to be added to fares such as £1 single from any SYJR station to London, third class, or £1.68 (£1 13*s*. 8*d*.), first class in 1923.

Popular trains

Not all SYJR passenger services ran empty in the 1920s. On Saturday mornings the platforms at Maltby would be nearly full, as passengers awaited the arrival of the 8.06 or 11.51 to Doncaster or the 9.31 to Worksop. Ticket receipts would be about £5 (equivalent to £165 in 1999), compared with a normal weekday of about one pound.

The line was also busy during Doncaster race weeks and especially in September when the St Leger was held, although this might involve another bus trip from Doncaster station. Evening excursion trips to Leeds and Nottingham were also run and well patronised. Even more popular were the 10 or 12 seaside excursions organised each year by the miners. Excursions were the only passenger services ever run over the Firbeck branch line, the first of which took place in July 1929 when 2,500 miners and members of their families went on a day trip to Blackpool. Special permission had to be obtained from the Ministry of Transport, whose inspectors imposed severe restrictions. These included the padlocking of all points, a maximum speed of 16 kph on curves and scarcely much faster on the rest of the line so 5 am departures were not unknown, and special steps and lighting were provided at Firbeck colliery yard. These trips were a regular feature of the social life of the coalfield until 1966. Harworth miners did not organise such trips until the 1950s. Cleethorpes and Skegness were popular destinations. One excursion train from Worksop to Bridlington, Filey and Scarborough in the mid-1960s hauled by an English Electric type '3' (later class '37') picked up at Shireoaks, Dinnington and Maltby with a return fare of £1. The return trip was not completed until after 2 am.

Undoubtedly the most famous passenger on the SYJR was the 10th Earl of Scarbrough, through whose estate at Sandbeck the line ran and who in return, as noted, had established virtually a legal right to a passenger service to Maltby.

A view along the platforms at Tickhill. *C. England*

Whilst in residence at his London house the Earl sent his laundry hamper back to Sandbeck via the SYJR twice weekly. If travelling along the line he always bought his ticket upon arrival at Maltby, and he was careful to check the change.

Almost equally famous in the locality was the Revd Sydney Spencer Claude Tickell, vicar of Stainton near Maltby (1914-1926), a living then in the gift of the Earl. He was noted for his tireless writing of letters to the press, which he always signed 'Claude S. Tickell', and for his love of wild animals. Many of the letters were about the animals. The vicarage at Stainton was surrounded by a wire fence 3 m high, inside which Mr Tickell kept a small menagerie including a pony and a donkey. When he was transferred to a living in Wiltshire, Mr Tickell had to hire a horse-box which he measured with great care to ensure the animals suffered no discomfort, before it was drawn away southwards by an SYJR train for the first part of its trip. The staff at Maltby lost a great *raconteur* when Mr Tickell left.

1926 Coal dispute

With the outbreak of the coal dispute, or lock-out on 1st May, 1926, the third major one in the history of the SYJR (and with more to come in the next 60 years), the line closed down completely once again, and all staff were laid off until the coal trains resumed almost five months later. Coal movements along the SYJR fell from 1.65 m t in 1925 to 960,000 in 1926, whilst in the same years the number of passengers fell from 32,600 to 7,864, of whom a mere 34 paid first class fares. Net profits from the line, shared between the LNER and the LMS also declined sharply from £36,463 to £12,638.

With 16,000 Nottinghamshire miners back at work by the end of September and almost 3,600 in Yorkshire, limited coal trains began running on the SYJR again in October 1926. On 30th November, Yorkshire miners officially resumed work. However the Committee showed no urgency to restart the passenger service. In April 1927, the elderly Sir Hugh Bell, Chairman of the LNER and a colliery owner and Rt Hon. Rupert Beckett, a director of the LNER and chairman of the *Yorkshire Post*, met the Earl to request the permanent withdrawal of the passenger service, but the latter stood firm. Not until 27th July, 1927, 15 months after the previous withdrawal, did passenger trains, two trains per day in each direction, reappear but with no Saturday 'specials'.

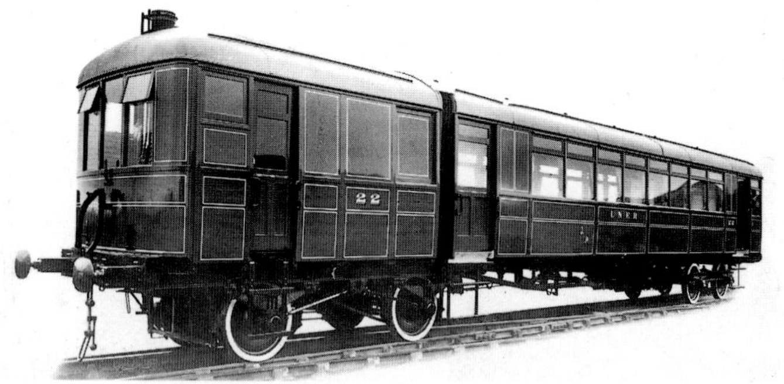

An official photograph of Sentinel steam railcar No. 22, acquired by the LNER in 1927.

Terminus for passengers

In an editorial on 29th July, 1927, *The Worksop Guardian* expressed the great exasperation and frustration which had been inflicted upon would-be passengers of the SYJR during the previous 17 years.

> The reinstatement of the passenger service (poor as it is) on the SYJR, which came into operation on Monday is at any rate a move in the right direction. The line, which was the unfortunate child of many rivalries, is now part of the LNER system and connects Doncaster, Maltby and Worksop. Primarily it is intended for mineral traffic yet, running as indicated through a well-populated district, it could be made to serve the needs and interests of the general community. Unfortunately this it has never done, nor under existing arrangements is it likely to do. Two passenger trains a day is the service offered and these run at the most inconvenient times, viz., departing Doncaster at 9.7 and 1.35 and Worksop at 11.17 and 3.40. These hours may suit the needs of the few, but they do not meet the needs of the many. No wonder the Companies concerned plead that the passenger service does not pay. How can they expect it with a meagre and indifferent service such as this? We are glad to see that Tickhill Urban Council has decided to press for a more generous consideration of public requirements. Other authorities in the district should follow suit. Then probably the management will see the sweet reasonableness of the request and set themselves out in a businesslike fashion to make the line of some use to the district through which it runs.

The Committee did make one gesture to try to improve the economic viability of the passenger service. A series of experimental runs were undertaken with a Sentinel steam railcar. Unfortunately it had two serious drawbacks. Firstly it set fire to the grassy banks of the deep cuttings and secondly it was too light for the steep gradients, and therefore useless for towing the horse-boxes which were a feature of the service. The LMS's diesel railcar, with a top speed of only 67 kph, would have been no better, spending two-thirds of its experimental year undergoing repairs.

These railcar failures undoubtedly helped to resolve the minds of Committee and, from July 1929 the service was reduced to one train at midday running from Worksop to Maltby and back, thus meeting its minimum legal obligation. Only Tickhill UDC protested at the ending of the Doncaster-Maltby trains and this was because it feared that local tradesmen would lose their parcels service. However on being assured that parcels and livestock service would be maintained and told of passenger service losses of £2,500 in 1928 (equal to £90,000 in 1999 prices), the Earl of Scarbrough finally withdrew his objections and the regular passenger service ceased from 2nd December, 1929.

Why closure?

The irregular nature of the service offered during the previous 19 years and the enthusiasm shown by the Committee for shutting it down - almost in 1917-1920 - and totally whenever there was an coal dispute, showed all too clearly that it regarded the service as an expensive and regrettable luxury which interfered with the real business of moving coal. Indeed the SYJR was only one small part of some 2,650 km (1,656 miles) of UK branch railways which lost their passenger services permanently between 1922 and 1947. This was a total closure figure which many rail managers and others believed should have been much higher.

Overall railway running costs doubled between 1913-1938, whilst charges both for passengers and freight rose by only 50-75 pc. Thus the LNER's passenger revenue and total profits declined by 35 and 50 per cent respectively between 1923-1933. Even by 1929, its passenger revenue had fallen 18 pc since 1923, which may explain its attitude to the SYJR passenger trains.

It is tempting to believe that, with the exception of Maltby whose location the Earl had chosen, the inconvenient siting of the stations at Dinnington and Tickhill - neither within 2 km of the centre - showed at the very least a disregard for future passengers' needs, if not a deliberate attempt to deter them. During construction a relatively slight re-alignment of the line, to the east at the latter two, and to the west at Maltby (with the Earl's agreement) could probably have halved these inconvenient distances, at least.

Even so, without a radically different approach, it is difficult to see how the SYJR could have ever run a consistently profitable service. The high proportion of miners living locally meant that, despite a daily absenteeism rate of 15 per cent nationally in the 1920s, this group would be unlikely to travel on weekdays. Another deterrent was the decline in miners' earnings which fell by a (UK) average of 50 pc between 1920 and 1923, and a further six pc by 1928. Meanwhile, agriculture slid back into depression after 1920, reducing farmers' incomes. Furthermore, the line served only one main centre of population, Doncaster, which had to compete with Rotherham and Sheffield for the attention of the people of the smaller places along the line. Only Tickhill with a population of less than 2,300 in 1931 was truly and solely within the orbit of Doncaster. The steady increase in trolley- and motor-bus services, cheaper, more frequent and more convenient, was the lingering death-blow to the service, whilst the motor-car had virtually wiped out first-class passengers by 1924.

Analysing the figures

The Committee justified the withdrawal by pointing to the bus service between Doncaster, Tickhill and Worksop of the East Midlands Motor Co., of which the LMS and LNER had recently become joint owners, and in which the latter's shareholding by 1938 was £120,000, amongst a road transport portfolio of £3m.

What the Committee didn't publicise was that, when passenger services closed, in the unusually profitable year of 1929, and with eight collieries (five, heavily) able to access the line, its net receipts from the SYJR totalled a little over £80,000, equal to almost £3m in 1999 prices.

Thus a loss of say £1,000 per annum on a 1922-type passenger timetable would have reduced this profit by scarcely more than one per cent. But the idea of a 'social' railway subsidised for the benefit of the passengers lay at least four decades ahead and certainly would never have entered the collective minds of the Committee although the Earl had pointed out that a profitable passenger service surely had never been anticipated.

During the 1930s the evening excursions and seaside trips continued so that each year several thousand passenger continued to be carried over the SYJR, including over the northern section *en route* to Bridlington. In the summer of 1935 an attempt was made to restart Saturday services from Maltby to Doncaster and Sheffield, but heavy losses ended this operation in 1937, which never appeared in *Bradshaw's Monthly Rail Guide*.

Passengers carried on the SYJR, 1929-1938

	1st class	*3rd class*	*Passenger revenue (£)*
1929	272	8,557	291
1930	-	8,956	160
1931	-	8,132	103
1932	-	6,935	110
1933	-	6,230	74
1934	-	9,918	176
1935	-	19,128	336
1936	-	15,086	193
1937	-	6,082	130
1938	-	8,246	314

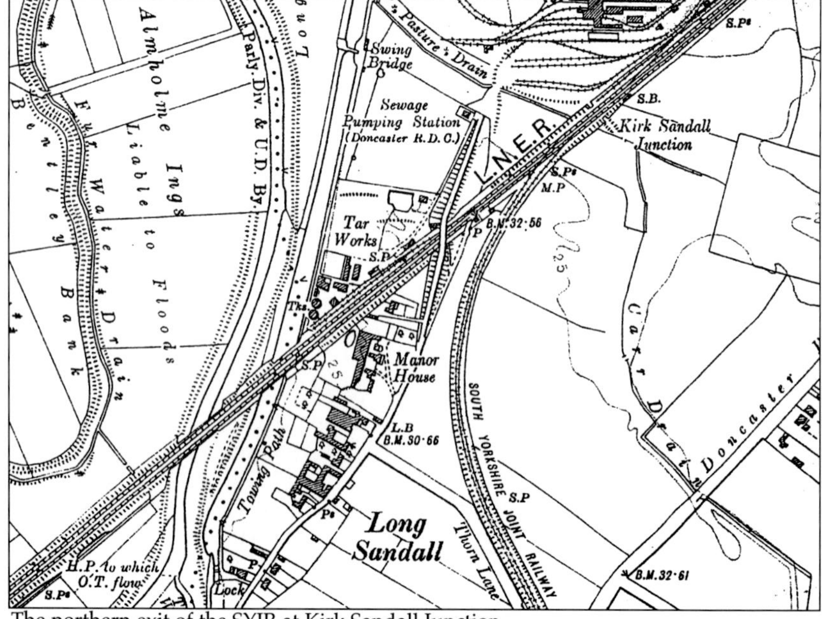

The northern exit of the SYJR at Kirk Sandall Junction.

Reproduced from the 6", 1931 Ordnance Survey Map

Chapter Nine

The SYJR and Coal Traffic, 1926-1939

The Great Depression

Between 1926 and 1939, the British coal industry suffered an intense and protracted depression unequalled by any other industry, to be followed by six years of war, during which all available coal was desperately needed. In 1920 with coal prices soaring, the labour force had peaked at an all-time record of nearly 1.25 million. Home demand was static around 200 m t, but following the two boom years of 1922-1923 and the revaluation of the pound against gold in 1925, exports went into a general decline.

The Humber had taken almost 14.5 m t of the last categories in 1913 (exports of 8.88 m t, coastwise of 2.6 m t, and 3 m t for merchant shipping and fishing vessels). By 1920, having totally lost revolutionary Russia, the premier 1913 market, the latter total had fallen by 83 pc, considerably reducing SYJR-hauled tonnages. Amongst the SYJR collieries, in 1920, coal shipments to the Humber from Dinnington were down to 55 k t, Maltby to 65 k t, Rossington to 18 k t and Yorkshire Main to 21 k t. After Humberside export increases to 9.3 m t in 1923 and 6.5 m t in 1929, shipments declined again to around 3-4 m t in the 1930s, with coastwise remaining at about one m t throughout the era. Consumption by merchant ships and fishing vessels added a further 2.5-3 m t pa. In summary, in the best year of 1923, almost 13.8 m t went by rail to the Humber, including that originating on the SYJR, whilst 10 years later the total was less than 7.5 m t.

Strike-prone

Coal was a highly labour-intensive industry facing a generally falling demand, especially from abroad, and in which average pithead selling prices after 1920 fell from £1.72½ (£1 14*s*. 6*d*.) p t to 65p (13*s*.) in 1928, recovering to only 70p (14*s*.) in 1936. Rather than seeking to increase productivity and find new markets, the coal-owners believed that only by wage reductions, longer hours, lay-offs, restricted output and further colliery closures could the industry remain profitable. The results were poisonous, creating great insecurity and resentment amongst the miners, who became convinced that only total nationalisation could solve the industry's problems.

Furthermore, work in the deep mines around Doncaster was hotter and harder and therefore more suited to younger miners. Many such young men were actively recruited by company agents to move to Doncaster (and the East Midlands generally) from the declining coalfields; Welshmen to Rossington and Scots and 'Geordies' to Maltby and many other areas. Despite World War I service in the army, many had then become unemployed, so they were angry and politically motivated and looking for trouble.

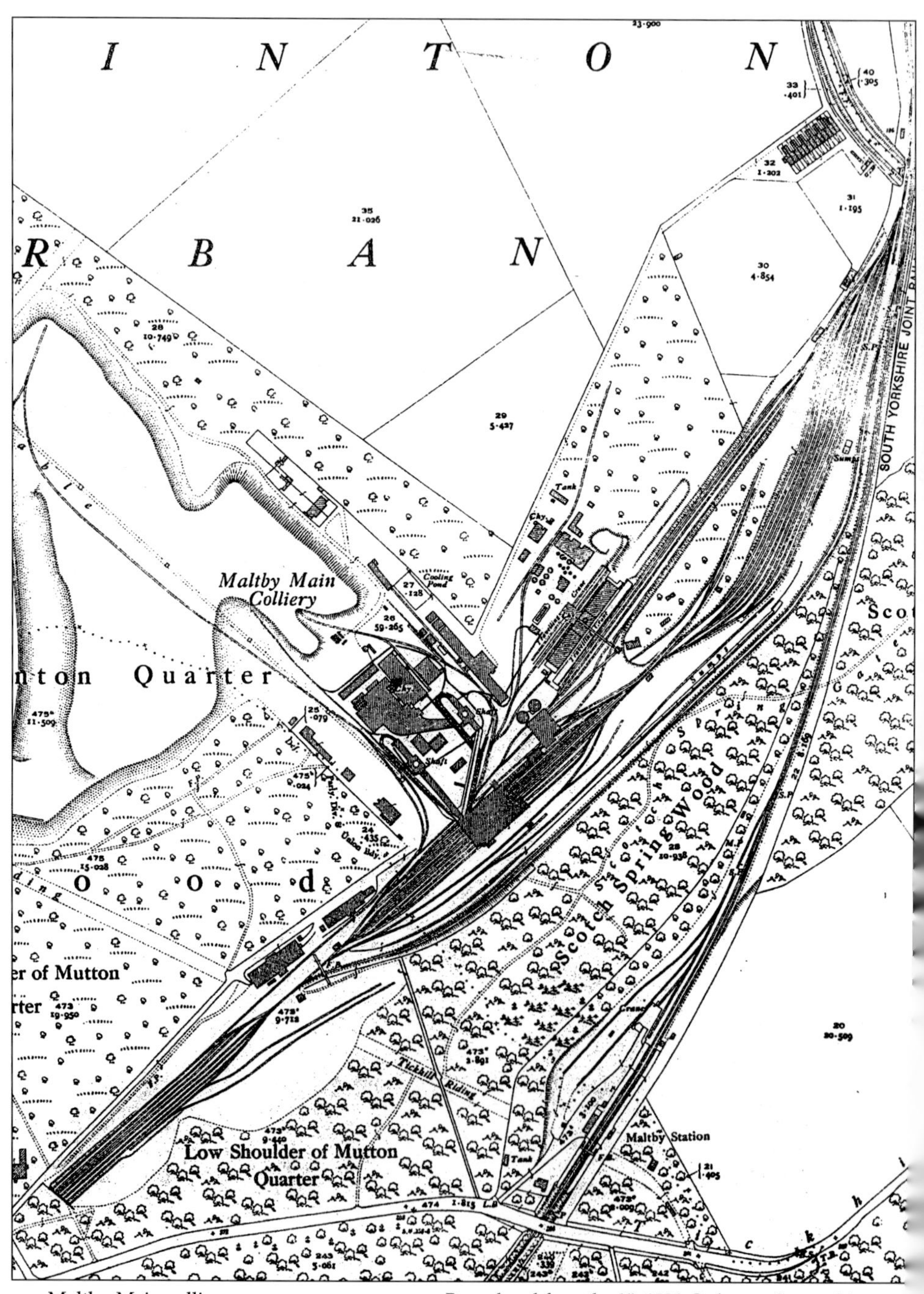

Maltby Main colliery. *Reproduced from the 6", 1929 Ordnance Survey Map*

Coal mining was unsurprisingly eight times more likely than any other industry to have serious disputes, shown most notably in the summer of 1926, which lost 146 million working days and closed the SYJR completely for five months, with the passenger service, as noted, remaining closed for 15 months.

Between 1927-1936, between 28 and 39 pc of all labour disputes were in the coal industry. From 1937 -1946 this percentage rose, but not steadily from 40 to 60 pc. The highly militant miners of the South Yorkshire (especially Doncaster) coalfield were always amongst the first to strike and the SYJR one of the very first lines to feel the impact of any prolonged action.

Furthermore, the fragmented state of ownership and depressed markets meant a reluctance to invest. Excluding the cost of new sinkings, capital investment in UK coal mines between the wars totalled about £107 m. Yet by reason that oms grew by only 14 pc between 1925 and 1936, compared with 118 pc in Dutch and 54 in Polish mines, this was clearly insufficient. The depressed state was shown also in average weekly earnings of coal miners in Yorkshire, which fell from 92p per shift (i.e. per day) in 1921 to 50p in 1928, rising to 63p in 1938, with an overall fall of 52 pc between 1920-1933.

The shift system could involve working theoretically from 6 am to 2 pm (for 51 pc of South Yorkshire miners) or 2 pm to 10 pm (31 pc) or 10 pm to 6 am (17 pc). However the actual time spent at the coal face, where half of all mine employees worked, was about 6¼ hours, by reason of the average 94 minutes time it took them in South Yorkshire to descend in the cage and then walk 1.77 km to their work-place at the coal-face.

SYJR-accessing collieries

Following the 1926 coal dispute, almost 17,700 workers were employed at the eight collieries accessing the SYJR, according to the *Colliery Yearbook and Coal Trades Directory* for 1928, which gave approximate annual production figures in some cases:

Dinnington	1,900 underground	520 surface	800,000 tons
Firbeck	1,431	206	500,000 tons (developing)
Harworth	776	174	
Markham Main	2,129	264	
Maltby	1,650	400	600,000 tons (developing)
Rossington	2,000	500	600,000 tons (developing)
Thurcroft	1,883	363	
Yorkshire Main	3,000	500	one million tons

In the high production year of 1929, the output of the SYJR's neighbouring colliery Silverwood reached the huge total 1.32 m t, unbeaten until 1992.

The result of falling demand was that, between 1914 and 1937, but mostly after 1926, more than half the UK's 3,000 (mostly small) collieries closed. Most closures were in the older fields such as South Wales, Scotland, Lancashire and Durham, but there were also some in West Yorkshire and in the Barnsley area of South Yorkshire. Inevitably these numerous closures also meant a huge decline in the UK mining work force - by almost 37 per cent between 1920-1935 - whilst the number of unemployed miners reached a record 39 per cent in 1932.

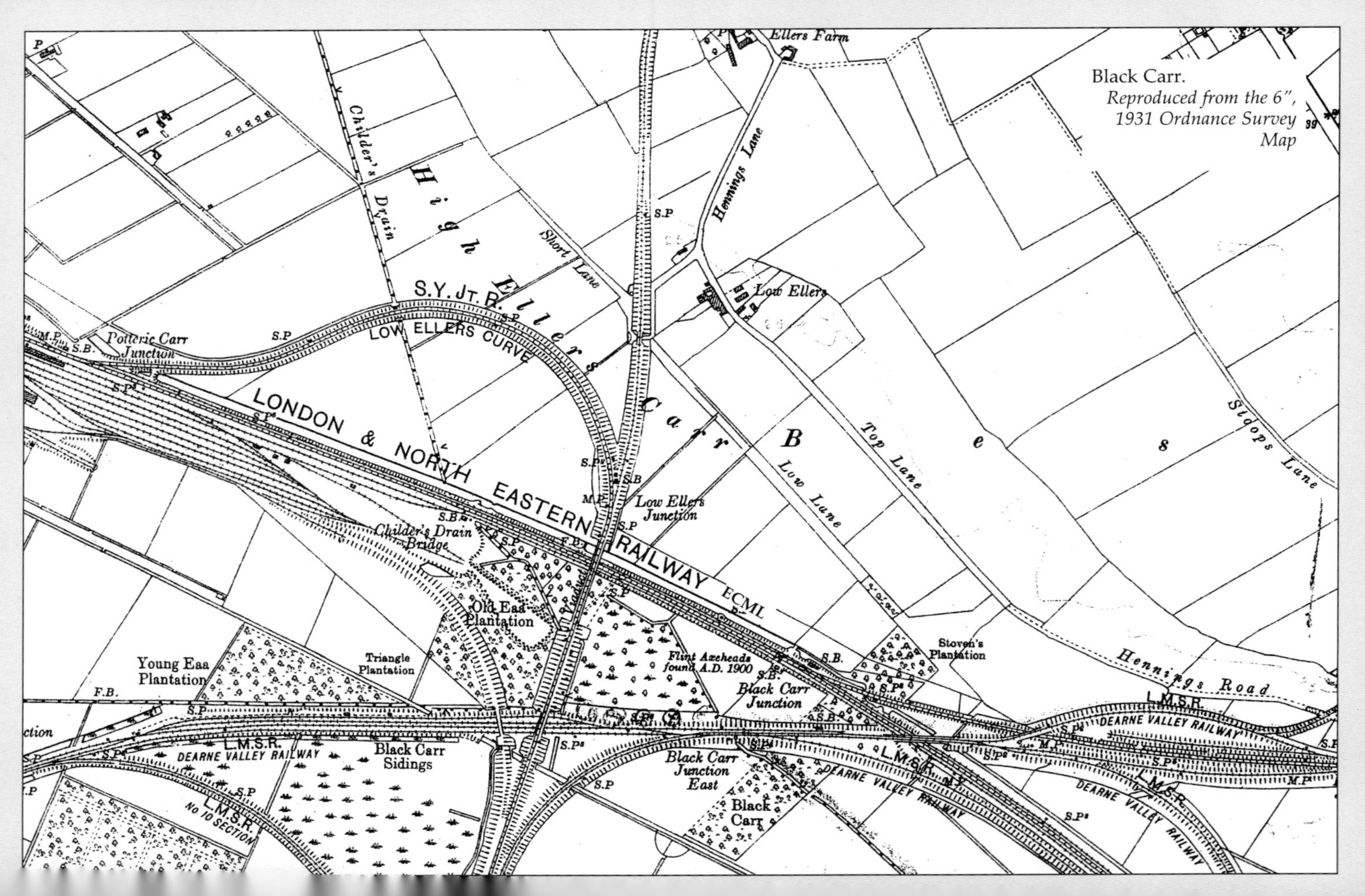

Black Carr.
Reproduced from the 6", 1931 Ordnance Survey Map

Maltby colliery about 1933. *NCB*

Dinnington colliery about 1934. *NCB*

Doncaster affected

By contrast, including those in the South and East of the county, and all those along and close to the SYJR, 29 new collieries opened in Yorkshire during the first quarter of the 20th century. However, in the troubled aftermath of the long dispute in 1926 and the world economic depression beginning in 1930, even Doncaster was affected and no new collieries were opened thereafter. Within a 13 km radius of the town, 16 collieries produced between 10 and 12 million tons annually and being new operations could produce coal at between 6p (1*s.* 2½*d.*) and 20p (4*s.*) per ton less than in older areas.

Although they were amongst the most efficient and productive in the country, providing unending train-loads for the SYJR through working the best seams, yet surprisingly little mechanisation had been introduced. In 1927, a total of only 1.66 m t of coal or 12 pc of output in South Yorkshire was machine-cut, compared with 53 pc in Scotland and 27 pc in West Yorkshire. However throughout Yorkshire this did rise to 56 per cent in 1938, still slightly below the national average. The number of (underground) mechanical conveyors in South Yorkshire collieries likewise rose from 1,200 to 8,000 between 1927-1939, moving out 82 pc of production.

By the latter date the new deep collieries, including those accessing the SYJR, were beginning to dominate the coalfield. They produced 50 per cent of all South Yorkshire output, of which 50 pc in turn was from the prized Barnsley seams and 22 pc, Parkgate. Eighty per cent of South Yorkshire miners in 1938 worked in large collieries (more than 1,000 employees).

Quotas and amalgamations

The various UK coal-owners (including the SYCOA) were given the opportunity to work in harmony rather than in competition and to rationalise production. This policy was legalised by the Mining Industry Act of 1926 and made compulsory by the second Labour government's Coal Mines Act of 1930, with control of sales coming in 1936. The 1930 Act gave the miners a 7½ hour day, imposed quotas and minimum prices and sought to encourage exports. Alternatively, this could all be seen as a crutch which supported industrial inefficiency.

The two most notable local examples of amalgamations were the interconnections between the Sheepbridge and Staveley Co's. and the establishment of the Central Collieries Commercial Association (CCCA also known as the 'Five Counties Scheme').

As a result of the former links, two great colliery groups were formed, involving six of the eight collieries which accessed the SYJR. The first in 1927, was a partial amalgamation, usually known as Denaby and Cadeby Amalgamated Collieries and capitalised at £5.9 m, but under a holding company, Yorkshire Amalgamated collieries (henceforth, YAC). It brought together Denaby and Cadeby, Dinnington, Maltby and Rossington collieries. The second group in 1937, Doncaster Amalgamated Collieries (henceforth, DAC) brought together Brodsworth, Bullcroft, Firbeck, Hickleton, Yorkshire Main and Markham Main collieries, in a £7.75 m merger. One advantage of such mergers was a more efficient and economic use of resources including the working of seams by connecting the galleries of adjacent collieries. DAC also set up an electrical 'ring main' amongst its collieries to supply current to each other and surplus energy to the Doncaster LNER 'Plant' works.

The Five Counties Scheme quota scheme immediately affected employment prospects in the area in the late 1920s and therefore indirectly the profitability of the SYJR. The coal owners of Derbyshire, Nottinghamshire, Leicestershire, Warwickshire and Yorkshire (of whom 60 were in South Yorkshire alone) and who controlled 90 out of 100 m t of the counties' production, had to agree upon a monthly quota for each colliery.

The combined Sheepbridge collieries had a quota of 1.629 m t in 1931, with various increases given until, in 1940, the system was scrapped. In 1937 the Five Counties allocation totalled almost 81.7 m t out of a UK output of 240 m t. The aim was to avoid producing loss-making and unsaleable coal, rather as internationally OPEC did with oil 35 years or more later. If a colliery reached its quota too soon, it was required to revert to a four- or even three-day week, and pay fines (15p - 3*s.* pt) on tonnage over the quota. For a variety of reasons it was not an efficient operation and acted against the consumers' interests. It also reduced the tonnages moved along the SYJR. Had there been a totally free market in coal, the SYJR's collieries would have produced more at the expense of the older coalfields, enhancing the profitability of the line.

In effect, in 1928-29 around 20-25 per cent of the 40,000 miners in the Doncaster area were working short-time because of quotas, although officially there was a shortage of labour. The situation became more serious in the deep depression years of 1932-1933 as demand fell and older men at Firbeck and Maltby were laid off. By 1938 the deep mines around Doncaster were estimated to be producing overall at only 60 per cent of capacity, contributing to the unemployment of more than 34,000 Yorkshire miners; some unemployed for many years, whilst more than 98,000 were still working. The Doncaster miners hated the quota scheme, (as no doubt did most SYJR employees) which stored up trouble for later.

Wages and strikes

Following a national ballot in 1935, in which Yorkshire miners voted by 82,733 to 4,169 to enforce a wages claim by strike action, an increase of 5p (1*s.*) per shift was secured. However, by reason of the quota restrictions, average earnings for all employees in the Yorkshire coal industry were by 1937, including allowances, less than £3 per week, for 252 shifts pa. The latter included the wages of boys, some as young as 14, who were employed as pit pony drivers. Low earnings of pit boys were one major reason why 95,000 Yorkshire miners struck for almost three weeks in July 1937, although by this date so-called lightning strikes to resolve grievances were becoming an unfortunate feature of the South Yorkshire coalfield - 57 at DAC and another 22 in 1938. Underground workers were of course paid more, earning in 1937 an average of £3.36 (£3 7*s.* 2½*d.*) per week (or £125 in 1999 prices) and 26p (5*s.* 2½*d.*) more a year later. This was about the same as an LNER signalman, itself no lightweight job, although as noted, easier on the SYJR.

Miners' transport at Maltby in 1930. *NCB*

Underground at Maltby. *John Goodchild Collection*

Danger underground

Mining remained a dangerous occupation, as the 1923 explosion at Maltby had shown. In 1931 at Barber Walker's Bentley colliery, just north of Doncaster, 45 men were killed in another explosion and during 1935-1936 at Yorkshire collieries, there were three more, killing 87 miners. In 1937 a total of 108 miners were killed in the county, whilst 25,600 were injured, requiring at least three days off work.

For the uninjured survivors, an increasing number of collieries were being provided with pithead baths. By the end of 1937 there were 29 in South Yorkshire, of which 11 also had canteens, whilst a further eight, all with canteens, were being constructed, providing total washing accommodation for almost 70,000 miners. Those at Maltby and Harworth were opened in 1926, Yorkshire Main 1930, Dinnington 1933, and Rossington and Markham Main in 1938.

Pithead baths could not wash miners' lungs and many thousands succumbed in later life to the disabling and untreatable disease, pneumoconiosis, which created severe breathing difficulties. It is brought about by prolonged inhalation of coal-dust particles less than 0.005 mm in diameter.

Doncaster pre-eminent

Changes in the market and in other coalfields meant that South Yorkshire increased in relative importance within the UK. In 1913, South Yorkshire had produced 9.6 pc of UK coal; by 1925, 12.7 pc; in 1935, 13.1 pc and by 1938, 13.4. Almost exactly half this output came from collieries producing less than 250,000 t pa, whilst only nine, all around Doncaster, were able to produce more than one m t pa.

Also indicative of Doncaster's importance as the centre of Yorkshire coal-mining activity was that, by 1927 three specialist companies which carried out boring, shaft sinking, freezing, cementation and tunnelling had established offices in the town. These were Blandford and Gee, the Belgian Foraky Co. and the Francois Cementation Co. There was also the Mining and General Stores Co. which supplied all manner of equipment and stores for the industry.

Boosted by the development of new deep collieries, production in South Yorkshire peaked at 33.5 m t in 1929, 21 pc higher than in 1913. The output in all Yorkshire, which had exceeded 43 m t by 1913, was more than 46 m t in both 1923 and 1924. Between 1922 and 1942, it fell below 40 m t only in 1926 and during the depression years of 1932-1934. Employment in all Yorkshire's mines reached peaks in 1913 (161,000), 1923 (187,400), pre-strike 1926 (193,700) and 1929 (172,700).

South Yorkshire Coalfield

	Employment	*No. of collieries*	*Production (m. tons)*
1913	96,572	184	27.7
1927	124,296		30.8
1929	119,157		33.5
1933	99,741		27.2
1938	98,383	121	30.5

The Yorkshire Main aerial ropeway in 1930. *John Goodchild Collection*

Firbeck colliery yard and engine shed. *Worksop Library*

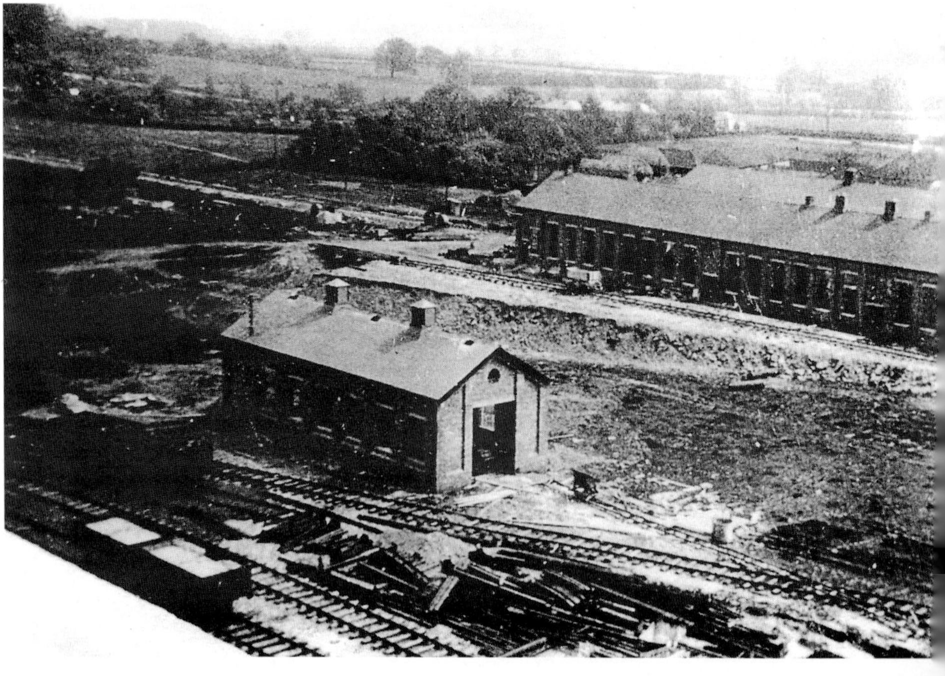

Thus over a period of 25 years (whilst in the later part its production was being deliberately restricted), South Yorkshire increased both its output and workforce, albeit with fewer collieries, whilst UK output declined by 21 pc and the total workforce by 30 pc. OMS in 1938 was 1.28 t in South Yorkshire, 11 pc above the UK average.

This enhanced performance of the South Yorkshire coalfield was almost entirely the result of the new deep collieries, such as those accessing the SYJR and of which Maltby and Yorkshire Main were the highest producers. However, with total inclusive operating costs of 70p (14*s*.) p t, profitability of only 6p (1*s*. 2½*d*.) p t (equal to £2.30 in 1999 prices) placed Yorkshire slightly below the UK average of 7p (1*s*. 5*d*.) for each of the 227 m t produced in 1938. Despite complaints of high rail freight charges, YAC, including Dinnington, Maltby and Rossington, made an overall profit of £245,600 (or £9 m in 1999 prices) in 1938-1939.

By contrast, Harworth whose 2,285 miners in 1935 produced 632,000 t and provided fuel for the *Flying Scotsman* locomotive, was wracked by a county inter-union dispute in 1936-1937, with the workforce declining to 1,319 and output to 363,000 t.

SYJR colliery production figures (,000 t-rounded down)

	1936	*1937*	*1938*	*1939*	*1940*
Dinnington	550	709	622	588	589
Firbeck	587	425	530	594	574
Maltby	1,005	1,052	999	1,012	935
Markham Main	728	732	718	781	919
Yorkshire Main	923	939	974	1,140	n/a

UK average colliery output in 1937 was 117,000 t.

SYJR traffic in the 1930s

By reason that it served only deep, productive collieries, the SYJR remained a very busy and profitable line, particularly following the large extra increments of production at Markham Main, Harworth and Firbeck from the mid-late 1920s. Despite only 1.3 m t being raised in all Yorkshire during the actual months of the 1926 coal dispute, one m t originated during that year on the SYJR, at a charge of £26,472 and thereafter the net profits of the line rose rapidly between 1927-1929 from £56 to £63 and £81 thousand pounds, the last equal to £3m in 1999 prices.

By 1928 and 1929, the originating tonnages on the SYJR had risen to almost 2.5 m t and 2.95 m t respectively, with the weekly record then standing at almost 70 k t, created during the harsh winter of the latter year. Assuming it was nearly all moved, this record output would have required about 20 trains per day (on a 6-day week). By October 1930, originating tonnage was around 60,000 pw or 2.8 m t for the year.

During the remainder of the inter-war period, from along its 48 km, there originated, including during the worst depression years of 1932-33, never less than 2.26 m t. The decline in SYJR coal traffic between 1929-1933 was 22 pc, but by 1937 it had regained 16 pc of this loss. Importantly, the SYJR increased its share of originating coal freight on Britain's railways from 0.44 pc in 1913 to 1.3 pc in 1929, maintaining the latter through 1938.

The annual gross earnings of the SYJR from 1929-1938 mostly exceeded £100,000 (equal in 1999 prices to about £3.8m or £79,000 for *each* of the 48 km of the line). This last figure was more than twice the earnings per km for coal trains on the national rail network. Each ton cost 20p (4s.) in freight charges, throughout this period, of which the SYJR, as noted received 5p (1s.), with the balance going to the two 'parents'.

SYJR coal traffic, 1929-1938

	M T originating	*Gross earnings (,000 t)* £	*Net receipts (,000 t)** £
1929	2.94	119	81
1930	2.80	119	77
1931	2.48	110	73
1932	2.26	99	63
1933	2.29	100	66
1934	2.41	102	67
1935	2.27	105	70
1936	2.61	105	81
1937	2.66	112	72
1938	2.57	120	77

During the late 1930s, the SYJR was open to traffic on weekdays for 16 hours - from 6.00 am to 10.00 pm. A total of about 36 trains (full and empty) per day ran along its lines, taking total annual coal exports of about 1.4 m t to Grimsby, Goole, Hull and Immingham, the last being Britain's largest facility, having a capacity of 18,000 tons per day. Coking fuel for the steelworks at Frodingham, near Scunthorpe, and at Staveley was also dispatched. Domestic coal in either direction went onto the DVR to Crofton Junction and beyond, or southwards via Worksop and Kirkby.

Administrative changes

The growth of coal movements from the collieries along the line after the end of the coal dispute in 1926 and the opening of Markham Main, Harworth and Firbeck in the mid-1920s meant more signalmen were required. It also put an increasing burden on line's administrative staff and so in July 1929 the SYJR moved its offices from Bank Chambers to a larger set at Lancaster House, in West Laithgate, Doncaster, taking on an extra clerk. The SYJR offices remained there until Nationalisation. In the October 1930 *LNER Magazine*, R.T. Munns noted that 'the functions of this office are naturally rather varied' and that 'the SY(JR) is staffed for traffic purposes by three stationmasters, four clerks, 28 signalmen, nine shunters, six porters and four number-takers, supervised by Mr W. Briggs, with a staff of six'.

* Rounded up.

This was a grand total of 61, six more than in 1914.

Aware of the growing importance of the South Yorkshire coalfield and particularly of the Doncaster area which had displaced Barnsley as its centre, the LNER established its main Minerals' Manager's office in the town in 1928. By reason that they shared several joint lines, the LMS and LNER also established in 1930 a committee to oversee these, including the SYJR.

Overall, however, by reason that the rest of its network was very much less profitable per km than the SYJR in generating traffic, the LNER was shedding staff; of its 202,000 employees in 1923, of whom only 7,000 were women, 12,000 went between 1923-1929 and a further 24,000 by 1933, including many by outright dismissal, as the economic depression deepened. This reduced its total wages bill from £36 m to less than £28 m, between 1923-1933.

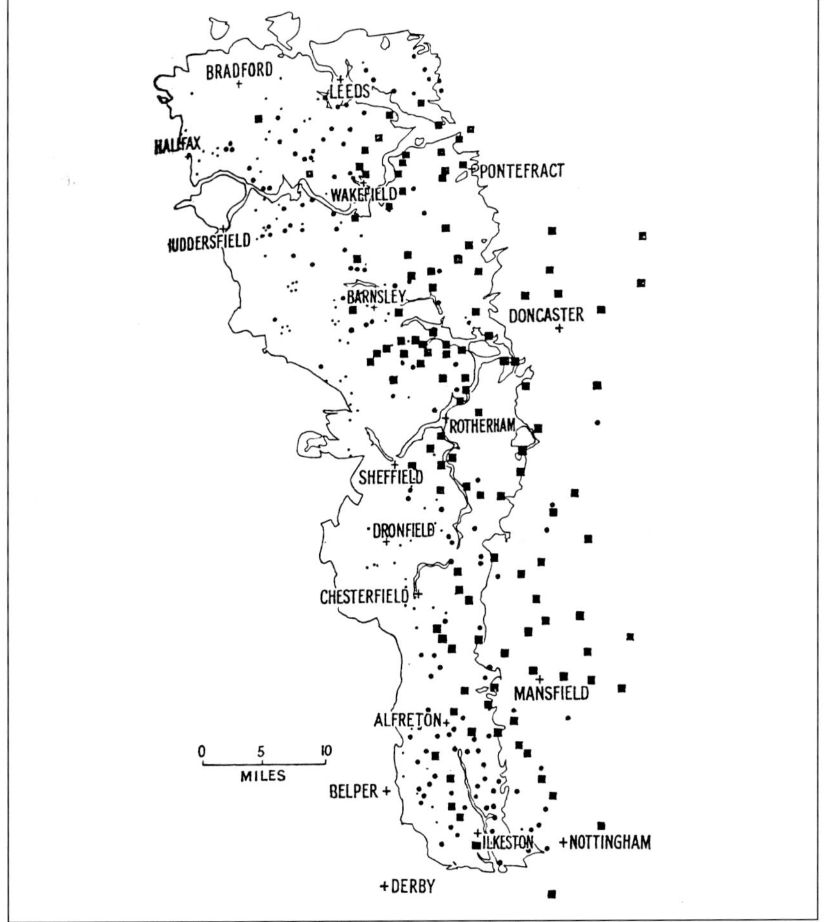

Map of the coalfield in the 1930s (collieries indicated by dots relative to size of workforce).

Chapter Ten

The SYJR at War II: 1939-1945

Coal trade, 1939

The outbreak of war in September 1939 did not radically change the situation in the UK coal industry, especially the abrasive industrial relations in South Yorkshire/SYJR collieries. With the loss of some export markets, which totalled 36 m t in 1939, more UK coal was released onto the home market, supplemented that year by an increased output reaching 231 m t.

However, it was noted as early as October 1939 that following, but not a result of, a call by the Secretary of Mines for 270 m t of production in the next 12 months, South Yorkshire collieries 'were getting back to full-time working'. Furthermore with the heavy loss of miners into the forces and other work, extra labour was being required at some places.

As the war became a struggle for national survival, two industries - the armed forces (including armament manufacturing) and agriculture - became paramount. All others, like coal and rail, were made either subservient to the needs of arms and agriculture or were, like car factories, turned over to the war effort. Thus by 1943, only three per cent of UK coal was exported, whilst 24 pc each went to public utilities, and to coking and gas and around 17 pc each to domestic consumers, to industry and to the railways. In effect therefore, almost all coal production was used and needed for the war effort, directly or indirectly, with e.g., 70 tons of coal being needed to make one tank.

The railway situation

The railways soon came under pressure. Under government direction from the start, i.e. The Railway Executive Committee (REC) - already an advisory body since September 1938 - took over administration a year later. Britain then had more than 32,328 km of railways, 21,600 locomotives (LNER, 6,491), 43,000 passenger carriages (LNER, 12,268), 650,000 freight wagons (LNER, 256,000) and nearly the same number of the last, privately owned, such as the 3,800 of the Sheepbridge Co. Overall in 1939, this gave the system a potential capacity considerably greater than its current traffic and it was therefore able to expand considerably to meet the wartime demands made upon it.

During the previous 15 years the rail companies had invested (gross) more than £280 million in the network. Allowing for depreciation and the backlog of World War I maintenance, this was about £160 m less than was required, so in terms of renewals, the railways were barely adequate for the heavy task ahead. The SYJR, especially its south-east 'branches' was by UK standards a 'new' railway and less in need of anything other than routine maintenance.

The task of the railways, whose own demand for coal was rising, was threefold. First to move freight, including coal, raw materials and foodstuffs to where they were needed. Coal was by far the heaviest and bulkiest commodity, but declining from 65 pc of total freight in 1938 to 55 pc in 1943. Second, rail had to move military units and their equipment as required, with the LNER alone moving 8,000 troop trains and 2,000 military freights between September 1939 and June 1940. Third with much reduced services, to move many more passengers.

The main task of the SYJR was first to move coal from its originating collieries and to provide pathways for any other traffic, such as coal convoys and military 'specials' which needed to use it. Difficulties in meeting all the above tasks soon arose.

Wagons and weather

The first fuel and rail crisis of the war was weather-induced. It began with sharp falls in temperatures in December 1939, followed late in January 1940 by widespread and very heavy snowfalls, causing very serious hold-ups and congestion on both roads and railways. More than 2,500 km of lines were blocked with 300 snow-ploughs in action, 59 on the ECML alone. The SYJR and its colliery sidings were blocked, which in turn forced cut-backs in coal production and lost DAC 30,000 tons per week in February. The whole situation was exacerbated also by staff illness and, in early February, by floods and landslides.

At the end of February, the railways had to organise several special weekends of extra trains to clear the backlog, which included moving 7,000 loaded 12 ton wagons in 140 trains out of the Doncaster area, including along the SYJR. The REC began to organise the weekly dispatch southwards of more than 140 coal trains of which 100 were sent by the LNER, divided between ECML (75) and the GNR & GER Jt line (25). By early March a total of one million loaded wagons (10 m t) had been dispatched south by the LNER and the LMS.

Despite the savings made by the pooling of all private and rail company wagons in September 1939, the 'wagons and weather crisis' cost more than 4.75 m t lost production in 1940 in the UK, although other factors increased this loss to almost 21 m t. These included various lightning strikes by 20,000 miners in February and March, including a one week dispute involving Markham Main's 2,300 men.

Coal in decline

The UK coal production increase to 231 m t during 1939 was not maintained, although it reached 224 m t in 1940, of which Yorkshire's output of 45 m t was the highest since 1929. The latter figure was helped by Markham Main's 919,000 t, a 17.7 pc rise over 1939, whilst Maltby, which had averaged more then one m t pa in 1936-1939 slipped back to 935,774 in 1940. From 1941, the UK fuel situation became dire as coal production fell year-by-year to only 184 m t in 1945.

As early as September 1941, the coal crisis became one of low production, not wagon shortages. One important reason for this, although not as serious as in 1914-18, was a declining workforce, which in 1941 stood at 109,000 in South

Yorkshire (31 pc of whom were in the concealed coalfield). Many thousands of young miners left in the first months to join the armed forces, including 130 Territorial Army members at Dinnington colliery.

Many miners also went to work in munitions in the new Royal Ordnance Factories (ROF), often built in the coalfields such as one at Maltby, next to the SYJR. Some Maltby miners 'moonlighted' there, alongside wives and daughters, instead of doing a colliery shift. Wages in ROF were higher and the work was less arduous, compared especially to that in small, declining collieries in the older coalfields. Some 800 of the latter producing less than 5 m t pa worked difficult seams which spread resentment amongst the now older miners.

This work and an agreement to suspend the fatal accident agreement, such as at DAC, led to a rise in serious accident rates. HM Inspector of Mines for Yorkshire noted in 1940 alone there had been a 32 pc rise in fatal accidents, whilst in the UK there were 937 fatalities (90 pc underground). Although by 1945 this number had declined to 553, in 1942 there were still 114 miners killed in South Yorkshire collieries and 319 seriously injured.

Government action

The serious fuel crisis led to the establishment in 1940 of the Yorkshire Joint Productional Coal Committee, (YJPCC), on which sat both miners and coal owners. It quickly identified two serious problems; first was absenteeism (rising from 6.4 pc in 1938 to 11.2 p c in 1942). Under the Essential Work Order (EWO), this could and did lead to fines or even jail sentences, as could a refusal to work underground. Second was lightning, unofficial strikes for which Doncaster was, as noted, becoming particularly notorious. Both problems remained serious throughout and long after the war.

By 1941, the South Yorkshire coalfield was short of 11,000 miners. Around the SYJR, Dinnington was 250 short and Firbeck, 100, whilst Maltby had 400 fewer than in 1939, Yorkshire Main, 127 and Thurcroft, 200. Surprisingly , Markham Main had 40 miners *more,* which partly explained its increased production (1939-1941) of 2,500 t pw.

Under emergency legislation, the Ministry of Labour banned the recruitment of miners into the armed forces and sent some 30,000 ex-miners back to the mines. In August 1942, YMA secretary, W.E. Jones, was given leave of absence to become Director of Labour for the Yorkshire coalfield, principally to reduce unofficial strikes and long weekend absenteeism, but he met with little success.

Absenteeism, Yorkshire's Regional Coal Controller told miners, was reducing output from deep mines by 8,000 t pw each. Churchill himself addressed a special miners' conference in London seeking co-operation, but in vain. No more effective was a visit to the Doncaster coalfield by King George V1 and Queen Elizabeth in February 1944. Absenteeism rose to an average 16.3 pc in 1945, with Yorkshire face-workers at 23.8 pc third highest in the national rankings. The SYCOA publicised such figures widely.

In June 1942, the Ministry of Fuel and Power was established to secure increased coal production, targeted at 234 m t pa. It took over operational control (but not financial control or ownership) of all coal mines, almost coinciding with the taking over of all coal seams by the Coal Commission (Coal Act 1938). For this the coal owners received £66.45 m compensation of which £10.3m went to Yorkshire.

By August 1943 the severe fuel shortage led to one in ten young men at 18, unless chosen for aircrew or submarines, being selected by ballot to work as miners. Known as 'Bevin boys' after the Minister of Labour, Ernest Bevin, 22,000 were chosen by 1945. Most were reluctant and many ill-disciplined, with 500 refusing to comply and 143 being imprisoned. Bevin boys were paid £2.20 (£2 4*s*.) per week, but after a strike by 150 at Doncaster in January 1944, this was increased to £3 pw with rises at 19 and 20 reaching £3.50 (£3 10*s*.).

Harworth employed these young recruits, as well as some Belgian miners, but as in all SYJR collieries, the workforce was overwhelmingly local men who either walked or cycled to work. Of the 2,200 miners at Maltby in 1941, 1,900 lived in the town, 120 at Tickhill and 40 at Braithwell, but many went to work on the Maltby Miners' Transport Co. which ran its own buses.

Wage rises

Wage and cost of living increases were also awarded to retain, recruit and stimulate miners, beginning with 4p (10*d*.) per shift in 1939 and followed up to 1st July, 1941 by five more plus an attendance bonus, a grand total of 15p (3*s*.) (equal to a £25 pw rise in 1999 prices, assuming five shifts per week). From 1942 a guaranteed minimum of £4.15 (£4 3*s*.) per week for underground workers was introduced, but by then aircraft factory workers could earn £6. Thus by 1943, whilst all mine workers earned an average of £5.12½ (£5 2*s*. 6*d*.) per week, they were still only 59th in the earnings league table of 100 jobs. The underground minimum was raised to £5 early in 1944, enabling South Yorkshire underground workers to earn £1.25 (£1 5*s*.) per shift (equal to £30 in 1999 prices), but the Government refused to increase piece rates for skilled men.

1944 coal strike

Unsurprisingly, further industrial unrest in the coalfields followed, including a strike - which was technically illegal - first by 15,500 men in February and then by 90,000 Yorkshire miners, from 16th March. This included all 13 collieries close to Doncaster, which employed a total of 30,000 men and naturally included those on the SYJR, but excluding Harworth and Firbeck. UK production lost two m t in the first quarter of 1944, with much of this from South Yorkshire and more than twice the losses of each of 1942 and 1943.

Both Ernest Bevin and the local (Doncaster) Communist party mistakenly blamed 'Trotskyists' and urged the miners to go back. Rossington men returned before the Easter holidays and the remainder immediately afterwards on 11th April, but only after the Government stepped in with more money and miners went onto the highest occupational minimum wage. By August 1944, almost 700 stoppages involving more than 450,000 miners had lost almost 2.2 m days work.

Daisy worked at Firbeck colliery from 1923 to closure and demolition in 1968. *Chris Booth*

Right: A Hunslet 50 hp passenger locomotive at Bentley colliery. *LAMA*

Left: A Hunslet 2 hp locomotive a Rossington collier in August 1939. *LAM*

Overall, according to Yorkshire's future Labour Prime Minister, Harold Wilson a state of 'guerilla warfare' existed in some collieries between the workers and management. Nigel Clark blames locally poor relations between the miners and MFGB/NUM officials. He noted that following the introduction of national pay scales, the MFGB became the National Union of Mineworkers on 1st January, 1945 after pithead ballots. Forty pc of Yorkshire miners *abstained*, a negative reflection of how miners viewed their union's officials.

Mechanisation

The Ministry of Fuel and Power meanwhile was also deliberately encouraging increased mechanisation in high output areas, particularly the whole productive East Midlands coalfield, including SYJR collieries. It even arranged for 20 mine managers to go to the USA for training and in December 1943 it established a training centre for mines mechanisation in Sheffield. An advanced course was established at Sheffield University which since 1906 had awarded Diplomas in Mining and Bachelor of Engineering (Mining) degrees.

However, the small Leicestershire field was much the most successful with annual output rising from 323 t per worker in 1938 to 467 t in 1943. Yorkshire's absolute production total actually declined by almost 10 m t between 1940-1945, but still increased its relative share of UK production to almost 21 pc in 1945.

Mechanisation helped also to increase South Yorkshire's share of UK output as the percentage of its machine-cut coal, using both compressed air and electricity, rose from 56 per cent in 1938 to 77 pc (or 20 m t) in 1945. By this date also some 86 pc of coal output was also being power-conveyed to the shaft. Amongst SYJR collieries, Dinnington had installed power conveyors in 1931 and achieved 85 pc machine cut by 1940. In 1941 Firbeck was described in a detailed official inspection as 'modern and fully mechanised' but despite very good management it had 'considerable mining difficulties . . . unpromising seams . . . removed by washouts . . . 20 m rising faults . . . maintaining output . . . very difficult', all of which had plagued output and development since its opening. Also by 1941 at Yorkshire Main machines cut 56 pc of production but it was a deep, gassy mine with severe faults and temperatures as high as 36°C (96°F). The former figure was twice the percentage machine-cut at Markham Main, which also had problems with gas, faults and water ingress. Thurcroft's 652 face-workers dug out and loaded by hand 1,656 t pd, but machine cutting was introduced on the new Parkgate seam in mid-1942, despite its very high temperatures and severe faults. Similarly, Maltby, with no long-term development plans in 1941, also dug out and loaded by hand its daily production of 3,427 t. By 1944, however, at Maltby, new lower and level galleries were being excavated, so that diesel locomotives could be used to pull underground trains. This was particularly important since power haulage could increase by 10-fold the weight of each load conveyed. In 1939 the first diesel locomotive engines had been approved for use in coal mines. Improved models appeared in 1941 and 1945. Rossington was one of the very first to operate these. Various American mining machines were also obtained under 'Lend-Lease' and by the summer of 1944 some 228 had been received, but only 84 were installed and working nationally, including some at DAC. Although by 1942 some power loading units and pneumatic stowing machines (roof supports) were being installed in SYJR collieries, implementation was slow, with only 0.6 pc (145,585 t) of South Yorkshire production being power-loaded in 1945.

Unsurprisingly therefore, one result of mechanisation was that almost 140 UK mines ceased to use pit ponies between 1938 and 1945 and the total number employed declined from 32,000 to 23,000. In 1941, Dinnington still had 49 ponies, Maltby 25, and Yorkshire Main 28. The number of under-16 boys underground who cared for the ponies fell in the same period by 57 pc, to less than 12,000 nationally by 1945. This was partly the result of low wages and the opportunity to earn more elsewhere, but also because of a fall in the birth-rate in mining areas after 1926.

By the end of the war, surprisingly in view of the 'certainty' of nationalisation, DAC carried out a very thorough review of technical reorganisation. It announced a programme of increased mechanisation and electrification, new roadways, and the use of (underground) locomotives to haul convoys of tubs each containing 2.5 tons of coal or of fast wire-rope haulage where locomotives could not be used. Total capital investment was estimated at £2.2 m (about £48 m in 1999 prices), of which about £300,000 would be spent at each of its three SYJR collieries. This would reduce costs variously by 17-24p (3*s*. 5*d*.-4*s*. 10*d*.)per ton and increase daily production by 450 t at Firbeck, 775 t at Yorkshire Main and 820 t at Markham Main. All of this was good news for SYJR revenues.

Open-cast mining

Meanwhile as an emergency measure, the Government began to encourage open-cast mining which by 1947 totalled more than 34 m t, including 10 m t from Yorkshire. Only 15 kms west of the SYJR at Maltby, lay the best UK site, the exceptional 1,600 ha Barrow-Wentworth seams of Barnsley coal where production began in January 1943. Opencast coal was retrieved from the close to the surface by drag-line excavators and then loaded directly into trucks at the rate of 100 t ph. These took it to a local colliery (not Maltby) for screening, preparation and dispatch by rail haulage, so the SYJR serving only deep collieries played no part in this work.

South Yorkshire's performance

By 1945, there were in operation some 121 collieries in South Yorkshire. They employed a total labour force of almost 95,000 (79 pc underground), of whom 12,000 worked in the mines of DAC and 16,000 of YAC. Six of these two combine's collieries, employing a total of about 15,000 miners, accessed the SYJR. Despite a total wartime decline in output from almost 32.27 m t in 1940 and 28.9 in 1942, South Yorkshire still produced 25.2 m t or 14.46 pc of the 1945 UK total. Output per man year (OPMY) was down to 265 t in 1945 (still 13 pc above the UK average), compared with a peak of 331 t in 1940. By contrast, Harworth recovering from the 1936 union strife, with more miners and mechanisation, increased its face oms from 3.1 t in 1940 to 3.8 in 1944, producing a total of 563,000 t in 1946.

By reason of shortages and inflation, the selling price of UK coal at the pithead had risen in 1944 by 90 pc above the 1938 price of 84p (16*s*. 9½*d*.) to £1.60 (£1 12*s*.) per ton. A year later in South Yorkshire it had risen to £1.75 (£1 15*s*.). Wages had risen by 80 pc between 1938-1944, whilst oms was down by almost 10 pc. Thus, even with a subsidy, DAC made a profit of less than 5p (1*s*.) per ton in 1944 (or £1.25 in 1999 prices).

Of South Yorkshire's 25.2 m t output in 1945, almost 5 m t went to gasworks, 5.8 to coke ovens, 3.56 for household use and 3.63 each to industry and the railways. Surprisingly, by reason of future sales trends, only 1.72 m t was going to generate electricity. A further 3.45 m t was consumed by the collieries, the miners and by other customers. Meanwhile, the output of Barnsley seams which in Yorkshire in 1938 was 17.4 m t had declined to 42 pc of total output, with one forecaster in 1943 predicting total exhaustion in 30-50 years, the lower figure being exactly right for Silverwood, Thurcroft, Maltby and Dinnington. By 1973 it had declined to 6.7 m t for all Yorkshire; this indicated that more miners would have to work deeper and hotter seams within a few years.

Railways under stress

Paradoxically, despite the wartime declines both in coal production and in the coal and coke traffic originating on the LNER, the latter falling from 74-63 m t between 1938 and 1944, the net ton-miles of UK coal trains actually increased from 8.3 bn to almost 9.3 bn in those same years. This was the result of an increase by 30 pc in the average length (from 73 km to 96 km) of overall coal freight journeys. By 1945, 73 pc (or 106 m t) of all saleable UK coal produced was moved exclusively by rail. These wartime increases were due partly also to the more efficient organisation of block trains running from collieries to distribution centres, with wagons arranged in strict order to avoid unnecessary shunting. Overall, UK rail freight traffic rose by nearly 50 pc between 1938-1944.

To make the task of the railways even more difficult, passenger traffic also greatly increased - by 68 pc in these six years, each train carrying twice as many passengers. This was the result of reduced services, of urban evacuations and of millions having to work away from home in both military and civil occupations. To undertake all these extra duties Britain's hard-worked railway locomotives were by 1944 burning a total of 15.2 m t, or 18 pc more coal than in 1939, much of it of inferior quality. Such were the problems of coal supply to locomotives that the REC set up a special committee in 1942 to try to deal with it.

Coal convoy trains

The threat of submarines also made the railways' situation increasingly difficult through the decline in coast-wise coal traffic. Rising from 7.2 m t in

Aerial view of Harworth colliery in 1946.
John Goodchild Collection

1923 to 14.6 in 1938, a large percentage of coal traffic had been moved by coastal shipping from the Tyne, Wear and Humber ports (SYJR output) to the Thames, whilst rail movements had fallen by 30 pc. By reason of both the takeover of ports by the Royal Navy and the threat of enemy action, which eventually sank 11 LNER-owned ships of various types, coal shipments from the three main Humber ports declined from 5 m t in 1938 to less than 1.5 m t by 1943.

To replace this lost coastal traffic and some previously road-borne coal, 7,757 special coal trains, commencing on 29th February, were run in 1940 from all the Scottish, Northern and Midland coalfields. This included the SYJR collieries, whose trains now began to use the southern exit much more. The number of these specials increased to 10,034 trains in 1941 but fell to 8,345 in 1942, during which years further extreme weather conditions struck. By the end of 1944, their total number had reached 41,500, an average of 23 per day every day for almost five years.

However, by reason of both enemy air action and illegible labelling on wagons, many convoy trains could be and were legally diverted (by an Order in Council of October 1940) from their intended destinations, without compensation and causing all manner of administrative problems. To move these specials, every available line was used, with pathways being created mainly by cancelling passenger trains. It has not been possible to discover how many convoy trains were directed southwards down the SYJR.

The historian (Crump) of the LNER at war, however, described the local situation at Doncaster as 'a nightmare to keep engines and crews balanced', not helped by the LNER's Doncaster district office moving 13 km south down the ECML to Bawtry where it remained for several months after the end of the war. By February 1941, however, the whole UK network was operating officially as one unified system.

Railway degradation

The wartime demands of 1939-1945 upon the rail system were exceptional and further depleted seriously the condition of the system, with £30 m worth of war damage and a £150m shortfall in maintenance and renewals (equal to about £4.6 bn in 1999). Severe shortages of skilled labour and materials reduced the number of new locomotives built during the war to less than 1,300, of which the Doncaster 'Plant' produced 50 of the LMS Stanier-type 2-8-0 after 1941. The 'Plant' also continued a reduced level of maintenance work during the war on about 1,200 locomotives.

Whilst LNER locomotives had become 260 pc more reliable between 1923 and 1938, as measured by the decrease of breakdowns, by 1946 this reliability measure had fallen by 54 pc, to below 1929 levels. This clearly indicated both overuse and under-maintenance. Thus at the end of 1943, some 3,100 locomotives were 'off the road', a situation which must have affected SYJR operations from time to time. So also must the almost 100,000 wagons which were standing unrepaired at the end of 1944, including long lines on the northern reaches of the SYJR's neighbouring line, the ex-GCR & H&BR Jt.

A Markham Main private owner wagon at Berkhampstead on 11th May, 1940. *H.C. Casserley*

A Maltby wagon at Berkhampstead 13th May, 1948. *H.C. Casserley*

A private owner wagon from Firbeck Main is seen in the station yard at Berkhampstead on 5th October, 1947. *H.C. Casserley*

A Firbeck Main wagon is seen at Stafford on 7th September, 1951. *H.C. Casserley*

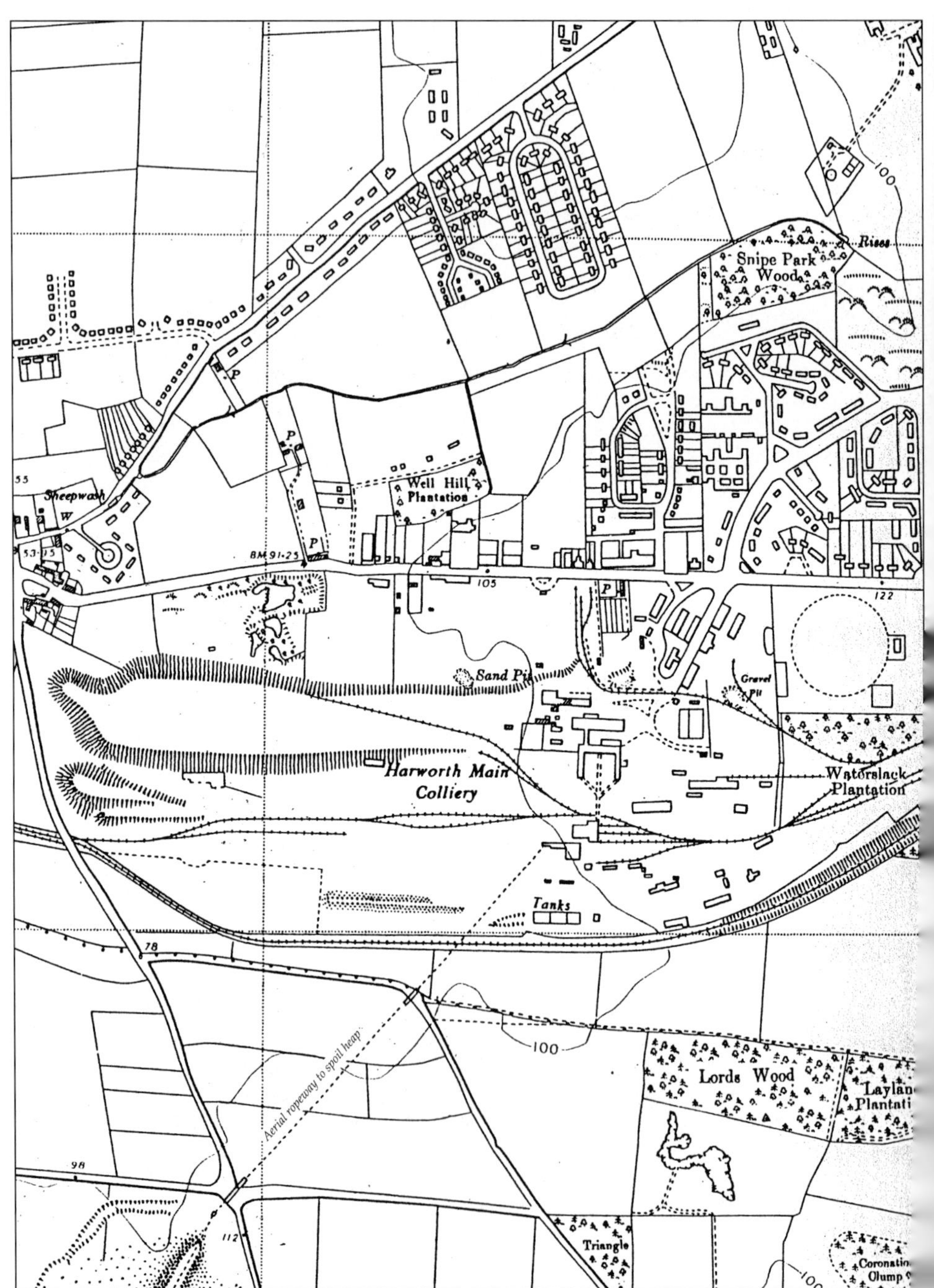

Harworth colliery. *Reproduced from the 6″, 1948 Ordnance Survey Map*

Despite the overwhelming importance of maintaining locomotives efficiently for the war effort, the Doncaster Plant had also, beginning in 1939, converted 150 vehicles for use as hospital trains and later prepared a nine-vehicle train for the C-in-C Home Forces. Its main new task was to convert itself partly into a munitions factory. It turned out tank hulls, armour plating, naval gun mountings and artillery breech rings, pontoons and engine parts for both aeroplanes and submarines. The LNER's munitions work was valued at almost £8.3 m (or more than £200 m in 1999 prices), whilst the LMS did about 2.7 times as much. A further £4.6 m went on LNER emergency works to help the coal convoy trains.

Financial implications

By reason of a huge increase in their business, the railway companies' net receipts rose to more than £105 million by 1943, compared with an average of only £39.5 m between 1935-1937. However the railways' net receipts were guaranteed and limited by the Government at the latter figure, giving the LNER a wartime annual net revenue of £10.13 m and the LMS £14.74 m.

Railway workers' pay appears to have been less of an national issue than for miners, perhaps because of better industrial relations than in the mines. By 1945 the average UK rate of pay for signalmen in industrial areas, such as along the SYJR, which by reason of the blackout had become more stressful, had risen to £5.72½ (£5 14*s.* 6*d.*) pw (or £127 in 1999 prices), compared with £3.70 (£3 14*s.*) in 1939. With Sunday overtime, a junior fireman could take home £3 pw in 1942, whilst experienced locomotive drivers were on a basic £6.32 (£6 6*s.* 6*d.*) pw in 1945. Station masters, grade 4, such as those at Maltby and Dinnington on the SYJR, who had been paid £230 pa in 1939, were on £90 pa more in 1945 (barely £7,000 pa in 1999 prices).

SYJR's wartime performance

The SYJR's wartime net revenue of £74,465 pa, was included in the above payments made to its two parent undertakings from the government control pool. By 1945-1946, the SYJR's net revenue had risen to almost £82,000, (or £1.8 m in 1999 prices), which clearly indicates, by reason of 27 pc wartime inflation, a decline in coal traffic since the late 1930s.

Overall, despite serving only deep, increasingly mechanised collieries it is clear that, given the overall decline in output and productivity in the coal industry during the war years and supported by the financial figures above, there was a corresponding, but unrecorded decline in the SYJR's originating traffic after 1940. However, the extant figures for one week's output in mid-September for each of the eight years, 1937-1944 at Markham Main reflect clearly the war-time decline in output. From 16.5 k t, they went successively to 15.3, 12.6, 19.6, 17.3, 16.1, 15.7 and 13.2 k t, a fall of 32.4 pc between 1940 and 1944. If the decline in SYJR originating coal traffic between 1938 and 1944 had mirrored exactly this colliery's production, then the former's 1944 figure would have been 2.22 m t or two pc lower than the trough of 1932.

The greatest decline was traffic to Humberside where, in early 1946, total LNER coal exports had recovered to only 51 k t pw. Southbound coal convoy trains might have replaced some of this latter traffic on the SYJR and, by reason that more of its own coal traffic went southbound, particularly to munitions and steel works and gas and generating stations, the line was kept busy and productive during the war. The very powerful, reliable and slow-running ex-NER 'T2' class 0-8-0s proved particularly valuable for this heavy work, competing for space on main lines with the many other extra south-bound coal, freight and military 'special' trains.

Additional duties for the SYJR included the servicing of new local war industries, such as the ROF next to Maltby colliery and occasionally acting as a feeder line both to and from the ECML and to the Midlands and for traffic diversions. The latter undoubtedly would have included returning empty coal wagons, diverted via the Harworth-Scrooby branch onto the SYJR.

Despite all these wartime duties, opportunities for track renewal on the SYJR declined during the war as spending on this item fell from £8,197 in 1940 to £4,675 in 1943 and to £3,629 in 1944, but it is unlikely that the managers would have imperilled safety. Minor works included £2,000 spent on alterations and extra wagon accommodation at Dinnington colliery in 1944, to which the colliery company contributed the majority, whilst DAC had spent £503 on a sidings connection at Firbeck in the previous year. The SYJR made a singular contribution to the iron and steel shortage in 1944, by agreeing to dismantle the passenger footbridge at Tickhill station, scrap value £281, after removal costs.

Like many other small communities throughout the UK, the SYJR colliery villages took in evacuees, Harworth took 230 children from Great Yarmouth in June 1940. Many more evacuees went to Doncaster, as this writer recalls and about 300 also went to each of Armthorpe, Dinnington and Firbeck, whilst ROF workers lodged in Maltby. Another local contribution by Dinnington was the use of its institute as an air-raid personnel centre and as a hospital, whilst Harworth allowed local military units to use its pithead baths.

By 1946 however, according to one former Tickhill porter, the SYJR had returned fully to its basic function and there were 'absolutely no passenger trains' to be seen using the line. Despite this, an attempt was made to spruce up the neglected line after the end of hostilities. A contract worth £3,506 (£77,000 in 1999 prices) was signed in 1946 with Shirley Painting services to repaint 31 bridges between Dinnington and St Catherines, and in 1947 a further £1,435 contract was signed with Arundel Contractors to clean and paint the three stations.

At the station master's house at Maltby, in April 1947, a hot water system and bathroom were installed, but even so his rent was increased to only £7.16 (£7 3*s.* 2*d.*) pa.

Further large-scale refurbishment of the system was announced in mid-1945, with the LNER's plans to withdraw 1,000 old and obsolete locomotives over the next five years and replace them at the rate of 100 per year, mostly from the Doncaster 'Plant', with new steam models. One year later the 2,000th locomotive built there since 1867, a modernised Pacific type, steamed out from the 49 ha site, watched by many of its 5,410 employees. In its 25 years, the LNER built 1,434 locomotives at Doncaster.

Bombs on Doncaster

The SYJR was on the Luftwaffe's secondary target list and on 16th January, 1941 36 one kg incendiary bombs were dropped next to the line in the Ellers Rd area of south Doncaster, whilst another 36 fell south-west of the SYJR's northern exit. On 28th April, 1944 34 10 kg HE bombs were dropped near Potteric Carr Jn, north of the ECML. Otherwise the line remained untouched. In all a total of 147 wartime enemy bombs fell on and around Doncaster, killing 20 persons and wounding 83, whilst destroying or damaging 895 buildings. By contrast the whole UK rail network was hit more than 9,000 times, destroying eight locomotives, 3,300 wagons and 637 passenger coaches, with much more lesser damage.

Plane crashes

Bombs were not the only objects falling from the sky which could have disrupted the SYJR during the war. Eleven British military aircraft crashed in the vicinity of the line (but not on it) between 1940 and 1944. Fortunately most of the air-crews survived these crashes, amongst them the Polish crew of a Wellington bomber from RAF Finningley, which ran out of fuel and crashed into the River Don. The Poles baled out safely at Kirk Sandall, close to the SYJR's northern exit. This area saw three crashes, one six months earlier than the Poles, involving another Wellington from RAF Burn (near Selby) and on 30th October, 1944 a Halifax crashed at Edenthorpe, quite close to Markham Main colliery.

Wellington bombers and crews *c*.1940. Three Wellingtons crashed near the SYJR during World War II. *Royal Air Force Museum*

By contrast with the Poles, the whole crew of a Lancaster bomber from RAF Lindholme was killed on 28th September, 1943 near Cockhill House, Old Edlington, about 3 km north of the line at Maltby. Surprisingly, this area also had seen two previous crashes. The first was also close to Cockhill, on 28th November, 1940 when an Anson from RAF Spittlegate suffered engine failure. On 17th February, 1943, a Defiant from RAF Digby also suffered engine failure and made a forced landing further east at Carr Lane, Wadworth.

It appears that as far as these crashes were concerned lightning strikes thrice! There were two west of Maltby (Hellaby) - on 26th May and 17th November, 1942, involving respectively a Hampden from Jurby (I of Man) and a Wellington from Finningley. A third, south of Maltby - at Slade Hooton and the earliest and closest to the line - was on 13th October, 1940 when a Whitley bomber ran out of fuel. South Anston, by contrast, was the site of only two crashes, the first on the 16th January, 1942 when a Stirling from RAF Mildenhall made a belly-landing after running out of fuel, but mercifully all the crew were saved. Eight months later a trainee pilot in an Oxford from RAF Leconfield also crashed there.

Railwaywomen at war

Even more than in 1914-1918, the SYJR like all Britain's railways relied upon women staff, including a clerk and a porter at Tickhill station and a signaller at Dinnington station who was still there in 1962. By January 1944 the LMS had 100 women platelayers at work. The main reason for employing more women was that 98,000 railwaymen (and 3,000 women) eventually joined the armed forces. Interestingly, 861 UK railwaymen also became miners during the war. This was a severe loss of personnel at a time of greatly increased military and industrial activity on the railways, exacerbated by petrol shortages for road transport. By 1943 some 16 pc of the UK's 762,200 railway employees were women. The LNER's female staff rose from 7,000 to almost 27,400 between 1940-1945, although many resigned soon after VE Day.

Chapter Eleven

Nationalisation and Retrenchment, 1947-1973

Commanding heights

The Labour Government elected in July 1945 with a 146-seat majority was determined to nationalise amongst other 'commanding heights of the economy' the rail and coal industries, despite the threat of national bankruptcy brought about by the cost of the war.

The immense potential size of the coal industry appeared to offer it a bright future. In 1946 *The Rapid Survey of Coal Reserves and Production* officially estimated that there were 20.5 bn t of developed coal reserves in the UK which could be worked during the following century. Of these almost 6.8 bn t were in the East Midlands field and about 700 m t were the prized Barnsley seams in South Yorkshire, many already worked by collieries along the SYJR and transported on the line. These 20.5 bn t would allow 200 m t pa - the new UK target - to be raised for the next 100 years. This total seemed to offer an assured and 'profitable' future for the SYJR and the collieries which accessed it. (It should be noted that the SYJR's annual financial performances ceased to be calculated specifically after 1939.)

The 1946 Coal Industry Nationalisation Act assessed the total value of the industry at £164 m (equal to £3.6 bn in 1999 prices), of which the Yorkshire coalfield at £35.7 m was the most valuable area. Of the latter sum, DAC (including SYJR-accessing collieries of Yorkshire Main, Markham Main and Firbeck) was valued at £5.8 m, whilst YAC (including SYJR -accessing collieries of Maltby and Dinnington - plus Rossington) were valued at £3.37 m. Barber Walker's Nottinghamshire and Yorkshire holdings (including Harworth on the SYJR) were valued at £2.7 m. Various subsidiary valuations and other costs almost doubled the total compensation to £309 m.

The Nationalisation of Britain's railways on 1st January, 1948 was also considered 'inevitable', following increased government control and regulation since 1914 and particularly since 1939. The whole network and its rolling stock were in a desperately run down state, with war damage and disinvestment totalling around £200 m or £4 bn in 1999 prices. Notwithstanding the past and future notional large profits generated by the SYJR's coal trains, there were even rumours that the LNER was going bankrupt. It seemed clear that only the taxpayer could afford to take on the large task of UK rail modernisation, which was not announced until 1955 and then given grudgingly and with no clear long-term aims.

The newly established British Transport Commission (BTC) through its subsidiary, the Railway Executive, took over all the assets of the railways (henceforth BR), including the SYJR and, for the huge sum of £43 m, it also purchased more than half-a-million small, unbraked and obsolete, privately-owned coal wagons. With a vague overall objective, but no clear plan, of achieving 'transport integration', BTC also took over the canal network and the ports, including those which exported SYJR coal on the Humber, and 41,000 road vehicles, of which 11,000 were originally owned by the railway companies.

An underground roadlayer checks the super-elevation of the rails on the curve.
John Goodchild Collection

The cost of transport nationalisation was £1.065 bn, of which the rail value was more than 97.6 per cent, paid for in freely negotiable government stocks (3 pc 1988 British Transport stocks). Overall, it was not considered an excessive compensation, unless one based it on the future profit potential of the network, which was doubtful from the start without major reforms to take account of post-war economic realities.

National Coal Board

Meanwhile on 1st January, 1947, to rejoicing amongst the miners, who would soon work a basic 37.5 hr, five day week, the industry became state-owned, run by the National Coal Board (henceforth, NCB). Many of the same Directors and managers were in charge of the NCB, so 'workers control' was not a possibility and the militancy of Yorkshire miners continued. Indeed, later in the summer of 1947 a strike, originating in Grimethorpe, became a lock-out, spreading to 60 collieries, resulting in 873,000 t lost.

The eight collieries which had accessed the SYJR, were in the NCB's No. 3 Division (North-Eastern, renamed the Yorkshire Division on 1st January, 1963), headquartered in Sheffield, but they were in different areas and sub-areas.

Approximate workforces and output, where available, were listed in the 1947 *Colliery Year Book and Coal Trades Directory*.

No. 1 Worksop
Area (A):
Harworth: 1,527 underground and 403 surface. Output 814,500 t pa
Maltby: 1,950 underground and 400 surface. Output 645,500
Thurcroft: 1,375 underground and 240 surface. Output 547,000
Area (B)
Dinnington: 1,100 underground and 400 surface. Output n/a
Firbeck: 1,500 underground and 400 surface. Output n/a

No. 2 Doncaster
Area (A)
Yorkshire Main: 1,900 underground and 500 surface. Output 735,000
Area (B)
Markham Main: 2,150 underground and 400 surface. Output 770,000
Rossington: 1,610 underground and 540 surface. Output 790,000

If the above production figures were correct and if the average output of Firbeck and Dinnington, as in 1955, did approach that of all the eight (629,000 t compared with 689,000 t), this meant that in 1946 the SYJR was still moving a tonnage comparable with the mid-1930s. However, by reason of a decline of more than 20 pc in South Yorkshire production between 1940 and 1946, of Barber Walker's in-house history giving Harworth's 1946 output as 563,000 t, (less than 70 pc of the *Colliery Yearbook*'s figure), and Rossington having lost direct access to the line this seems very unlikely.

Also in sub area (B), but beyond the SYJR's reach, at the then north-eastern limit of the concealed coalfield, were Hatfield (1,940/420 men - 712,000 t) and Thorne (1,970/500 men - 690,000 t).

Class 'O4' 2-8-0 No. 63637 in Dinnington colliery sidings in June 1962. *Ray Williams*

Steam locomotion at Markham Main in the form of 'O1' class 2-8-0 No. 63670 on 23rd March, 1963. *Geoff Warnes*

Modernisation

Given the UK's economic problems and the wartime degradation of both the coal and railway industries, no large pay increases were likely there. In mining, oms was unsurprisingly lower in 1946 than in 1937. An estimated £300 m was needed for urgent modernisation, and up to £600 m by 1950, (or £11.55 bn in 1999 prices). Yet, with coal providing more than 90 pc of Britain's energy, the Government wanted cheap fuel for industry. BR naturally wanted to move as much coal as possible, although it was probably undercharging for this, since freight rates in real terms were 22 pc cheaper in 1956 than in 1939.

Moreover selling coal cheaply deprived the NCB of investment capital, which in each of its first five years never exceeded £30 m, so coal remained in short supply and by 1949 UK coal consumption was only 191 m t. Nevertheless it soon became obvious that science and technology were playing an increasing role in the industry and the sheer hard physical labour was slowly lessening.

Poles and Hungarians

In addition to capital, 40,000 extra miners were needed and were offered average earnings of £8 pw. Despite the overall decline in the total workforce, even in 1946 the South Yorkshire NUM opposed the employment of 1,000 former Polish soldiers, ignoring their heroic wartime contributions, but citing language and subsequent safety risks. Finally they agreed, if Poles and other foreigners were paid union rates and would be the first to be dismissed in the event of redundancy.

Harworth was one of the SYJR collieries which took on Poles - signs in Polish were erected - and also a number of ex-German POWs. In 1957 the NUM was to give the same reasoning about Hungarians, refugees from their failed uprising.

Despite these capital and labour shortages in 1949, the NCB earned £481 m in sales, whilst expenditure was £451 m (£300 m in wages). Out of the £29 m operating profit, interest charges had to be met. Exports of coal raised £50 m in much needed foreign currency but also perpetuated domestic rationing until the end of the 1950s.

Yorkshire's contribution

With estimated reserves of almost 4.3 bn t or 21 per cent of the UK total, Yorkshire production in 1949 at 42.1 m t, made it the largest NCB division. Almost half this output came from the concealed coalfield around Doncaster and from the other collieries along the SYJR. In the 1950s 'King Coal' still reigned here, with 70 pc of all male workers in Dinnington and Maltby being miners, as were 32.4 pc in Doncaster and 18 pc in Rotherham. Arguably therefore, the SYJR was the main artery in the heart of the most important division of the NCB. Trailing considerably behind Yorkshire in production, were the Nottinghamshire and Derbyshire division with 32.5 mt, and South Wales, 22.8 mt.

Noting Yorkshire's divisional profits of 22.5p (4*s*. 6*d*.) per ton in the 1950s, the Ministry of Fuel optimistically estimated its collieries would achieve an output of 50 m t by 1961-1965, out of a planned UK total of 240 m t. This was endorsed within the Second Plan for Coal (1956), which scheduled investment by 1965 to reach £865 m. The low cost, high productivity East Midlands coalfield was to receive increased capital funding, thus ensuring that the SYJR and its collieries would remain very busy and profitable in their primary role.

Post-war record

Much of the NCB's optimism was based on increasing productivity, which rose by 18 pc from 3.29 t oms in 1952 to 4.0 t in 1960 (and by a further 12 pc to 4.55 t, in 1962). This was achieved by both increased mechanisation and a reduction in the labour force. Between 1952 and 1960 the percentage of UK coal cut mechanically rose from 79 to 92 pc, power-loaded coal from less than 4 pc to almost 60, whilst power-conveyance rose from 85 to 96 pc. Total capital investment was £462 m between 1947-1955 (about £8.3 bn in 1999 prices), but was still less than planned.

Nevertheless, by 1955 it enabled the 700,000 miners working in the UK's 850 collieries to achieve a post-war production record 225 m t, to which those accessing the SYJR contributed more than 5.5 m t (2.5 pc of the total). Almost 75 pc of Yorkshire coal went out by rail, but as always much locally raised went out directly via the ECML, GNR & GER Jt and DVR, so it is therefore reasonable to assume that in 1955, but not in 1946 as noted above, the SYJR was originating around 2.5 m t coal freight, equal to the annual average of 1929-1938.

1955 Yorkshire strike

Remarkably, this 1955 record was achieved despite major strikes that year, of locomotive drivers and in early May the largest disruption in the Yorkshire coal industry since 1926. It began with a fillers' dispute - probably the most militant of all trades - at Markham Main, which was probably the fourth most militant colliery in Yorkshire. It was centred firmly on Doncaster which had seven of the most stoppage-prone collieries in the county, if not the UK, and from where flying pickets spread out.

The strike quickly involved 115,000 miners in the Yorkshire coalfield at 96 collieries, including all those on the SYJR. This strike contributed most to the county's total loss of production of 1.85 m t, or 12.2 t per man in 1955 and probably denied the SYJR a post-war freight record.

Encouraged by the success of this tradition, and despite being able to earn up to £20 pw (equal to £300 in 1999 prices) at the face, Yorkshire miners were involved in more than 1,100 disputes, mostly short stoppages of work or 'go-slows' in 1956. There were another 1,000 in 1957, prompting a joint NCB-NUM investigation into some of the most strike-prone collieries, including Markham Main and Rossington. In these two years approximately 78 pc of all labour stoppages were in the UK coal industry, much higher even than during World War II and, with South Yorkshire leading the way, the SYJR/BR suffered the consequences as usual in lost shipments and revenue.

The vital market

Despite these strikes, the UK's coal consumption reached 213 m t in 1956-1957, an all-time record, exceeding by a considerable margin even that of the record production year of 1913, when more than 30 pc had been exported. More optimistically for the future of the SYJR and its collieries, more than 13 pc of the Central Electricity Generating Board's (henceforth, CEGB) capacity was located in the NCB's Yorkshire division in 1960, making it the former's largest generating area. The CEGB was established in 1957 to replace the former Central Electricity Board of 1926.

Overall, UK coal sales to these generating stations, which had risen from 3 m t in 1903, 14.7 m t in 1937 and to 23.5 m t by 1945, then doubled by 1957. By the latter date, several more large coal-fired stations were being constructed or planned to open locally in the next 10-15 years. Thus in 1957, via BR's huge obsolete wagon fleet, the NCB was supplying 46.5 m t to the CEGB, 37.48 to industry, 28.77 to domestic users, 30.78 to coke ovens and 26.4 to gas works. Collieries themselves consumed 7.1 m t and the railways 12.2, the last down by three m t from 1945 and declining. Naturally, the superb steam and gas coal from the SYJR's collieries sold well in these markets.

The human cost

Such achievements came with a price, however. From 1947, there was an increasing emphasis on safety, with some 31 Central Mines Rescue Stations in the UK, of which six were in the Barnsley, Doncaster and Rotherham areas, close to the large, deep SYJR collieries. Nevertheless, in 1949 for example, 469 UK miners were killed, including 238 by falls and 109 by haulage mishaps, whilst 2,180 were injured sufficiently to require hospital treatment. Mercifully, this death toll was only 50 pc of the 1940 total and with many subsequent closures of older collieries and the substitution of machines for men on dangerous jobs, the UK mortality figure fell much further. It was 313 in 1960, 217 in 1966, 82 in 1970 and continued downwards thereafter. Pneumoconiosis remained a serious problem, affecting about 12 pc of miners, with 4,000 new cases in the UK annually in the 1950s and almost 3,000 in the early 1960s, but falling to 624 in 1969.

An underground view at Maltby colliery during modernisation in 1957.
John Goodchild Collection

Maltby colliery exterior in 1957. *John Goodchild Collection*

BR's coal freight

In 1948, more than 58 pc of the rail freight in Britain was coal and coke, a total of 161 m t transported at a rate of 69p (13*s*. 10*d*.) per ton, over an average 89 km haul. Between 1948-1953 total BR freight rose from 273 to 289 m t, whilst net receipts rose from £22.4 m to £37 m. The expansion of the coal industry up to 1957 made this freight the largest part of BR's gross earnings, exceeding £111 m and even in 1959 providing a notional profit of £24 m.

Despite these earnings, BR was already into its third year of operating deficit, which reached £99 m in 1962. Nevertheless, a disproportionate share of this BR coal freight - around 5.5 m t in 1955 - and therefore its earnings, still emanated from the eight collieries accessing the 48 km of the SYJR and its connecting lines.

However, by the latter year, one local councillor claimed that Dinnington colliery, then producing 3,000 t per day, would be totally exhausted within 12-15 years. The NCB said 30 years, but the lower forecast proved true, as also for the Barnsley seams at other local collieries. Another Doncaster colliery, where 2,400 miners were producing 14,000 t pw, was closed in 1956. Thorne had seen 20 years of increasing water ingress, eventually at more than 7,000 lpm or four tons of water for every ton of coal extracted. Despite concrete tubbing costing £250,000, further flooding in 1958 constantly put back reopening.

Less seriously, distribution of Markham Main coal via the SYJR was briefly interrupted by a landslip just north of the A18, for three days in the winter of 1958-1959, followed by three months of 16 kph speed restrictions, The clay embankment had been virtually liquified by heavy rain causing both the landslip and a movement of the track, both vertically and horizontally. Restoration was accomplished by tipping wagon loads of ashes onto the track until it was re-levelled and also onto the embankment, broadening it to reduce the gradient.

By this time, the shortage of coal - around 15-20 m t pa since 1947 - which the NCB had been addressing, came to an end suddenly in the economic recession of 1957-1959. Coincidentally with BR's financial troubles, the NCB also found demand falling by 20 m t over two years. Stock piles grew to more than 35 m t by the end of 1959, or 17 pc of the year's output, partly due to the success of the miners and the NCB managers in increasing output and productivity.

In 1960, despite this glut, the output of the collieries accessing the SYJR exceeded slightly that of 1955, with 5.6 m t, thus ensuring that coal traffic on the line remained heavy and profitable, despite increasing road competition.

Maltby reconstructed

The principal reason for these high SYJR output figures was capital investment. In addition to the £462 m (1947-1955) noted above, which the NCB invested in the UK, another £790 m was spent between 1956 and 1964, a combined total equal to about £20 bn in 1999 prices. Maltby colliery received £3 m between 1947-1961, for major reconstruction, including complete electrification of the colliery - winding gear, lighting and ventilation, the last incorporating a new

The coke wharf and colliery buildings at Harworth in 1958. *D. Stanyard*

Harworth colliery from the ovens office in 1958. *D. Stanyard*

system of 'methane drainage' in 1956 to remove firedamp quickly from the workings. Also in 1956, it was deepened to 833 m to access the seams (estimated at 34 m t) of Swallow Wood and Haigh Moor. Power-loading which had begun at Harworth in 1950, came in 1954-55 to Maltby, Markham Main and Yorkshire Main but not until 1962 at Rossington. By 1959, 70 pc of Maltby's output was being power-loaded.

Whilst 2,606 men at Maltby had produced 1.012 m t in 1939 (opmy, 388 t), by 1948 the 2,088 miners were getting only 682,700 t (opmy, 326t). By 1960 the modernisation programme was beginning to bear some fruit and 1,918 miners increased opmy to 427 t. Although the latter was only 10 pc higher than in 1939, possibly the result of disruptions caused by the long modernisation programme, nevertheless output in 1960 was more than 820,000 t. Maltby was one of only three SYJR collieries to exceed that total whilst between 1958 and 1961 profits rose from 55p (11*s*.) to £1.70 (£1 14*s*.) p t. Thurcroft had brought into production the difficult Parkgate seam and 1,800 men exceeded 500,000 t in production in both 1955 and 1960. However, the difficult working conditions in the 'Parkgate era' (1942-1972) created militant workers. In the 1950s a £1 m reconstruction of Yorkshire Main increased annual output to 914,000 t, whilst reserves were estimated at 82 m tons.

Competitive energy sources

Meanwhile, the NCB's senior management was facing competition from foreign coal imports, whilst alternative energy sources were increasing. By 1959, coal was supplying 10 pc less of total UK energy than it had in 1950. Cheap oil available from UK refineries encouraged the CEGB to begin using it rapidly after 1955 and 13 generating stations were using 5.5 m t in 1962.

The expansion of electricity generation in turn encouraged industry to move from coal to electrical power. Householders slowly followed suit, encouraged by the move to high-rise buildings and the July 1956 Clean Air Act. This Act was designed to prevent another 1952-type killer 'smog' (smoke + fog) and was also a clear acknowledgement of the serious effects of fossil fuel air pollution. As a result of this Act and further legislation in 1968 smoke emissions from coal-burning declined from 2.32 m t in 1956 to 0.26 in 1985.

There was further competition for coal. The first 'Dutch' North Sea gas began to be extracted in 1959 and the 'British' in 1967, whilst liquified Saharan gas had arrived in 1964. The UK coal-gas industry used 26 m t of coal in 1957 (including 33 pc of Yorkshire's output), but with declining coal sales, it faced eventual extinction (1977). Gas-fired generating stations were another much later threat.

Meanwhile, the UK Atomic Energy Authority published plans in 1954 to construct nuclear power stations and three years later the target was 5,000-6,000 MW of capacity, only to be reduced by 50 pc in 1960. By 1965 nuclear capacity from the first two 'Magnox' stations (1956 and 1959), was only 2.3 pc of total UK electrical generation. However, with more building and others planned, there were in operation by 1969 13 small nuclear power stations producing 12 pc of UK electricity. The NCB faced losing up to 40 m t of sales by 1975, so the long-term threat, even to the SYJR and its collieries was clear.

Two views of construction during rebuilding at Harworth colliery on 22nd February, 1959.
(Both) Bassetlaw Museum, Retford

Harworth colliery viewed from the bridge on the Harworth-Blyth road in the summer of 1959. A line disappeared behind the coke heap (*right*) which continued to Scrooby.
D. Stanyard

BR modernisation

In 1955 BR's over-optimistic £1.24 bn Modernization and Re-equipment Plan was published, of which £210 m was to be allocated for freight services, including new marshalling yards. Steam locomotion was to be replaced by diesel and electric haulage for which £150 m and £185 m respectively was allocated. The number of steam locomotives on the network declined belatedly by almost 5,000 between 1951 and 1959. Nevertheless, BR still managed to build more than 1,400 new ones between 1948-1960, but none at the Doncaster 'Plant' after 1957. Coal sales to BR accordingly declined from 15 to nine m t pa between 1947-1960.

On the SYJR, the first diesels, the 1,365 hp, 104 t Brush type '2' (later class '31'), a good locomotive of limited pulling power arrived in 1963, followed in 1964 by 1,750 hp English Electric type '3' (later class '37') which had a good, if noisy engine. In 1965 the 2,750 hp Brush type '4' (later class '47') arrived, ideal for this work but prone to slippage without sanding equipment. Also used between Worksop and Dinnington were BR Sulzer types '2' and '4' (later class '25' and '45'), but both were poor performers and 'accident prone'. All made their own small contribution towards the extinction of the BR market for coal in 1969.

Steam locomotives, which came variously from the depots at Doncaster Carr, Retford GN, Hull Dairycoates, Frodingham and Wakefield (Belle Vue), lingered on the SYJR and its colliery sidings until 1966 and even later in a few yards. Amongst the last types running on the SYJR were ex-GCR/LNER 'O4s' and ex-LNER 'O2s', 2-8-0 WD 'Austerities' and ex-LMS '8F' class 2-8-0s.

An ex-War Department 'Austerity' 2-8-0 at Markham Main colliery sidings in January 1963.
David Thorpe

Ex-LNER 2-8-0 'O2/2' class No. 63937 approaches Firbeck Junction with a coal train from the Maltby direction on 23rd July, 1963.
M. Mitchell

Coal contraction

Faced with falling sales in 1958, the NCB suspended Saturday working at all collieries, including those along the SYJR, to reduce overtime and output. Occasionally, even weekend maintenance was curtailed, as at Harworth, but its coking plants ran for 7 x 24 hrs, with all bunkers full on Fridays. UK coal rationing, introduced in World War II, ended for all customers.

In January 1959 the NCB announced the first 12 colliery closures, but 34 were actually closed and 47,000 miners made redundant in this swathe. There were rumours of more to come, but none on the SYJR.

Overall between 1957-1962, the number of NCB wage earners declined by 22 pc from 710,000 to 556,000, a downward trend affecting employment at collieries accessing the SYJR also. Open-cast production which had risen from 12 m t in 1950 to a peak at 14.3 m t in 1958, was cut back to 7.3 m t by 1962.

Scots and 'Geordies'

Yorkshire's total production in 1959 was 41.9 m t. The 50 m t pa postulated in the Revised Plan for Coal (1959) was reduced by 10 pc. However, the NCB naturally continued to favour the low-cost, high productivity East Midlands coalfield at the expense of high-cost ones. By the late 1950s, it was encouraging miners to move from the latter to the former, establishing a 'Pick your Pit' campaign, using mobile offices. By 1966, some 7,000 men, including many 'Geordies' had moved, particularly to the East Midlands. At Maltby, where 200 houses were specially built and a Caledonian Working Men's Club set up, 52 Scots arrived in 1963 alone. This project began to run down after the 1965 Redundancy Payments Act.

The importance of the Yorkshire coalfield in the 15 year post-war period can be gauged from the small number of the county's colliery closures. Whilst through 1951, 1957 and 1962, the UK colliery totals fell from 901 to 841 to 669 respectively, an overall decline of 26 pc, the comparative Yorkshire totals were 115, 108 and 105, a decline of only nine pc, all in the older western coalfield. Furthermore, whilst the total number of NCB employees declined by 22 pc between 1957 and 1962, the favoured East Midlands coalfield lost only five pc of its workforce. Thus by 1961, as the centre of gravity of the industry moved eastwards, the deep collieries around Doncaster were employing 1 in 3 of all South Yorkshire miners compared with 1 in 20 sixty years earlier. Each had an average workforce of almost 1,700 compared with less than 900 in the older, smaller mines of the Barnsley coalfield. Nevertheless, despite Doncaster's growth and importance, the total number of miners in the concealed coalfield was only 27,000 in 1961, some 7,000 fewer than in 1941. Furthermore total coal production in Yorkshire fell below 40 m t in 1961 and by a further 5 m t during the next decade.

A battery driven underground train at Maltby colliery in 1964.
Archives and Local Studies, Rotherham Central Library

The Robens' decade

Faced with a crisis in the coal industry, the Government appointed a former Minister of Labour, (Lord) Alfred Robens as Chairman of the NCB (1961-1971). Robens developed policies to try to compete with the other energy producers and rescue the coal industry's finances - which required £60 m pa profit to pay interest charges. First, he accelerated the closure programme of loss-making collieries to cut costs, especially wage totals. Second, he invested more in new machinery for productive collieries, including those along the SYJR, aiming by improved productivity to reduce the price of coal and increase sales, particularly to the CEGB.

Even in 1960, before Lord Robens took over, 44 collieries had closed or merged. Thirty-two followed in 1961, resulting in more than 22,000 redundancies, the number increasing throughout the 1960s. Large-scale closures began to affect Yorkshire in 1965 and by 1969 there had been another 200 UK closures. The return of a Labour Government in 1964, beset by economic problems, but with an abundance of energy resources, had brought no relief to coal. The National Plan of 1965 merely promised reduced production, more closures and more job losses. During the Robens' decade, there was an overall decline from 698 to 292 UK collieries, and from 583,000 workers to 283,000 (representing one closure every nine days and 30,000 jobs lost pa). Remarkably, amidst this contraction only one SYJR colliery was closed.

Eventually, the SYJR was affected in December 1968, with the closure of Firbeck, geologically-troubled since its opening day. By 1969, the total number of miners at the seven SYJR 'survivors' had fallen to just over 10,000, compared with almost 15,000 at eight locations in 1946. Coal freight originating on the SYJR in 1968 had also fallen to 2.1 m t or 153,000 tons below 1932, the lowest point of the 'Great Depression', and it fell even further in both 1969 and 1970 following the loss of Firbeck and major coal strikes in both years.

Administrative changes

In 1964 BR's Eastern Region had been reorganised into five divisions with one centred on Doncaster, into which naturally the SYJR fell. Three years later, the five-tier management structure of the NCB was also reorganised - into three levels, creating 17 intermediate areas. Yorkshire, with 100 collieries in eight smaller areas, employing 100,000 miners and producing 41 m t in 1966, was important enough to hold four of these intermediate areas.

Two of these new areas were served by the SYJR - Doncaster with 13 collieries, 22,500 miners and 9.7 m t output, but losing nearly a quarter of a million pounds in 1965-1966, and South Yorkshire, with 10 collieries, 14,500 miners, 5.6 m t output, but £1.3 m in profit. In addition to the six collieries in these two areas, which accessed the SYJR, so also did Harworth and (temporarily) Firbeck, in the new North Nottinghamshire area, whose 18,000 miners produced 8.4 pc of UK coal output.

As part of this re-organisation, Coal House, a tower block, was opened in Doncaster in 1966. It employed some 1,000 Yorkshire and National HQ staff (the National Computer Centre) dealing with purchasing, production and other matters. It also became a highly convenient target after 1969 for the region's militant striking miners.

NCB Investment

Robens' second major objective was increased productivity, of which about 20 pc was achieved simply by the many closures and the remainder by expanding the investment programme. In 1967, he chose 50 core mines, almost all in the East Midlands coalfield, to spearhead an increase in output from 35 to 60 m t pa. These would principally supply the CEGB through new automated technology, described below. Under Robens, the NCB invested a total of £810 m, equal to more than £12 bn in 1999 prices.

Since 1950, the NCB had already been investing heavily, including at SYJR collieries, much of it on new machines such as (by 1966), 693 Anderton shearers, 294 Trepanners and 158 Rapid Ploughs. Thus as early as 1960, as noted, more than 92 pc of coal was cut mechanically. Technical improvements included automation and even remote (face) operation in a few places. Self-advancing powered roof supports were also introduced on new faces. At the coalface, loading was mostly (63 pc in 1960) done manually onto trains, which hauled 100 t, or onto conveyor belts, of which there were 7,400 km in the UK by 1971.

However in March 1966, the National Power-Loading Agreement was signed by the NCB and the NUM, which ended piece-work for some 200,000 miners and resulted by 1971 in single machines cutting and power-loading 93 pc of UK coal.

In the Doncaster area alone, the NCB had invested £56 m between 1947 and 1970 (equal to about £750 m in 1999 prices), spending heavily, and variously along the SYJR. A new face of 180 m length cost about £175,000 in new machinery. In the 1960s for example, Maltby's Barnsley seam was equipped with Huwood slicers, working the 150 m longwall face on a three-shift day and achieving a face oms of 11 t, a total of more than 1200 t pd.

Dinnington had 1,751 miners of whom 1,372 worked underground in 1962. Of the latter, 580 were at the coalface and their oms of 5.8 t had improved by 21 pc since 1959. Even this was 3,000 t pw below the NCB's target, resulting in a £29,000 loss in 1963. In 1961 the old coking plant had been closed and proposals were considered in 1966 - but not carried through - to merge Dinnington with neighbouring Thurcroft, allowing all coal to be wound up at the latter, with manriding and facilities at the former, but reducing total employment by 500. In 1965 Dinnington station buildings suffered their second fire and were demolished.

Good output results continued to be achieved elsewhere along the SYJR. At Markham Main, the workforce declined by one-third between 1966-1969, increasing productivity by a matching 33 pc and making the first profits since nationalisation. In one week in 1969, Rossington achieved a record output of 27,866 t. The SYJR's neighbour, Silverwood, produced more than one m t that year and again in 1972, one of only five collieries in Yorkshire to do so. By the latter year, Yorkshire Main which then accessed only the SYJR, operated five faces, two of Barnsley, on which four shifts were worked, and three of Swallow Wood, all producing an annual profit of one million pounds.

In 1972-3 Markham Main was working a four-shift day, although soon to be reduced to three, and had three Barnsley faces operating, soon to be four. Rossington operated five Barnsley faces. Adjacent to the latter, at Maltby, where in 1971 a new coal preparation plant costing £1.5 m opened, a South Yorkshire record of more than 31,500 t output in one week was achieved in 1973. This helped to push its year's production to more than one m t. Maltby was about twice as productive in oms as either Thurcroft or Dinnington, where a new vacuum filtration plant to dry coal by steam was being installed. At all three, the Swallow Wood seams were being opened, but the last two had serious problems.

During the Robens' decade productivity, measured by opmy, increased by 52 pc from 305 t to 463 t whilst total UK output declined from 184 to 133 m t or by 27.5 pc. In the longer term between 1947 and 1975, as a result of the closures of small operations, the average production per UK colliery rose from 192,000 t pa to 466,100. The majority of collieries accessing the SYJR produced well above the latter figure, as indicated in the following table. This all helped to make the whole East Midlands coalfield very successful with a total operating profit of £265 m between 1947-1971, perhaps £4 bn in 1999 prices.

South Yorkshire coalfield - SYJR production figures (,000 t rounded up)

	1955	*1960*	*1965*	*1970*	*workforce in 1970*	*main seam*
Markham Main	692	682	746	648	1,700	Barnsley
Rossington	760	857	906	902	1,900	Barnsley, Dunsil
Yorkshire Main	869	826	1,096	704	1,900	Barnsley, Dunsil
Maltby	659	820	854	666	1,600	Barnsley, Haigh Moor
Dinnington	683	639	541	406	1,000	Barnsley, Haigh Moor
Thurcroft	550	501	388	309	900	Parkgate, Haigh Moor
Harworth (Notts)	685	698	667	513	1,200	Barnsley
Firbeck (Notts)	621	610	493	closed	-	
Totals	5,500	5,600	5,700	4,100		

Electricity market

Without the active and joint co-operation of BR, the NCB and the CEGB in one particular sector, the decline of coal and coke freight rail traffic could have been much worse, as Robens noted. This co-operation was for rail and coal the outcome of three pressures. First BR's need, in the wake of the devastating Beeching Report of 1963 threatening a large reduction of UK rail services, to further modernise, rationalise and try to reduce losses. Second was the NCB's battle to increase sales into the now most important, expanding and eventually, almost sole market, electricity generation. Third, to meet the rapidly rising post-war demand for power, the CEGB decided that tried and tested coal-fired stations fuelled cheaply were the answer, rather than limited capacity, untried Magnox nuclear plants. Thus it required regular coal deliveries, which generally increased in annual totals until the record peak 'burn' of 1979.

UK generating capacity grew by 25 pc to 37,000 MW between 1960-1964 alone, including the stations of High Marnham (1,000 MW) on the Trent, commissioned in 1959 and Thorpe Marsh (1100 MW), 8 km north-east of Doncaster (1963), with both requiring three m t pa. of mostly local coal. A further 20,000 MW was commissioned, including larger coal-fired units (each of about 5 m t pa) at West Burton (1967), Ratcliffe (1968) and Cottam on the Trent (1969); Ferrybridge 'C' (1966) and Eggborough (1968) on the Aire and Fiddler's Ferry (1971) on the Mersey. During 1968-1969, with this assured market, the NCB was able to raise coal prices by up to 40 pc.

Furthermore, in July-November 1969 the massive generating complex of Drax A & B, on the Ouse was finally approved, designed to produce a total of almost 4,000 MW or 10 pc of maximum English demand. Commissioned in stages between 1974 and 1986, Drax was served by a re-opening of about 6 km of the old H&BR main line eventually requiring around nine m t pa and, providing work for thousands of miners, including those along the SYJR. The approval for Drax and other stations also decided the NCB to assist with their supply by developing the 1,000 m t reserves of the Selby coalfield, which by the late 1980s was supplying 8 m t pa to Drax and other local stations.

On the downside for coal, the 1967 White Paper had emphasised future nuclear and natural gas generation of electricity and the Government could have chosen to fuel Drax with natural gas from the Ekofisk field. It did not but Drax was the last major coal-fired station to be commissioned, although building the second stage did not begin until 1978.

Nuclear-, oil- and gas-fired stations became the long-term preferred options, despite the fact that the nine Magnox nuclear reactors, which had cost £750 m by 1970 (equal to £6.8 bn in 1999 prices) were suffering corrosion problems. Indeed, Robens claimed that coal-fired stations operated 25 pc more cheaply than nuclear ones, by reason that the former were one third cheaper to build. Furthermore, the new Advanced Gas-Cooled reactor (AGR) programme was approved in 1965 but fell well behind schedule, as technical problems developed. Designed to produce 8,000 MW by 1976, the first, Dungeness 'B', was not commissioned until 1985.

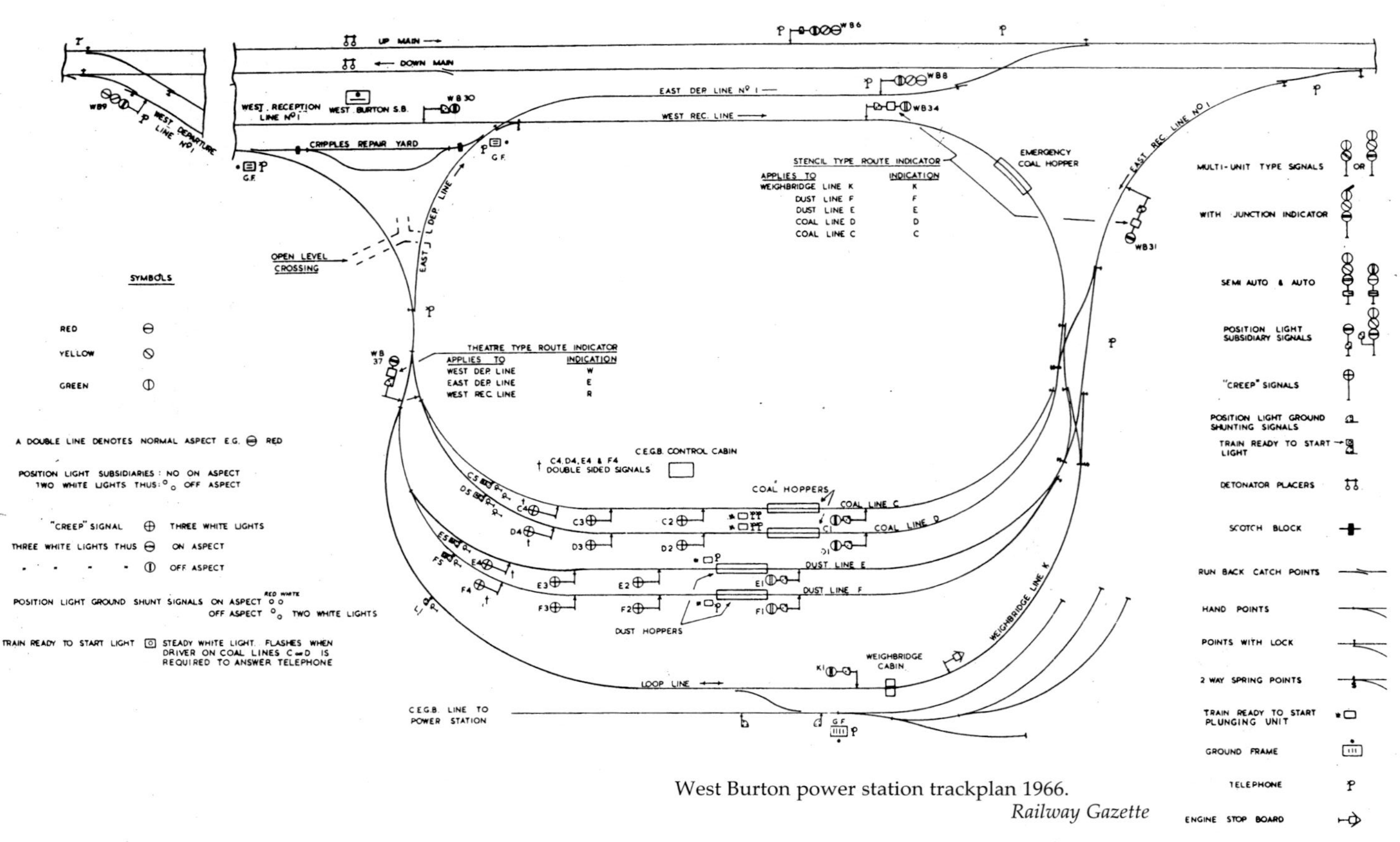

West Burton power station trackplan 1966.

Railway Gazette

Layout of tracks, signals and coal hoppers for "merry-go-round" trains at West Burton Power Station

Mechanised coal depots and Immingham Bulk Terminal (IBT)

To cater for major users, including the growing electricity market, which were in both their vital interests, BR and the NCB initiated three new joint developments. The first in 1963 was to replace 4,000 small coal depots with 80 large and 300 smaller, mechanised ones to handle block trains instead of single wagon loads and by 1970 these were handling 5 m t pa. By 1965 the nine freight sidings at Doncaster had been reduced to three, handling 1,800 wagons daily. Doncaster Up Decoy and Worksop undertook block train work with 16 t coal wagons originating from SYJR collieries, including Firbeck, until it closed.

Also initiated in 1963 and in operation by 1970 was the new £11.5 m IBT, a joint venture by the NCB, BR, the BT Docks Board and after 1967, British Steel, whilst bulk chemicals were also handled there. Immingham had been a major SYJR export outlet since 1912. The new IBT handled bulk cargos of coal exports (then 1.25 m t pa) and iron ore imports.

IBT coal trains originating at SYJR collieries assembled in the Worksop freight yards, travelling via Gainsborough Trent Jn, but used the SYJR as an emergency diversion route. If it was closed, diverted trains travelled via Sheffield (Attercliffe) and Doncaster. At IBT trains unloaded non-stop at 'creeping' speed (0.8 kph/½ mph) under the control of unloading signals, but it could hold up to five trains in the sidings in the event of any delays or other problems.

Between 1971 and 2001 total tonnage handled through IBT increased from 1.18 m t to 19.1 m t. However, whilst coal exports declined rapidly from 1984 and ceased in 1990, coal imports began in 1985, peaking at 2.7 m t in 1996.

Merry-go-round trains

In January 1964, BR and the CEGB signed a long-term agreement (for at least 10 years) for the conveyance of train-loads of coal to the new, large coal-fired generating stations. In September 1965, BR and the NCB introduced merry-go-round trains (henceforth, m-g-r), to provide a constant and efficiently handled supply of coal to these generating stations, to the IBT and to new integrated steelworks such as at Scunthorpe. The last was also supplied partly by SYJR coal, including combined train-loads from Thurcroft and Dinnington collieries.

The first English m-g-r service ran in Nottinghamshire, between the new (1961) state-of-the-art Beavercotes colliery and West Burton, hauled by re-geared class '47s' (2,750 hp Brush type '4'). By the 1980s each train consisting of 45 x 32 t wagons (5.56 m wheelbase) was loaded automatically from overhead bunkers at the collieries in an hour or less, with each wagon being weighed automatically before and after. Each train ran round a circular loop at the generating station, and each wagon was unlocked and unloaded automatically via their three bottom-opening doors into large hoppers. After further weighing, the doors were re-closed and locked, also automatically. By 1968 West Burton could accept 100 trains in a five-day week with an average discharge time of 38 minutes.

Brush type '2' (later class '31') No. 5835 waits to depart from Dinnington colliery, 7th October, 1971. *C.A. Allenby*

A pair of class '20s' Nos. 20072 and 20187 pass Dinnington Colliery Junction signal box, coming off the Thurcroft branch on 15th January, 1992. *Chris Booth*

This type of operation in a very basic, non-automated form had been established for SYJR and other trains at Hull docks before 1914, later in a more sophisticated form at the LMS's Stonebridge Park generating station and by Yorkshire coal merchants for reloading trucks in 1931.

By 1965, BR had 2,744 m-g-r wagons on order to cope with the expansion of this new service. These included large-capacity 45 t HAA wagons, which were built at British Rail Engineering in Shildon in Co. Durham, the first ones starting service on the SYJR in the same year. By 1981, the BR fleet of m-g-r wagons had increased to 10,565 with 460 being built.

The maximum for steam-hauled coal trains was 448 gross tons (28 x 16 t wagons) raised to 544 and 576 gross tons for class '31' and '37' diesel locomotives, each pulling 34-36 wagons. By contrast a South Yorkshire m-g-r could pull 30 or even 34 x 51 t (34 t payload) wagons giving a train-load of up to 1,556 gross tonnes. Most used 30 x 32 t wagons. However, it required two class '20', '31' or '37s', all used on the SYJR between the 1960s and 1990, to pull an m-g-r, whilst Thurcroft was invariably served by class '20' from Worksop. The long-wheelbased class '45' was banned from the SYJR after several derailments at Maltby.

When the class '47' and later, in 1975-1983, the '56' and '58' (3,300 hp) were introduced, each could handle a m-g-r single-handedly, although the latter was prone to wheel-slip. By the 1990s, classes '59' running between Maltby, and Ferrybridge and Drax and '60', hauling imported coal to West Burton and Cottam, had appeared on the SYJR.

Class '47s' usually hauled only 30 wagons, but fewer on Trans-Pennine trains to Fiddler's Ferry or for departures from Maltby or Harworth collieries. Trains from Worksop to Immingham (class '47') via the SYJR could pull 32 wagons if given extra assistance between Worksop and Dinnington. Importantly, m-g-r wagons also had Westinghouse dual auto air braking systems, adopted as standard by BR from 1965, to replace vacuum braking. All drivers underwent special training, SYJR guards eventually becoming redundant and the task of controlling heavy trains on the steepest SYJR gradients became much easier.

Whilst lacking the romance of the temperamental steam locomotive (and 40°C footplate temperatures), diesels made the driver's work easier with their more predictable performance. The comforts of the diesel included air-conditioning in the cabs of class '56' onward, although not without initial teething problems. Diesels were also up to two-thirds cheaper to run than steam and for this job, drivers were paid, in November 1965, with 2.65 hrs overtime, about £17 pw net. This rose to an average of about £42 (1974), £69 (1979), £155 (1988) and to more than £500 pw by the end of the century.

Following their introduction in 1970, automatic overhead bunkers (rapid-loading systems) were installed at a cost of about £250,000 each - rising to one million pounds by the mid-1980s, to handle m-g-r trains at high production collieries such as Rossington (1971), Maltby (1976) and Silverwood (1978). All were approached up an incline which could cause slippage and necessitate a rerun. However their rate of installation was quite slow in South Yorkshire compared with Nottinghamshire and the new Selby field. Some collieries preferred to load with huge powered shovels. By 1983, some 37 rapid-loading systems with a total annual loading capacity of 40 m t pa had been installed in East Midlands collieries.

Similarly the introduction of m-g-r trains increased. By 1972 there were 148 daily m-g-r trains, mostly in the East Midlands, Yorkshire and Lincolnshire including those originating on the SYJR. They supplied the Aire, Ouse and Trent generating stations with 60 pc of their increasing needs. Both Harworth and Maltby sent several daily trains to West Burton, whilst other 'coal formations' were tripped into Worksop Up Sidings from where they were shuttled to both West Burton and Cottam, as the need arose. Rossington also served West Burton, using the former GNR & GER Jt line, and Thorpe Marsh, which was also served by both Hatfield and Yorkshire Main. The latter used the old GCR and H & BR Jt line until it was finally closed in 1970.

By 1984, the large South Yorkshire collieries were supplying Drax, Eggborough and Ferrybridge with 300 train loads per week totalling 300,000 tons. This was much the heaviest national m-g-r flow, with more to come when Drax 'B' came on stream. All this local m-g-r activity came under the control of the Freight Manager (Coal) at Doncaster, using a TOPS central computer system.

M-g-r trains were far more productive than those using the old wagons. Each generating station could be serviced by 200 wagons compared with 2,000 using traditional methods. The NCB gained by rapid loading, BR by rapid transit and the CEGB by rapid discharge. However, *non-stop* trains (at 0.8 kph) were not always possible by reason of occasional queues of both arrivals and departures, especially at West Burton and Cottam. One cause of such delays was broken belts, which carried away the arriving coal at generating stations. Thus overall each wagon made only 25 pc of the journeys originally envisaged in the planning stage. A typical driver's shift was one trip of nine hours, but two trips if it was very short, such as between Hatfield colliery and Thorpe Marsh. Train crews could even disembark for a meal at the generating station whilst the train discharged.

M-g-r signalling

At West Burton generating station, to where the first m-g-r trains were routed, and to which many thousands more from the SYJR would run, a new power-operated signal box opened in October 1964 between Trent and Clarborough Jns. The *Railway Gazette* (7th January, 1966) described how it operated 28 routes by individual keys, 15 points machines and also released four ground frames. All were worked from a key/switch desk which gave the operator a diagrammatic, illuminated view of the track circuit layout. Each point and signal had its own switch on the desk. The running signals were multi-aspect, amongst which the main-line signals worked automatically when the box was closed.

From this box, trains could be signalled from either track of the main line into the station's reception lines, until accepted by the CEGB controller. Both operations were done through pressing plungers, the latter sending trains into either one of the two Coal (unloading) or Dust (loading) lines, or onto the weighbridge line. All operations and staff are protected by signals and fail-safe systems, even allowing the train to be halted in mid-unloading, by 'creep signals'. Apart from Dust trains which tended to go round twice to top up, the departure system was similar, including signal-side plungers to indicate whether the train was departing for Gainsborough, Retford or to the 'cripples' siding (for damaged wagons).

Nuclear threat

In 1967 as noted above, government policy began to favour nuclear power stations and one was authorised at Hartlepool, in the Durham coalfield, although it did not start producing electricity until 1989. In an editorial on 20th October, 1967, the *Railway Gazette* forecast that this 'marks the beginning of the end for the m-g-r'. After the current coal-fired generating stations were built, with 40-year life expectancies, it asserted, coal production would begin to decline in the 1980s. The newer nuclear stations with 25 year lives would take over base load provision. The *Gazette* concluded that the following decade (the 1970s) would be 'the hey-day of the m-g-r'. Apart from failing to forecast the mass arrival of natural gas-powered stations in the 1990s, this was a far-sighted prediction. Stewart Joy (1973) thought the late introduction of m-g-r trains and other unspecified 'railway-inflicted handicaps' were responsible for their unrealised potential.

SYJR timetable, 1969-1970

In 1969-1970, the SYJR was open on weekdays from 5.40 am at both ends and until 6.30 pm at Kirk Sandall, 8 pm at Low Ellers and 9.20 pm at Brancliffe. Thus Dinnington station signal box was open from 5.30 am to 9 pm. At this time a weekly total of about 400 train paths were time-tabled to use some part or all of the line, running at maximum speeds of 40 kph or in the case of Maltby colliery, the Harworth line and most curves, 25 kph. The last limit also applied to the 5 km branch line at Rossington colliery which had been be severed from the SYJR. Whilst some timetabled services had been suspended, many others were for locomotives hauling empty wagons back to collieries.

All trains to or from Markham Main used Kirk Sandall or the ECML at Potteric Carr, but never ran further south on the SYJR. However Markham did supply domestic coal to Scotland in air-braked Speedlink wagons, forming up train loads in Doncaster's Up Decoy Sidings for evening departures. By reason of recent line closures, no trains from Thurcroft or Dinnington delivered loads other than southwards, exiting at Brancliffe. However trains did depart from Maltby, Harworth and Yorkshire Main collieries, both northwards and southwards; from the last via the SYJR mainly to Keadby generating station. Trains with empties to Rossington could no longer move off the SYJR directly, but had to run from St Catherine's onto Black Carr West and then be propelled through Black Carr East into the colliery yard. Furthermore whilst many trains ran on only one, two or three days each week, the remainder ran on five or six days each week.

WEEKDAYS **WORKSOP TO KIRK SANDALL JN AND BRANCHES** F162

Mileage M	C	M	C	M	C	DOWN	0D49	8D85	8E89	8D49	0D34	9K09	9K06	8D82	9K60	8E71	8E71
							05 47 EBV from Doncaster Bank	05 02 from Scunthorpe	04 30 from Kirkby	To Immingham R.S.	LE to Stainforth			To Scunthorpe	To Doncaster Belmont	06 30 from Kirkby	05 22 from Toton
							MX			MX	SX			SO	MO	MO	MX
0	0					**WORKSOP SIDINGS** ... dep						06 10	06 25				
0	27					Shireoaks East Jn						06X15	06X30				
1	35					Shireoaks Station			05 36			ML	ML			07 35	07 35
2	30					Brancliffe East Jn			05 41			06 25	06 40			07 40	07 40
5	58					Dinnington Colliery Jn. ... arr			05 55							07 54	07 54
		0	0			... dep						06 38	06 53				
		2	7			**THURCROFT SDGS.** ... arr											
6	51					Dinnington & Laughton ... arr			SUSPENDED MO								
						... dep											
11	19					Maltby ... arr											
						... dep							07 14				
11	62					Maltby Colliery South ... arr						07 00					
						... dep											
12	5					Maltby Colliery North ... arr											
						... dep							07 17				
13	49	0	0			Firbeck Jn 'A'							07 22				
		3	29			Harworth Colliery ... arr							07 39				
						Harworth Glass Bulbs ... dep									07 42		
						Harworth Colliery G.F. ... arr									07 47		
		0	0			... dep									07 49		
		3	29			Firbeck Jn 'A' ... arr					After working 05 55 from Scunthorpe				08 06		
						... dep									08 20		
14	69					Tickhill & Wadworth ... arr											
						... dep											
17	46	0	0			St. Catherines Jn ... arr		06 29									
						... dep		06 31							08 37		
		0	60			Black Carr Sidings West ... arr											
						... dep		06 39									
		1	75			Yorkshire Main Sidings ... arr		06 48									
18	31			0	0	Low Ellers Jn ... arr	06 03										
						... dep	06 04								08 41		
				0	51	Potteric Carr Jn									08*58		
20	17					Markham Main Colliery ... arr	06 12										
						... dep				06 39	07‖45			08 47			
23	4					**KIRK SANDALL JN** ... arr											
						... dep				06 51	07 56			08 59			

Working timetable, May 1970.

WEEKDAYS **WORKSOP TO KIRK SANDALL JN AND BRANCHES**

DOWN	9D38	9D37	9K16	9K10	8E90	9K07	9K10	9K10	9K10	9K16	9K16
	To Normanby Park	08 50 Yorkshire Main to Scunthorpe			08 00 from Kirkby						
			MSX	SO	SO		M ThO	TFO	WO	MSX	MO
WORKSOP SIDINGS ... dep			08 45	08 45		09 32	09 58	09 58	09 58		10 10
Shireoaks East Jn			08X50	08X50		09X37	10X03	10X03	10X03		10X15
Shireoaks Station			ML	ML	09 16	ML	ML	ML	ML		ML
Brancliffe East Jn			09 00	09 00	09 21	09 47	10 13	10 13	10 13		10 25
Dinnington Colliery Jn ... arr			09 15		09 35						10 40
... dep			09 17	09 13		10 00	10 26	10 26	10 26	10 42	10 42
THURCROFT SIDINGS ... arr			09 31							10 56	10 56
Dinnington & Laughton ... arr											
... dep											
Maltby ... arr											
... dep						10 18	10 44		10 44		
Maltby Colliery South ... arr				09 38				10 48			
... dep	08 30										
Maltby Colliery North ... arr											
... dep	08 34					10 21	10 47		10 47		
Firbeck Jn 'A'						10 26	10 52				
Harworth Colliery ... arr						10 43	11 09				
Harworth Glass Bulbs ... dep											
Harworth Colliery G.F. ... arr											
... dep											
Firbeck Jn 'A' ... arr											
... dep	08 39								10 52		
Tickhill & Wadworth ... arr											
... dep											
St. Catherines Jn ... arr		09 07									
... dep	08 53	09 09							11 06		
Black Carr Sidings West ... arr											
... dep									11 11		
Yorkshire Main Sidings ... arr									11 20		
Low Ellers Jn ... arr											
... dep	08 57	09 16									
Potteric Carr Jn											
Markham Main Colliery ... arr											
... dep											
KIRK SANDALL JN ... arr											
... dep	09 12	09 31									

F163

WEEKDAYS **WORKSOP TO KIRK SANDALL JN AND BRANCHES** F164

DOWN		9D03	8E52	9D03			8D82	8D87		9K16	0D01	9D53	8D03	8E55	9D18	8E74	9K17	0V815	0M11		
		10 57 Markham Main to Doncaster Belmont	10 00 from Kirkby	11 20 Markham Main to Doncaster Belmont			To Doncaster Belmont	10 50 from Scunthorpe			13 12 LE Markham Main to Carr Loco	13 40 Yorkshire Main to Normanby Park	13 00 from Scunthorpe	11 00 from Kirkby	To Scunthorpe	12 00 from Kirkby		EBV	EBV		
		SX	MC SO	SO						SO	MX			MC SO		MC SO		SX	T& ThO		
WORKSOP SIDINGS dep										11 25					11 50		12 48				
Shireoaks East Jn										11X30					11X55		12X53				
Shireoaks Station			10 57							ML				11 48	ML	12 48	ML	13 05			
Brancliffe East Jn			10 59							11 40				11 50	12 05	12 50	13 03	13 08			
Dinnington Colliery Jn arr			11 13							11 55				12 04		13 04		13 21			
dep										11 57					12 18		13 16		13 43		
THURCROFT SIDINGS arr										12 11							13 27				
Dinnington & Laughton arr																					
dep																					
Maltby arr																					
dep																			14 03		
Maltby Colliery South arr											After working 10 31 from Immingham				12L42		SUSPENDED	After working 10 58 from Toton			
dep															13L58						
Maltby Colliery North arr																					
dep																			14 09		
Firbeck Jn 'A'																			14 14		
Harworth Colliery arr																			14 30		
Harworth Glass Bulbs dep							11 08														
Harworth Colliery G.F. arr							11 13														
dep							11 15														
Firbeck Jn 'A' arr							11 32														
dep							11 46								14 07						
Tickhill & Wadworth arr																					
dep																					
St. Catherines Jn arr								11 57				13 57	14 08					—0M95 on TFO	After working 12 36 TO from Maltby 12 15 ThO Harworth to Bristol		
dep							12 03	12*06				13 59	14 10		14 21						
Black Carr Sidings West arr																					
dep								12 16					14 18								
Yorkshire Main Sidings arr								12 25					14 27								
Low Ellers Jn arr		11 08		11 31							13 20										
dep		11 11		11 34			12*13				13 22	14 06			14 25						
Potteric Carr Jn		11 20		11 42			12*29				13 28										
Markham Main Colliery arr																					
dep																					
KIRK SANDALL JN arr																					
dep												14 22			14 40						

Working timetable, May 1970.

WEEKDAYS **WORKSOP TO KIRK SANDALL JN AND BRANCHES**

DOWN	0K40	8E76			9K20	8E77		9K08		9D26		9D61		8E74	9D27		9K43	9K61		8E55	
	EBV	13 00 from Kirkby				14 00 from Kirkby				17 14 Markham Main to Doncaster Belmont		To Normanby Park		14 33 from Toton	To Keadby P.S.			To Doncaster Belmont		18 05 from Toton	
	MW FO	MC SO			T& ThO	MC SO		SX		SX				SX			SX			SX	
WORKSOP SIDINGS dep	13 41				13 45			15 43							16 25		16 55				
Shireoaks East Jn	13X45				13X50			15X48							16X30		17X00				
Shireoaks Station	ML	13 48			ML	14 48		ML						16 19	ML		ML			20 12	
Brancliffe East Jn	13 49	13 53			14 00	14 50		15 58						16 21	16 40		17 10			20 17	
Dinnington Colliery Jn arr		14 07				15 04								16 35						20 31	
dep	14 01				14 13			16 11							16 53		17 23				
THURCROFT SIDINGS arr																					
Dinnington & Laughton arr																					
dep																					
Maltby arr					14 33																
dep					14 47			16 29													
Maltby Colliery South arr	14 21														17L15		17 45				
dep												17 08			17L44						
Maltby Colliery North arr																					
dep					14 53			16 32				17 12			17 49						
Firbeck Jn 'A'								16 37													
Harworth Colliery arr								16 54													
Harworth Glass Bulbs dep																		19 10			
Harworth Colliery G.F. arr																		19 15			
dep																		19 17			
Firbeck Jn 'A' arr					15 00													19 34			
dep					15 09							17 17			17 54			19 48			
Tickhill & Wadworth arr					15 18																
dep																					
St. Catherines Jn arr																					
dep												17 31			18 08			20 05			
Black Carr Sidings West arr																					
dep																					
Yorkshire Main Sidings arr																					
Low Ellers Jn arr										17 25											
dep										17 27		17 35			18 12			20 09			
Potteric Carr Jn										17 35								20*23			
Markham Main Colliery arr																					
dep																					
KIRK SANDALL JN arr																					
dep												17 50			18 35						

F165

WEEKDAYS — KIRK SANDALL JN TO WORKSOP AND BRANCHES

F166

M	C	M	C	M	C	UP		8D84	0D49	9K60	8D85	8M55		8D86	8M06§		9K38		9K48				
								04 15 from Normanby Park	05 47 EBV Doncaster Bank to Markham Main	05 51 from Doncaster Decoy	05 02 Scunthorpe to Yorkshire Main	To Toton		05 55 from Scunthorpe	To Kirkby								
									MX	MO													
0	0					**KIRK SANDALL JN** arr																	
						dep		05 37			05 55			06 59									
2	67					Markham Main Colliery arr					**06*06**			**07 10**									
						dep					**06*15**												
				0	0	Potteric Carr Jn			05 57	06 01													
4	53			0	51	Low Ellers Jn arr			**06 03**														
						dep		05 52	**06 04**	06 06	06 24	SUSPENDED MO											
		0	0			Yorkshire Main Sidings dep																	
		1	15			Black Carr Sidings West arr																	
						dep																	
5	38	1	75			St. Catherines Jn arr					**06 29**												
						dep		05 55		06 09	**06 31**												
8	15					Tickhill & Wadworth dep																	
						Firbeck Jn 'A' arr				**06 22**													
9	25	0	0			dep				**06 36**													
		3	29			Harworth Colliery G.F. arr				**06 55**													
						dep				**06 57**													
						Harworth Glass Bulbs arr				**07 02**													
		0	0			Harworth Colliery dep									Rep. No. 8M17 SO				**08 32**				
		3	29			Firbeck Jn 'A'		06 06											08 48				
10	79					Maltby Colliery North arr																	
						dep		06 13											08 55				
11	22					Maltby Colliery South arr		**06 17**															
						dep											**08 08**						
11	55					Maltby arr																	
						dep													08 59				
16	33					Dinnington & Laughton arr																	
						dep																	
				0	0	**THURCROFT SDGS.** dep																	
17	26			2	7	Dinnington Colliery Jn arr											**08 36**		**09 22**				
						dep						**07 20**			**08 55**		**09 01**		**09 47**				
20	54					Brancliffe East Jn arr											**09P35**		**10P21**				
						dep						07 35			09 10		**09 40**		**10 26**				
21	49					Shireoaks Station						07 38			09 13								
22	57					Shireoaks East Jn											**09X50**		**10X36**				
23	4					**WORKSOP SIDINGS** arr											**09 54**		**10 40**				

Working timetable, May 1970.

WEEKDAYS — KIRK SANDALL JN TO WORKSOP AND BRANCHES

UP		9D37		8D81	9K65		8M06		8D86	0D03	9K55	8M60		9K42	9D03	9K49	8M43	9K49	9D03	8D87	
		To Scunthorpe		09 05 from Doncaster Decoy			To Kirkby		08 55 from Scunthorpe	10 15 EBV from Stainforth		To Toton			To Doncaster Belmont		To Toton		To Doncaster Belmont	10 50 Scunthorpe to Yorkshire Main	
					MSX		SO		SO	SX	SX	MC SO		SO	SX	SX	MC SO	SO	SO		
KIRK SANDALL JN arr																					
dep									10 05	10 20										11 37	
Markham Main Colliery arr									**10 16**	**10 30**											
dep															**10 57**				**11 20**		
Potteric Carr Jn				09 11																	
Low Ellers Jn arr										After working 08 53 from Scunthorpe					**11 08**				**11 31**		
dep				09 19											**11 11**				**11 34**	11 52	
Yorkshire Main Sidings dep		**08 50**																			
Black Carr Sidings West arr																					
dep		09 00																			
St. Catherines Jn arr		**09 07**																		11 57	
dep		**09 09**		09 22																**12*06**	
Tickhill & Wadworth dep																					
Firbeck Jn 'A' arr				**09 35**																	
dep				**09 49**																	
Harworth Colliery G.F. arr				**10 08**																	
dep				**10 10**																	
Harworth Glass Bulbs arr				**10 15**																	
Harworth Colliery dep																**11 36**		**11 36**			
Firbeck Jn 'A'																11 51		11 51			
Maltby Colliery North arr																					
dep																11 58		11 58			
Maltby Colliery South arr																					
dep														**11 26**							
Maltby arr																					
dep																12 02		12 02			
Dinnington & Laughton arr																					
dep																					
THURCROFT SIDINGS dep					**10 10**						**11 35**										
Dinnington Colliery Jn arr					**10 24**						**11 49**			**11 54**		**12 25**		**12 25**			
dep							**10 30**				**11 51**	**12 10**		**12*24**		**12 50**	**13 06**	**13*16**			
Brancliffe East Jn arr											**12P25**			**12P58**		**13P24**		**13P50**			
dep							10 45				**12 30**	12 25		**13 05**		**13*41**	13 21	**13 55**			
Shireoaks Station							10 48					12 28					13 24				
Shireoaks East Jn											**12X40**			**13X15**		**13X51**		**14X06**			
WORKSOP SIDINGS arr											**12 44**			**13 19**		**13 55**		**14 10**			

F167

WEEKDAYS — KIRK SANDALL JN TO WORKSOP AND BRANCHES

UP		9K42	9K55	8M95	8V81§	8V81§	9K42	9K42	0D18	8D36	8M38	9K39	0D18	0D01	9D53	9K56	8M36
				● To Toton	To Bristol S.P.M.	To Bristol S.P.M.			11 50 LE from Doncaster Belmont	10 31 from Immingham E.S.	To Toton		12 50 LE from Doncaster Belmont	LE to Carr Loco	To Normanby Park		To Toton
		TO	SO	TFO	M ThO	WO	M WO	FO	SX	MX	MC SO		SO	MX			MC SO
KIRK SANDALL JN	arr																
	dep									12 20							
Markham Main Colliery	arr									12 31							
	dep													13‖12			
Potteric Carr Jn									12 05				13 05				
Low Ellers Jn	arr													13 20			
	dep								12 10				13 10	13 22			
Yorkshire Main Sidings	dep					12 04									13 40		
Black Carr Sidings West	arr				Class 9 to Dinnington C. Jn												
	dep					12 14									13 50		
St. Catherines Jn	arr								12*14						13 57		
	dep					13|19			12*33				13 13		13 59		
Tickhill & Wadworth	dep																
Firbeck Jn 'A'	arr																
	dep					Class 9 to Dinnington C. Jn											
Harworth Colliery G.F.	arr																
	dep																
Harworth Glass Bulbs	arr																
Harworth Colliery	dep				12 15												
Firbeck Jn 'A'					12 30	12 30			12 46				13 24				
Maltby Colliery North	arr																
	dep				12 37	12 37			12 53				13 31				
Maltby Colliery South	arr								12‖56				13‖34			SUSPENDED	
	dep	12 36						12 36				13 22					
Maltby	arr																
	dep				12 41	12 41											
Dinnington & Laughton	arr								After working 10 57 from Markham Main				After working 11 20 from Markham Main	After working 10 21 from Immingham			
	dep																
THURCROFT SIDINGS	dep		12 50													14 48	
Dinnington Colliery Jn	arr	13 04	13 04		13*04	13*04		13 04				13 50					
	dep		13*31	13 44	13L44	13L44	13 54	13*54			14 15	14 25				15 00	15 10
Brancliffe East Jn	arr		14P05				14P28	14P28				14P59				15P31	
	dep		14 10	13 59	13 59	13 59	14*39	14*39			14 33	15 04				15 36	15 26
Shireoaks Station				14 02	14 02	14 02					14 36						15 29
Shireoaks East Jn			14X20				14X49	14X49				15X14				15X46	
WORKSOP SIDINGS	arr		14 24				14 53	14 53				15 18				15 50	

Working timetable, May 1970.

WEEKDAYS — KIRK SANDALL JN TO WORKSOP AND BRANCHES

UP		8D03	9M11	9K40	8M33	0D61	9K40	8D88	9K83	8M59	9K41	8D09	9D26	9K50	9K29	0M07
		13 00 Scunthorpe to Yorkshire Main	To Garston		To Toton	EBV		14 20 from Normanby Park	16 35 from Doncaster Decoy	To Toton		14 52 from Scunthorpe	To Doncaster Belmont			EBV
			TThO	MW FO	MC SO		TThO			SX		SX	SX	SX	SX	SX
KIRK SANDALL JN	arr															
	dep	13 48						15 32				16 06				
Markham Main Colliery	arr											16 17				
	dep												17 14			
Potteric Carr Jn									16 42							
Low Ellers Jn	arr												17 25			
	dep	14 03						15 47	16 47				17 27			
Yorkshire Main Sidings	dep					14 50										
Black Carr Sidings West	arr															
	dep					14 59										
St. Catherines Jn	arr	14 08				15*05										
	dep	14 10				15*21		15 50	16|50							
Tickhill & Wadworth	arr															
Firbeck Jn 'A'	arr						15 40		17 03							
	dep								17*24							
Harworth Colliery G.F.	arr								17 43							
	dep								17 45							
Harworth Glass Bulbs	arr								17 50							
Harworth Colliery	dep		14 55											17 55		
Firbeck Jn 'A'			15 10			15 34	15 47	16 01						18 10		After working 18 05 from Toton
Maltby Colliery North	arr															
	dep		15 17			15 41	15 54	16 08						18 17		
Maltby Colliery South	arr					15 44		16 12								
	dep			14 56							17 55				19 33	
Maltby	arr						16 00									
	dep		15 21				16 32							18 21		
Dinnington & Laughton	arr					After working 13 00 from Scunthorpe										
	dep															
THURCROFT SIDINGS	dep															
Dinnington Colliery Jn	arr			15 24			16 58				18 23			18 44	20 01	
	dep		15 42	15 49	16 05		17 13			18 06	18 48			19 12	20 26	21 07
Brancliffe East Jn	arr		16P13	16P23			17P47				19P22			19P46	21P00	
	dep		16*23	16 28	16 20		17 52			18 21	19 27			19 51	21 05	21 21
Shireoaks Station					16 23					18 24						
Shireoaks East Jn			16X33	16X36			18X02				19X37			20X01	21X15	21X26
WORKSOP SIDINGS	arr		16E37	16 42			18 06				19 41			20 05	21 19	21 29

The productivity gains achieved by the miners and their managers and the collaboration of the NCB, BR and the CEGB both ensured that the SYJR remained an important and profitable line. However, the SYJR lost business to road transport which, in the absence of specialised railheads for bulk coal, had through 1950-1970 reduced from 75 to 60 pc the railways' freight share of Yorkshire's coal production.

Overall in 1970, BR was still hauling some 112.5 m t of coal and coke in 2,000 trains per week. Of this, 1.6 pc originated on the SYJR, compared with 0.44 pc in 1913 and 1.3 pc in both 1929 and 1938, indicating, by reason of the decline of the coal industry, a rise in the line's relative importance in the UK. This was despite 1970s proven coal traffic of 1.8 m t originating on the SYJR (i.e. excluding possible tonnages from Thurcroft and Yorkshire Main), being more than 20 pc below the 2.26 m t of 1932, itself the lowest point of the 'Great Depression'.

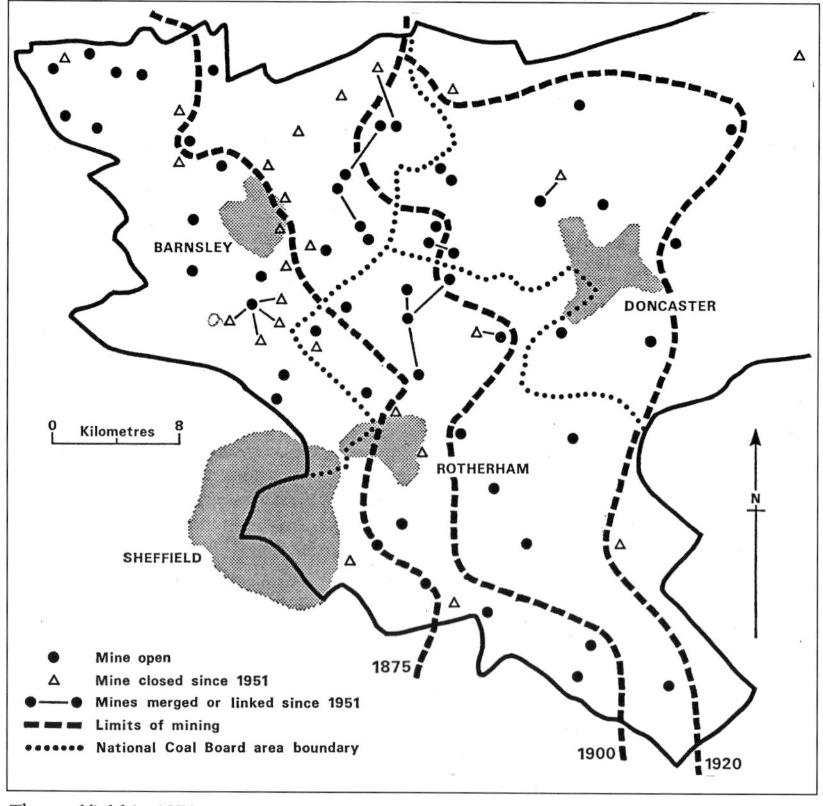

The coalfield in 1971. *Geography*

Chapter Twelve

The SYJR in the era of the Coal Strikes, 1969-1985

Flying Pickets

When Lord Robens took full command of the NCB early in 1961, he thought that the Doncaster coalfield was, 'despite its good coal reserves, troubled . . . stiff with mining as well as industrial relations problems'. In fact, within days (February 1961), he had to face what he called an 'unofficial ugly strike . . . spread by flying columns' to some 60 mines in the Yorkshire coalfield, including all those around Doncaster and some on the SYJR. It lasted two weeks and cost 800,000 t of lost production, which was not too serious given the stocks of unsold coal and had minimal effect on SYJR freight movements.

The absence of major strikes from 1961-1969 did not mean that the miners were happy. They watched oms rising (by 58 pc, 1961-1971), whilst wages lagged behind, so that by 1970 miners were only 17th in the industrial earnings league table. Furthermore by ending piece-rates, the 1966 National Power-Loading Agreement required some miners, such as in the Doncaster area, to take pay cuts. Many miners felt betrayed by the Harold Wilson's 1964-1970 Labour governments, even if the latter did write off £415 m of NCB's £960 m capital debt and introduce pensions for miners at 55 in 1967. Although not until 1965 did the closure programme threaten Yorkshire seriously, miners then watched it reach a crescendo of 55 closures and 55,000 redundancies in 1968-1969 and another 40 closures forecast in the coming year.

Rail closures

Almost equally angry, despite the writing off in 1968 of almost £1,300 m of BR's debt, were the rail unions. Railway workers were faced with closures also, totalling 9,245 km (5,777 miles) of track in the decade after 1961, including a number of coal lines in Yorkshire and North Nottinghamshire. The South Yorkshire Jn line to Wrangbrook closed in 1967. The rail link to the former Firbeck colliery was lifted in 1970, whilst Harworth, having lost its short link to the ECML at Scrooby in 1965, had access only via the SYJR. Also dismantled in 1970 was the GCR and H&BR Jt line from Gowdall to Braithwell Junction (as far south as the A631 road) and its southern spur to Silverwood colliery. This had been used for wagon storage for nearly three decades, but was so neglected as to be obscured by undergrowth with trees growing between the sleepers and even through the wagons. The DVR was closed in July 1966 west of Yorkshire Main to Barnburgh and was dismantled in 1972. Also dismantled was the section at the eastern end of the DVR which ran under the SYJR connecting it to the former GNR & GER Jt. The remaining short section of the DVR from Yorkshire Main to St Catherine's Jn was singled. In 1969-1970, the signal boxes at Thurcroft, Firbeck and Harworth collieries and at Harworth Jn and Tickhill

Kirk Sandall Junction signal box, 31st August, 1971. *M.A. King/Chris Booth Collection*

Low Ellers Junction signal box, 16th June, 1973. *M.A. King/Chris Booth Collection*

station were all closed as a result of systems up-gradings and line closures. Also closed to goods traffic were the SYJR stations at Tickhill (November 1964), Dinnington (May 1965) and Maltby (June 1965).

Regular coal strikes

By the end of the 1960s and despite growing inflation, the average wage in coal mining was less than £25 pw for underground workers and £20 for those on the surface. Meanwhile the colliery closure programme and miners' transfer schemes had brought more militants or 'extreme left wingers', according to Lord Robens, into the East Midlands coalfield and especially South Yorkshire. One symptom of lowered morale amongst Yorkshire's 75,000 miners was the average rate of absenteeism which by 1969 at 22 pc was well above the national average. Indeed it was worse than anything previous, except South Yorkshire's face workers in 1945 (23.8 pc).

In September 1969, the relative harmony in the coalfields ended with an unofficial strike at Cadeby quickly spreading to all Yorkshire's collieries and beyond, closing 140 out of the 307 UK mines. Lasting two weeks, the strike disrupted freight on the SYJR, which carried 175,000 t fewer than in the previous year. It lost a total 2.5 m t of UK production worth £15 m and some £4 m of miners' wages. However it did secure the full NUM claim of £1.37½ (£1 7*s.* 6*d.*) pw (£12.50 in 1999 prices).

Twelve months later the NUM tabled a 33 pc pay claim and a strike ballot gained 60 pc support in Yorkshire, but only 143,000 in favour nationally or 55 pc, below the NUM's required 66 pc for action. Nevertheless three weeks of unofficial strikes followed in October-November 1970. Centred on Doncaster, it was enforced by determined flying pickets, who picketed Coal House and brought all the 10 area collieries and all but one in the South Yorkshire area to a standstill. Another 2.8 m t (£21 m) of production and £5 m of wages were lost, bringing with it as always more disruption to SYJR movements. Later the NCB's original 10 pc offer was accepted by an almost 2:1 vote.

The 1969 and 1970 actions were a hint of things to come. In July 1971 the NUM tabled pay demands of 35-47 pc and the NCB offered less than 8 pc. The union then voted to reduce from 66 to 55 pc the necessary strike majority. With almost 59 pc in favour (but 75 pc in militant Yorkshire), the necessary majority was there for the first official miners' national strike since 1926.

This began with an overtime ban on 1st November, 1971 and became a full strike on 9th January, lasting until 27th February. All 280,000 miners at the UK's 289 collieries struck. The combination of cold weather, a blockade of generating stations by miners, supported fully by ASLEF members who moved 80 pc of fuel, and the closure of the Saltley coke depot forced power cuts. Coal traffic on the SYJR was brought to a halt by the NUM/ASLEF actions, a situation exacerbated by the run-down of unsold coal stocks to only 6 m t nationally.

As the strike lengthened, the pickets stopped members of NACODS, the safety and maintenance men's union, from entering Dinnington, an action which could have closed it for ever, given its technical difficulties and high costs. Similar action in February was taken by pickets at other SYJR collieries

St Catherine's Junction signal box, 16th June, 1973. *M.A. King/Chris Booth Collection*

Tickhill & Wadworth signal box, 16th June, 1973. *M.A. King/Chris Booth Collection*

Firbeck Junction A signal box, 26th July, 1972. *M.A. King/Chris Booth Collection*

Maltby Station signal box, 28th August, 1968. *M.A. King/Chris Booth Collection*

Tickhill station, view looking south towards Maltby on 26th May, 1975.
R.M. Casserley Collection

Maltby station, view looking north towards Tickhill on 26th May, 1975.
R.M. Casserley Collection

including Maltby and Thurcroft. The latter was another troubled operation where in 1970, the Parkgate seam was being replaced by Haigh Moor and by which time the workforce of 900 was producing only about 310,000 t pa. Also affected was Markham Main, following the death of one of its miners struck by a truck whilst picketing at Keadby generating station on 2nd February.

By 10th February, more than 1.6 m UK workers had been laid off and the country was only two weeks from a total shutdown. A State of Emergency was declared and the hastily-established Wilberforce Committee quickly awarded the miners a pay increase of £5 per week. On the 25th it was announced that all miners in South Yorkshire were returning to work. Later the NCB later announced an overall loss of £157 m for the year, but the Coal Industry Act of 1973 provided some relief, writing off some £450 m of debts and enhancing redundancy terms and various operational grants.

Despite the introduction of an incomes policy by the (1970-1974) Heath Government, the miners, particularly in South Yorkshire, believed that they could secure further pay increases. In July 1973 the NUM tabled a pay claim ranging from 22-46 pc and in October rejected a 13 pc offer from the NCB, followed by an overtime ban in November. SYJR operations and elsewhere were soon seriously affected by ASLEF's ban, in support of a pay claim, on Sunday, overtime and rest-day working, which began on 12th December, 1973. This action continued with one-day stoppages until mid-February 1974.

By this time, however, following the Arab-Israeli war in Autumn 1973, the oil exporters (OPEC) cut back shipments to the west by 25 pc (later to 15) and increased prices heavily. The Government called a State of Emergency, instituted a three-day week, referred the miners' claim to the Pay Board and called a general election for 28th February. The NUM voted 80 pc in favour of a strike, including large majorities at the SYJR's collieries, and struck on 10th February. On 4th March the General Election brought Harold Wilson back to Downing Street and a pay settlement well over twice the NCB's offer ended the strike. The South Yorkshire area's annual production fell by 2 m t to 7.56 m t, creating a loss of £10.7, compared with a previous year's profit of £1.7 m. The freight operations and revenues of the SYJR were severely but unquantifiably disrupted and reduced for the fourth time in six years.

Plan for Coal, 1974

In 1970, UK generating stations had consumed a record 76 m t of coal and three years later Yorkshire alone was supplying more than 20 m t pa to this market, with SYJR collieries amongst the most important sources. However, smarting from effects of the strikes, the CEGB wanted to reduce its long-term dependence on coal and, outside the mining areas, there was a the growing preference for nuclear-, oil- and even gas-fired stations. All this forced the NCB and BR to struggle to maintain their share of this market.

North Sea gas, however, provided only 12 pc of Britain's energy requirements and was regarded, according to Parker, as a 'premium fuel' and until the 1990s not to be used for electricity generation. Only 38 m t of North Sea oil came

This Wickham two-car unit, Nos. DB975005/6 formed the Eastern Region General Manager's saloon. It is seen here at Firbeck 'A' on 11th February, 1976 while working from York to York via the SYJR line to Harworth and then to Worksop and Retford.

E. Willoughby/Chris Booth Collection

Maltby Colliery South signal box looking towards Maltby station on 1st April, 1973.

M.A. King/Chris Booth Collection

Diverted due to engineering works, a Scunthorpe to Llanwern steel train passes Firbeck A signal box, *en route* towards Maltby on 5th January, 1976. *E. Willoughby/Chris Booth Collection*

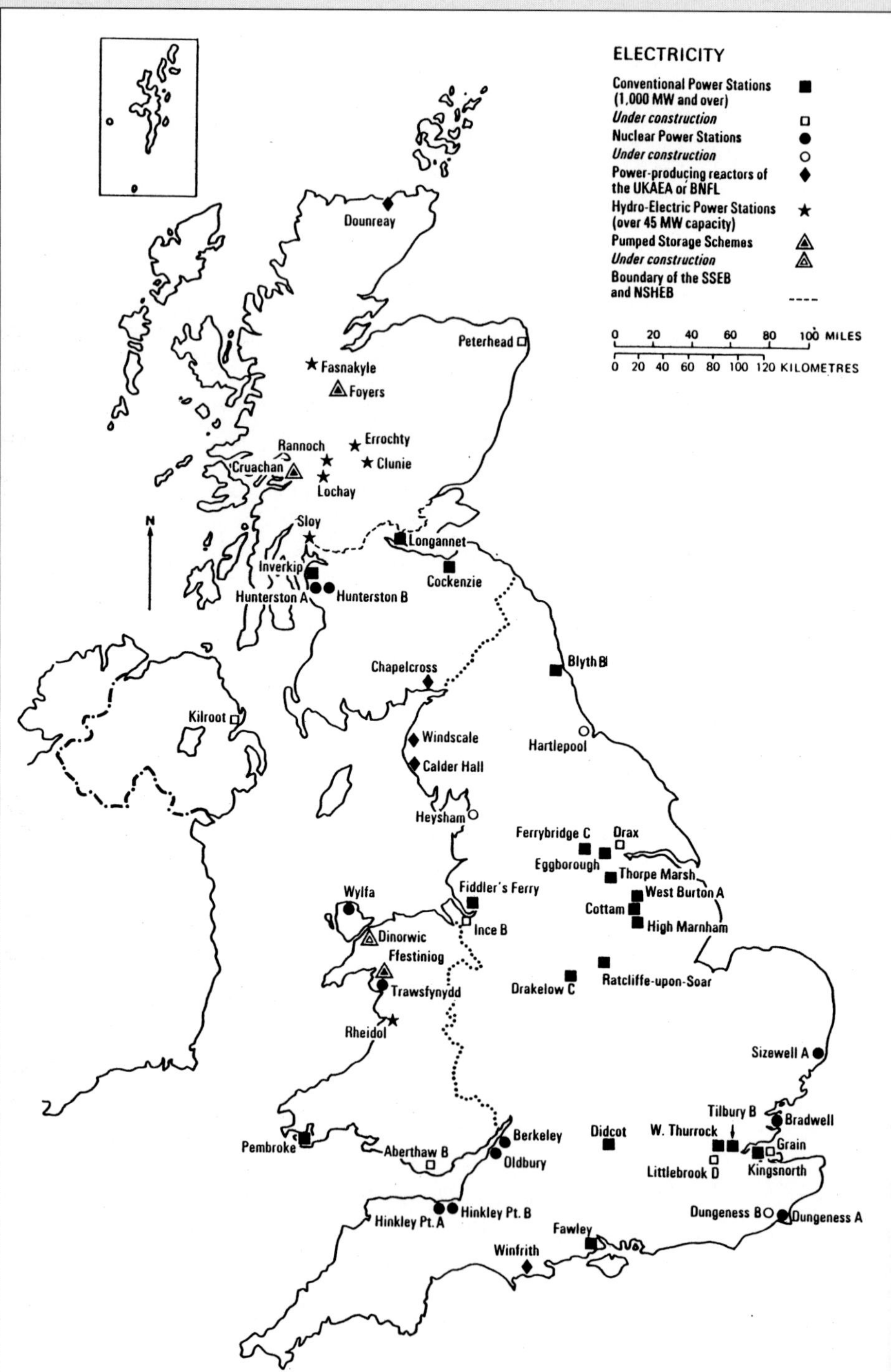

ELECTRICITY
Conventional Power Stations (1,000 MW and over)
Under construction
Nuclear Power Stations
Under construction
Power-producing reactors of the UKAEA or BNFL
Hydro-Electric Power Stations (over 45 MW capacity)
Pumped Storage Schemes
Under construction
Boundary of the SSEB and NSHEB
0 20 40 60 80 100 MILES
0 20 40 60 80 100 120 KILOMETRES
N
Dounreay
Peterhead
Fasnakyle
Foyers
Rannoch
Errochty
Cruachan
Clunie
Lochay
Sloy
Longannet
Inverkip
Cockenzie
Hunterston A
Hunterston B
Chapelcross
Blyth B
Kilroot
Windscale
Calder Hall
Hartlepool
Heysham
Ferrybridge C
Drax
Eggborough
Thorpe Marsh
Fiddler's Ferry
West Burton A
Wylfa
Cottam
High Marnham
Ince B
Dinorwic
Ffestiniog
Ratcliffe-upon-Soar
Drakelow C
Trawsfynydd
Rheidol
Sizewell A
Tilbury B
Bradwell
W. Thurrock
Grain
Berkeley
Didcot
Pembroke
Aberthaw B
Oldbury
Littlebrook D
Kingsnorth
Hinkley Pt. A
Hinkley Pt. B
Dungeness B
Dungeness A
Fawley
Winfrith

Map of generating stations, 1979. *HMSO*

ashore in 1977, whilst in that year also, nuclear power was producing no more than 14 pc of British electricity. Coal was still 'King' at the generating stations.

Moreover, oil prices continued to rise throughout the 1970s, from $13-$34 a barrel and with Labour Governments in power from 1974-1979, coal became favoured again. Initially therefore, the closures in the coal industry virtually ended and production stabilised in the late 1970s at around 122 m t pa with a total workforce of 230,000. Only six Yorkshire collieries, none on the SYJR, were closed between 1974-1981. By contrast *The Plan for Coal* of 1974 announced an expansion of output by 42 m t by 1980, including the development of new coalfields in the South Midlands and at Selby in North Yorkshire.

By the following year, the NCB was able to produce a profit of £34 m, whilst benefiting from £68 m of grants under the various Acts. The new Labour Government also helped BR with the 1974 Railways Act which wrote off £250 m debt and made grants available for the provision of facilities to increase freight haulage by rail. Thus by 1977, 80 pc of all rail freight, which included 94 m t of coal and coke, went by train-load, as distinct from wagon-load.

SYJR production, 1976

Overall by 1975-1976, the SYJR-accessing collieries were helping to raise Yorkshire's coal production to 26 pc of the UK total. During that year, Maltby produced 886,000 t, Yorkshire Main 604,000 and Markham Main 576,000, whilst Thurcroft and Dinnington were each around 340,000. But even combined with Harworth's production, this meant that less than 2 mt pa was originating along the SYJR, well below the average 1930s level. One reason for this was the 'loss' to the line since 1940 of virtually all shipments from Rossington, which was then producing more than one m t pa.

Despite this improved market for coal, especially electricity generation, total output in the Doncaster and South Yorkshire areas of the NCB fell by 1.5 and 18 pc respectively between 1971-1977. Both areas were in profit, the latter area helped by the investment of more than £4 m each for Thurcroft and Dinnington in 1974 for skip winding gear and coal preparation plants. In 1977, a new coking plant was opened at Thurcroft, which recovered 99 pc of coke production at the rate of 330 t per hour. By 1980 Thurcroft sent 98 pc of its output to the British Steel Corporation.

It is likely that the Queen was made aware of this hard-won achievement around her when, preparatory to her visit to South Yorkshire on 28th July, 1975, the Royal Train was stabled earlier that day (2.45-9.30 am) at Firbeck, requiring a strong police presence and special passes for rail workers. Following visits to Doncaster, Barnsley, Sheffield and Rotherham, she and Prince Philip visited Silverwood colliery on the 30th, descending 550 m and travelling 2.8 km to one of the four faces. There she hacked off a lump of coal as a souvenir.

89 million tonnes

By 1977, despite the competition from oil (16 pc) and nuclear (14 pc), almost 70 pc of the CEGB's output was still coal-fired, with consumption of more than 80 m t. This total then reached an all-time record of 89 m t in 1979, by which time Drax 'A' was fully on stream and further increases in world oil prices were giving coal a 40 per cent price advantage. Unsurprisingly, the NCB and CEGB were able that year to conclude a five year agreement for the provision of 75 m t pa at stable prices (of £37 pt in 1981).

From the point of view of their economic survival, the deep collieries of the East Midlands coalfield, including those on the SYJR and other BR operations, were fortunate that much of the local new capacity in the 1960 s was coal-fired. More worryingly for the long term, between 1951 and 1979 sulphur dioxide emissions from these coal-fired stations rose from 1.02 m t to a peak of 3.1 (58 pc of all UK emissions) although falling thereafter, whereas the UK total from all sources had been in decline since 1966, when it had peaked at 5.93 m t.

In a bid to increase productivity, the NCB proposed and the NUM agreed to negotiate local earnings schemes. Within two years average weekly pay at the coalface had increased by almost 50 pc from £85 to £125. The result was a noticeable improvement in UK productivity and output, the former by 14 pc oms between 1979-1983 and the latter by 4 m t between 1978-1981.

At Maltby for example, the 1,450 miners increased production from 780,000 t in 1979 to 950,000 t in 1981, mostly sent out on SYJR m-g-r trains. Less happily, but almost inevitably in a period of high inflation, average UK colliery operating costs had risen by 50 pc between 1973-1980. Unfortunately, this period also coincided with the beginning of a serious recession and industrial decline, especially in steel. Particularly devastated were neighbouring Sheffield and Rotherham, many works there being important customers of SYJR collieries. North Sea oil production, meanwhile, was rising steadily from 38 m t in 1977 to a peak of 126 m t in 1986, helping to increase the value of the pound and damage coal exports and industry generally.

The result of all these factors was a large and growing stockpile of unsold coal. No more coal could go to the CEGB which in 1976 had reached its maximum capacity of 58,677 MW, or almost 40 pc above maximum demand. Despite a government order in 1978 that two new advanced gas-cooled reactors be built, the CEGB reduced total capacity to less than 55,000 MW by 1983, by which time it was burning only 81 m t of coal.

The Ridley plan

In May 1979 the Conservatives, led by Mrs (later Baroness) Margaret Thatcher won the general election. Memories of the NUM's two defeats of the Edward Heath Government rankled and in 1978 Mrs Thatcher had asked Nicholas Ridley MP to begin preparing to defeat an anticipated and potentially devastating miners' strike. Ridley's plan involved keeping one year's supply of coal at power stations, converting others to dual coal/oil firing, contracting haulage firms with non-union drivers who would not be intimidated by pickets to move coal, cutting off social security to strikers and training special police units to deal with flying pickets. Some of these, including the virtual paralysis of the line, would be variously part of the experience of the communities along the SYJR in 1984-1985.

In 1980 a Coal Industry Bill requiring a completely self-financing NCB would, according to Arthur Scargill, the Yorkshire NUM leader, cause the closure of 50 collieries. Meanwhile, productivity and unsold coal stocks were rising and early in 1981 an NCB announcement of a plan to close 23 collieries led to unofficial miners' strikes. Unready yet to face a national coal strike, the Government yielded. The closure programme was stopped, coal imports slashed and £500 m in state aid was given to the industry. Nevertheless, mining jobs continued to disappear 'by stealth' at an average rate of 1,000 a month for the next 18 months. Simultaneously, the generating stations began stocking coal, acquiring a multi-million tonne reserve by December 1981, by which time Arthur Scargill had been elected President of the NUM with a 70 pc majority.

100,000 train loads

Despite the high output of East Midlands collieries, all was not well in the SYJR's area. Between 1977-1982, total output in the South Yorkshire and Doncaster areas had fallen respectively by 8 pc and 10 pc, with losses of 80p and £2.90 p t. By reason of technical problems, Dinnington had the highest costs amongst the SYJR collieries at £45 per ton, compared with the two 2001 survivors - Maltby and Harworth each at around £31-32. All the SYJR collieries were recording losses, as high as £22 per ton at Markham Main. Ironically the latter's immediate neighbour Rossington had the lowest costs at £27.7 pt.

An ever smaller percentage of the coal originating along the SYJR was now from the prized Barnsley seam, all but exhausted in the early 1980s. Swallow Wood, Parkgate and eight others were then the principal sources but, from Maltby, a £1.5 m survey had computed, 100 m t of reserves were accessible. This was theoretically equal to about 100,000 m-g-r train loads to be dispatched along the SYJR, assuming it could all be extracted economically!

Re-signalling at Doncaster

Overall by 1982, the five collieries with access to the SYJR (plus Rossington) were sending to generating stations up to 75 pc of their combined output of more than 4.8 m t pa. By reason that an ever larger proportion of this output also went by m-g-r and, notwithstanding the frequent industrial unrest and seemingly endless closures in both the coal and rail industries of the post-war period, the SYJR was still originating about 2 m t pa of coal freight and therefore managing to remain a profitable and important part of Britain's rail network with a good future.

To ensure these operations, SYJR signalmen had worked 12 hour days, but this soon began to change at the end of the 1970s with a major upgrading of signalling at Doncaster. A power signal box was installed there, which took over

Self-moving powered hydraulic supports, 1976. *Museum of South Yorkshire Life*

Passing Maltby Colliery North signal box is diverted 6J28, Whitwell Quarry to Doncaster train, hauled by class '31' No. 31284, as a sister engine waits in the colliery sidings with a Maltby to Worksop trip working in 1980. *B.E. Bates/Chris Booth Collection*

all signalling on the SYJR as far south as Firbeck Jn. The box at St Catherine's Jn had been closed in May 1977 and its functions taken over temporarily by Decoy No. 1 box. Also closed were the boxes at Maltby Colliery Sidings North in February 1978, Low Ellers (May 1979) and Markham Main sidings and Kirk Sandall Jn in February 1980. Firbeck 'B' box and the short stretch of line from Firbeck East Jn to Firbeck South Jn were abandoned in June 1983, meaning that Harworth trains could not proceed northwards unless they reversed at Firbeck West Jn. Earlier boxes closed on the line included Thurcroft Sidings (May 1969), Maltby Station (November 1972) and Dinnington Station (May 1973).

M-G-R safety

At Harworth, for example, instructions in the *Sectional Appendix to the Working Timetable and books of Rules and Regulations -SOUTHERN AREA -* (February 1982) and the *BR (Eastern Region) M.G.R. Train Working and Operating at Rapid Loading/Unloading Installations (Collieries, Power Stations etc.)* (February 1983) required that:

> Drivers approaching Harworth from Maltby surrendered their key tokens to the Firbeck 'B' box signalman who, in return gave it later to the driver approaching from Harworth, if the Firbeck 'A' box gave the all-clear. If not the driver collected a token from the auxiliary instrument fixed beside the signal leading onto the single line and phoned the 'A' box signalman from there. Guards were responsible for ensuring that trains approaching from Harworth stopped at the 'B' signal and were required to check if the train was clear of the trap points and inform the signalman at 'A' if he was inside the trap points.
>
> Approaching Harworth colliery, the guard had first to seek permission from the NCB weigh office staff to enter the loading area and obtain two radio sets, one for the driver, after which the NCB's mechanical shovel operator became responsible for the movement of the train, contacting the guard and driver by radio. The guard was responsible for informing the driver to stop at the radio pad.
>
> Strict radio discipline was maintained with the use of the words 'British Rail Guard to British Rail Driver' preceding all radio instructions, which had to be acknowledged. In the event of a breakdown of radio communications, the driver had to stop until these were restored. An initial radio test transmission was made before the train moved into the loading area, after which the train could move forward at 6.4 kph (4 mph).

Loading and weighing was carried out at a stop/start speed not exceeding the usual 0.8 kph, after which the train proceeded to the rear of the weighbridge and halted. The radio sets were then returned to the NCB staff after which the train was propelled to the departure line. Defective wagons were placed in the 'cripples sidings', which were controlled by NCB staff, who held the keys to padlocked points controlling access there.

The need for adhering strictly to such detailed safety regulations was illustrated by one incident at Firbeck in this period. A driver of an m-g-r (2 x class '20') out of Harworth exchanged tokens at Firbeck 'B' and passed over the West Jn towards Maltby. As he moved through the cutting with both locomotives 'working flat out' he noticed the pipe pressure falling, meaning either that a pipe had burst or the wagons had become separated. The braking systems applied automatically, becoming totally seized. The driver and the guard walked back down the line and found the last three wagons derailed. It transpired that the signalman had put the signal back to danger whilst the train was passing over the trap points and operated them, instead of waiting first to see the red light at the rear of the train. Trap points are designed to derail any unauthorised movement against a danger signal. One wagon was leaning drunkenly against the edge of the cutting and the other two had 'chewed up' the line and sleepers.

Battlefield positions

During 1982-1983, the scenario of a titanic NUM-Government battle slowly unfolded. In July 1982 the NUM Conference agreed to make a 31 pc pay claim, on behalf of its members whose average earnings were £154 pw. With the new super-pits in Leicestershire and Selby due to open, the NCB wished to close 30 existing collieries which employed 20,000 men. This rose to a hit-list of 46 one month later, with almost all closing in the next two years. The NUM announced an overtime ban in October, but only 39 pc of its 220,000 members voted to strike.

In April 1983, the NUM moved to a new purpose-built HQ in Sheffield, and Mrs Thatcher was returned to Downing St with an larger majority in June. In September she appointed a new Chairman of the NCB, the tough Scottish-American (Sir) Ian MacGregor, former head of British Steel. In October, another NUM overtime ban began, soon costing the NCB £2-3 m pounds per month. The colliery closure programme was accelerated, but still those on the SYJR remained sacrosanct. To soften the impact of closures, the Government offered younger miners either relocation or redundancy pay, whilst many older men could take an early pension and lump sum. Meanwhile the 'Ridley plan' was ready. Coal stocks exceeded 58 m t (but 40 per cent of these were held within collieries). Dual-fired generating stations were on stream and Police Support Units (PSU) totalling 10,000 men were on stand-by.

The Coalfield, 1984

At the start of the strike, there were still more than 54,000 miners in Yorkshire employed at 53 collieries, producing more than 26 m t pa. Of these, the most militant in Yorkshire were the 13,355 miners in the Doncaster area, which produced 5.8 m t pa, part of it from along the SYJR, and of which 75 pc went to CEGB stations. With absenteeism down to 11.5 pc, perhaps to compensate for the overtime ban of October 1983, and helped by £34 m investment in the previous year, productivity was still rising. At Yorkshire Main, a new Coal Preparation plant had been started and another was planned at Markham Main. Safety was good with the Doncaster area having only one fatality in 1982-1984.

In the South Yorkshire area, which had almost 14,000 miners producing 6.57 m t on the eve of the strike, some of it also originating along the SYJR, investment levels were high and all coal was cut and loaded by power. A huge development plan to increase production from 1 to 2 m t pa was in progress at Maltby where

1,400 men worked the Parkgate and Swallow Wood seams. At Dinnington, 920 men also worked on the Swallow Wood seam, as did the 850 men at Thurcroft, producing 550,000 t pa. Productivity was breaking new records with oms amongst face workers at 15.87 t at Dinnington, 16 at Maltby and 22.58 at Silverwood - no longer connected to the SYJR - where a new £2 m winding engine had been installed. Absenteeism in the South Yorkshire Area was down to 10.4 pc, but tragically six fatalities and 90 serious injuries had occurred in 1982-1984.

All this production in the two Yorkshire areas and 866,000 t from Harworth continued to benefit the SYJR greatly. Compared with the 20 pc which went by road and seven by water, about 73 pc of Yorkshire's coal production now moved by rail, a reversal of previous trends brought about almost entirely by the growth of m-g-r movements. The latter were going in larger 34 wagon sets, many hauled by class '56' and '58' diesels. In 1983 most of Yorkshire's coal went to CEGB stations, 80 pc by m-g-r, whilst exports via the IBT took 0.75 m t from the Doncaster area alone.

Strike in Yorkshire

In 1984, the imminent closure programme amongst the remaining 171 UK collieries appeared to be targeted at militant areas, but still none was on the SYJR. The first Yorkshire closure at Cortonwood colliery was, despite one million pounds of recent capital investment, announced on 6th March. This provoked an all-out strike from 9th March, under Rule 41 - allowing local strikes. Yorkshire's miners struck, including all those along the SYJR, except at Harworth, whose North Nottinghamshire Area's ballot was held on 15th-16th March. Unofficial Yorkshire pickets arrived outside Harworth on the 12th and were joined by local men, whilst large numbers of police arrived there and elsewhere in the county.

The strike which was to last a full year, cost around £6 bn, led to 10,000 arrests and left three dead and 1,000 injured. 100 collieries were closed soon after and 100,000 jobs lost, leaving the once-mighty NUM split and greatly weakened.

Overall by 14th March, 1984, the whole Yorkshire coalfield had closed down and 133 collieries throughout the UK were idle, either by voting or picketing. In neighbouring Nottinghamshire however, miners voted 20,188 to 7,258 or 73 pc against a strike. At Harworth, the vote was 753 to 312 (67.4 pc) against. No national ballot was held. Despite more than 2,300 Nottinghamshire miners initially striking, all its collieries were still in operation including Harworth, only 13 km south of militant Doncaster.

Mass picketing

Despite court injunctions, Yorkshire pickets assembled outside their own silent collieries and others still working. At Harworth, within easy reach of militant miners from neighbouring Markham Main and Rossington, large numbers of police were deployed. On 2nd May, 8,000 pickets arrived there crossing fields to avoid the police, who were drafted in to keep the majority of Nottinghamshire miners working throughout the strike.

WEEKDAYS — GAINSBOROUGH TRENT JNS TO TINSLEY AND SHEFFIELD,AND BRANCHES — YJ52

Mileage M.C.	Mileage M.C.	DOWN Up- Broughton Lane Jn to Shepcote Lane Jn.Nunnery Jn to Nunnery Main Line Jn			6D54	6J76		7E43	6M62	7M27			6D64		6D45	0J03	0D48		6D64	7D48			6M43	6M43		6M25
					22 48 SX M.G.R. from Immingham NCB Termnl	23 31 SX M.G.R. Immingham NCB Termnl to Shirebrook R.S.		20 44SX M.G.R. Avenue Sdgs to Immingham NCB Termnl	20 53 SX ABS Parkeston Yard to Widnes West Deviation	To Garston Speke Sdgs			01 45 COY from Peterboro West Yd		02 53 M.G.R. from Immingham NCB Termnl	LD	LD		04 16 COY from Peterboro West Yd	M.G.R. to ScntCHP			05 38 M.G.R. Immingham NCB Termnl to Avenue Sdgs	05 38 M.G.R. Immingham NCB Termnl to Barrow Hill		06 38 COY Kirton Lime Sdgs to Earles Sdgs
		TIMING LOAD			D	D		D	D	D			D		D	D	D		D	D			D	D		D
					MX AIR ■ Y	MX AIR ■		MX AIR ■	MX AIR ■	MSX			MX AIR ■		MX AIR ■	MTX	TWO		MO AIR ■	TWO AIR ■			MSX AIR ■	SO AIR ■		MFX AIR ■
			1																							
0.00		GAINSBOROUGH TRENT JNS	2			00 43							03 42		03 59				06 05				06 48	06 48		07 05
		West Burton C.E.G.B.	3										03 47						06 10							
		Cottam C.E.G.B. dep	4																							
4.70		Clarborough Jn	5		←	00 51							Maximum Speed 55 m.p.h		04 07	After working 00 35 from Garston Speke Sdgs							06 56	06 56		07 12
8.56		Retford Thrumpton S.B.	6		00 06	00 57									04 13								07 02	07 02		07 17
14.32		Manton Wood N.C.B.	7																							
16.49		Worksop West S.B. arr	8																							
		Worksop West S.B. dep	9		00X18	01 10			02X17						04X26								07 15	07 15		07 27
17.05		WORKSOP S.S. arr	10		00 22				02 20						04 30											MFX UNTIL 26 NOV AND FROM 20 MAR TWSO 29 NOV TO 17 MAR
		WORKSOP S.S. dep	11						02 35	03 39						04‖49	06‖07									
17.32		Shireoaks East Jn	12			01 12			02X39	03X43						04X53	06X10									
18.35		Shireoaks	13						ML																	
19.45	0.00	Brancliffe East Jn	14														06 13									
	3.28	Dinnington Colliery Jn	15														06‖25			06 50						
	9.32	Maltby Colliery Sth. S.B.	16																	07 15						
	9.55	Maltby Colliery Nth. S.B.	17														To work the 06 50 to ScntCHP			07 17						
	11.19	Firbeck Jn.A.	18																	07 23						
	15.16	St.Catherines Jn.	19																	07 37						
	20.54	KIRK SANDALL JN	20																	07 53						
22.33		Kiveton Park Colly	21						02 48	03 53						04 59							07 25	07 25		07 38
	0.00	Beighton Jn	22					01 38																		
		Beighton Depot	23																							
26.51	0.79	Woodhouse Jn arr	24					01RR45															07RR33	07RR33		
		Woodhouse Jn dep	25					02RR11	02 54	03 59						05 05							08RR*14	08RR14		07 43
28.13		Orgreave	26																							
30.19	0.00	Darnall	27						03 00	04 06						05 11										07 49
			28																							
	0.50	Attercliffe Jn	29							04 08						05 13										
		Broughton Lane Jn	30							04 12						05 15										
		Shepcote Lane Jn	31							04 14						05 17										
	3.48	TINSLEY N.Y. arr	32							04RR20																
			33							EF						Tinsley T.M.D. arr 05‖27										
	0.00	TINSLEY N.Y. dep	34							04RR45																
		Shepcote Lane Jn	35																							
		Broughton Lane Jn	36																							
		Broughton Lane B.O.C.	37																							
	2.78	Attercliffe Jn	38																							
30.74	3.27	Woodburn Jn	39						03 01																	07 50
		Nunnery Main Line Jn	40						03 03																	07 53
			41																							
39.70		Deepcar F.D.	42																							

Working timetable, 3rd October, 1983 to 13th May, 1984.

WEEKDAYS — GAINSBOROUGH TRENT JNS TO TINSLEY AND SHEFFIELD,AND BRANCHES — YJ52

Mileage M.C.	Mileage M.C.	DOWN Up- Broughton Lane Jn to Shepcote Lane Jn.Nunnery Jn to Nunnery Main Line Jn			6D54	6J76		7E43	6M62	7M27			6D64		6D45	0J03	0D48		6D64	7D48			6M43	6M43		6M25
					22 48 SX M.G.R. from Immingham NCB Termnl	23 31 SX M.G.R. Immingham NCB Termnl to Shirebrook R.S.		20 44SX M.G.R. Avenue Sdgs to Immingham NCB Termnl	20 53 SX ABS Parkeston Yard to Widnes West Deviation	To Garston Speke Sdgs			01 45 COY from Peterboro West Yd		02 53 M.G.R. from Immingham NCB Termnl	LD	LD		04 16 COY from Peterboro West Yd	M.G.R. to ScntCHP			05 38 M.G.R. Immingham NCB Termnl to Avenue Sdgs	05 38 M.G.R. Immingham NCB Termnl to Barrow Hill		06 38 COY Kirton Lime Sdgs to Earles Sdgs
		TIMING LOAD			D	D		D	D	D			D		D	D	D		D	D			D	D		D
					MX AIR ■ Y	MX AIR ■		MX AIR ■	MX AIR ■	MSX			MX AIR ■		MX AIR ■	MTX	TWO		MO AIR ■	TWO AIR ■			MSX AIR ■	SO AIR ■		MFX AIR ■
			1																							
0.00		GAINSBOROUGH TRENT JNS	2			00 43							03 42		03 59				06 05				06 48	06 48		07 05
		West Burton C.E.G.B.	3										03 47						06 10							
		Cottam C.E.G.B. dep	4																							
4.70		Clarborough Jn	5		←	00 51							Maximum Speed 55 m.p.h		04 07	After working 00 35 from Garston Speke Sdgs							06 56	06 56		07 12
8.56		Retford Thrumpton S.B.	6		00 06	00 57									04 13								07 02	07 02		07 17
14.32		Manton Wood N.C.B.	7																							
16.49		Worksop West S.B. arr	8																							
		Worksop West S.B. dep	9		00X18	01 10			02X17						04X26								07 15	07 15		07 27
17.05		WORKSOP S.S. arr	10		00 22				02 20						04 30											MFX UNTIL 26 NOV AND FROM 20 MAR TWSO 29 NOV TO 17 MAR
		WORKSOP S.S. dep	11						02 35	03 39						04‖49	06‖07									
17.32		Shireoaks East Jn	12			01 12			02X39	03X43						04X53	06X10									
18.35		Shireoaks	13						ML																	
19.45	0.00	Brancliffe East Jn	14														06 13									
	3.28	Dinnington Colliery Jn	15														06‖25			06 50						
	9.32	Maltby Colliery Sth. S.B.	16																	07 15						
	9.55	Maltby Colliery Nth. S.B.	17														To work the 06 50 to ScntCHP			07 17						
	11.19	Firbeck Jn.A.	18																	07 23						
	15.16	St.Catherines Jn.	19																	07 37						
	20.54	KIRK SANDALL JN	20																	07 53						
22.33		Kiveton Park Colly	21						02 48	03 53						04 59							07 25	07 25		07 38
	0.00	Beighton Jn	22					01 38																		
		Beighton Depot	23																							
26.51	0.79	Woodhouse Jn arr	24					01RR45															07RR33	07RR33		
		Woodhouse Jn dep	25					02RR11	02 54	03 59						05 05							08RR*14	08RR14		07 43
28.13		Orgreave	26																							
30.19	0.00	Darnall	27						03 00	04 06						05 11										07 49
			28																							
	0.50	Attercliffe Jn	29							04 08						05 13										
		Broughton Lane Jn	30							04 12						05 15										
		Shepcote Lane Jn	31							04 14						05 17										
	3.48	TINSLEY N.Y. arr	32							04RR20																
			33							EF						Tinsley T.M.D. arr 05‖27										
	0.00	TINSLEY N.Y. dep	34							04RR45																
		Shepcote Lane Jn	35																							
		Broughton Lane Jn	36																							
		Broughton Lane B.O.C.	37																							
	2.78	Attercliffe Jn	38																							
30.74	3.27	Woodburn Jn	39						03 01																	07 50
		Nunnery Main Line Jn	40						03 03																	07 53
			41																							
39.70		Deepcar F.D.	42																							

WEEKDAYS — GAINSBOROUGH TRENT JNS TO TINSLEY AND SHEFFIELD, AND BRANCHES — YJ54

DOWN SEE SPECIAL NOTES		0D80	7M20	6D50	0J03	0M59	9L92	7D80	6D61	0L53	6M59	8M29	6D63	0V56	6D43	6M70	6M56
		LD	11 58 Clipstone N.C.B. Ø to Garston Docks	10 59 M.G.R. from Immingham NCB Termnl	LD	14 15 LD from Tinsley T.M.D.	To Crofton Depot	M.G.R. to ScntCHP	COY to Lindsey Oil Refinery	LD to Healey Mills N.Y.	COY to Ditton BOC Sdgs	To Toton New Bank	14 14 from Immingham Recep Sdgs	LD	15 56 M.G.R. from Immingham NCB Termnl	ABS to Toton West Yard	15 05 M.G.R. Immingham NCB Termnl to Avenue Sdgs
TIMING LOAD		D	D	D	D	D	D	D	D	D	D	D	D	D	D	D	D
		SX	SX AIR ■ Y	SX AIR ■ Y	SX	TTHO	TO	SX AIR ■	MTTHO AIR ■ Y	THO	TTHO AIR ■	SX	SX	MWFO	SX AIR ■	SX AIR ■	SX AIR ■
	1		Ø -				CCE a/c										
GAINSBOROUGH TRENT JNS	2		11 52	12 21									15 34		16 58		17 15
West Burton C.E.G.B.	3		Ollerton				Timed To A										
Cottam C.E.G.B. dep	4		N.C.B.				Maximum		**13 00**								
Clarborough Jn	5			12 29			Speed Of		13 04				15 46		17 06		17 23
Retford Thrumpton S.B.	6			12 35			25Mph		13 09				15 54		17 12		17 29
Manton Wood N.C.B.	7																
Worksop West S.B. arr	8																
Worksop West S.B. dep	9			12X48					13X20				16X12		17X25		17 42
WORKSOP S.S. arr	10			**12 52**					**13RR24**				**16 16**		**17 29**		
WORKSOP S.S. dep	11	**12‖26**							**13RR44**			**14 51**		**17‖18**		**17 30**	
Shireoaks East Jn	12	12X29										14X56		17X22		17X34	
Shireoaks	13		12 41														
Brancliffe East Jn	14	12 32												17 24			
Dinnington Colliery Jn	15	**12‖44**						**13 12**						**17‖36**			
Maltby Colliery Sth. S.B.	16							13 37									
Maltby Colliery Nth. S.B.	17	To work			After			13 39		After				To work			
Firbeck Jn.A.	18	the 13 12			working			13 45		working				the 18 03			
St.Catherines Jn.	19	to ScntCHP			11 23 from			13 59		12 06 from				to			
KIRK SANDALL JN	20				Mtsorrel			14 15		Crofton				Westbury			
Kiveton Park Colly	21		12 50		Sdg					Depot				Up T.C.			17 52
Beighton Jn	22																
Beighton Depot	23				**13‖11**		**13 52**			**14‖28**							
Woodhouse Jn arr	24																**18RR00**
Woodhouse Jn dep	25		12 55		13 16		13X58			14 32							**18RR20**
Orgreave	26																
Darnall	27		13 02		13 23		**14 22**			14 38							
	28																
Attercliffe Jn	29		13 04		13 25		14 28			14 40							
Broughton Lane Jn	30		13 07		13 28		14 32			14 43							
Shepcote Lane Jn	31		13 08		13 30												
TINSLEY N.Y. arr	32		**13RRC13**			Tinsley	Darnall										
	33		**EF**		Tinsley	T.M.D.	arr 14PB14										
TINSLEY N.Y. dep	34		**13RR36**		T.M.D.	dep 14‖15											
Shepcote Lane Jn	35				arr 13‖40	14 25											
Broughton Lane Jn	36					14 28											
Broughton Lane B.O.C.	37					**14‖30**					**15 04**						
Attercliffe Jn	38										15 10						
Woodburn Jn	39					To work					15 12						
Nunnery Main Line Jn	40					the 15 04					15 15						
	41					to Ditton											
Deepcar F.D.	42					BOC Sdgs											

Working timetable, 3rd October, 1983 to 13th May, 1984.

WEEKDAYS — GAINSBOROUGH TRENT JNS TO TINSLEY AND SHEFFIELD, AND BRANCHES — SUNDAYS

DOWN SEE SPECIAL NOTES		7E78	8L22	6D52	6D67	0J03	7M79	7J14	8J14	6J73	8E36	6D60	8M33	6D54
		16 40 from Mtsorrel Sdg	To Healey Mills N.Y.	16 53 M.G.R. from Immingham NCB Termnl	16 06 COY from Peterboro West Yd	LD to Tinsley T.M.D.	To Garston Speke Sdgs			18 38 M.G.R. Immingham NCB Termnl to Shirebrook R.S.	18 10 COY Longport Jn to Worksop S.S.	20 46 M.G.R. from Immingham NCB Termnl	COY to Longport Jn	22 48 M.G.R. Immingham NCB Termnl to Worksop S.S.
TIMING LOAD		D	D	D	D	D	D	D	D	D	D	D	D	D
		MFO ■	SX	SX AIR ■ Y	SX AIR ■	SX	MSX ■	FO	FSX	SX AIR ■	MTHO ■	SX AIR ■	MTHO ■	SX AIR ■ Y
	1	CCE a/c												
GAINSBOROUGH TRENT JNS	2			**18*01**	18 07					19 45		22 06		23 51
West Burton C.E.G.B.	3				**18 12**									
Cottam C.E.G.B. dep	4													
Clarborough Jn	5			18 10	Maximum					19 53		22 14		23 59
Retford Thrumpton S.B.	6			18 18	Speed 55					19 59		22 20		00 06
Manton Wood N.C.B.	7				m.p.h									→
Worksop West S.B. arr	8													
Worksop West S.B. dep	9			18X31						20 12		22X33		
WORKSOP S.S. arr	10			**18 35**								**22 37**		
WORKSOP S.S. dep	11		**18 00**				**18 55**	**19 08**	**19 27**				**23 38**	
Shireoaks East Jn	12		18X04				18X59	19X12	19X34	20 14			23X43	
Shireoaks	13		**ML**				**ML**							
Brancliffe East Jn	14													
Dinnington Colliery Jn	15													
Maltby Colliery Sth. S.B.	16													
Maltby Colliery Nth. S.B.	17					After								
Firbeck Jn.A.	18					working								
St.Catherines Jn.	19					16 40 from								
KIRK SANDALL JN	20					Mtsorrel								
Kiveton Park Colly	21		18 16			Sdg	19 12	19 22	19 50				23 56	
Beighton Jn	22	18 08									21 09			
Beighton Depot	23	**18 14**				**18‖46**								
Woodhouse Jn arr	24										**21RR15**		**00RR09**	
Woodhouse Jn dep	25		18 26			18 51	19 19	19 28	20 02		**21RR35**		**00RR29**	
Orgreave	26													
Darnall	27		18 35			18 58	19 28	19 36	20 16					
	28													
Attercliffe Jn	29		18 37			19 00		19 38	20 22					
Broughton Lane Jn	30		18 41			19 03		19 42	20 27					
Shepcote Lane Jn	31		18 43			19 05		19 44	20 29					
TINSLEY N.Y. arr	32		**18 48**					**19 52**	**20 39**					
	33		EF			Tinsley		EF	RCL					
TINSLEY N.Y. dep	34		**21 30**			T.M.D.								
Shepcote Lane Jn	35					arr 19‖15								
Broughton Lane Jn	36													
Broughton Lane B.O.C.	37													
Attercliffe Jn	38													
Woodburn Jn	39						19 31							
Nunnery Main Line Jn	40						19 35							
	41													
Deepcar F.D.	42													

WEEKDAYS — TINSLEY AND SHEFFIELD TO GAINSBOROUGH TRENT JNS,AND BRANCHES — YJ58

UP

Down- Shepcote Lane Jn to Attercliffe Jn.Nunnery Main Line Jn to Nunnery Jn

Mileage M.C.	M.C.			7D45	8M33	7D55	7E43	0M27	6E94	7E89	7D72	6B64	7D74	7E47	7E56	0M63	7E47	7E47	7D53	0M04
				M.G.R. to Immingham NCB Termn	23 38 MTHO COY Worksop S.S. to Longport Jn	M.G.R. to Immingham NCB Termn	20 44 SX M.G.R. Avenue Sdgs to Immingham NCB Termn	02 45 LD from Shirebrook L.I.P.	02 57 COY Earles Sdgs to Kirton Lime Sdgs	00 35 from Garston Speke Sdgs	04 02 M.G.R. Thoresby N.C.B. Ø to Immingham NCB Termn	COY to Fletton C.E.G.B	05 53 M.G.R. Thoresby N.C.B. Ø to Immingham NCB Termn	18 00 WO COY Llandarcy to Tuxford C BP Devlpmt	20 57 FSX Garston Speke Sdgs to Mansfield S.S.	LD	18 00 MTTHO COY Llandarcy to Gainsboro L Rd BP Ex	18 00 WO COY Llandarcy to Gainsboro L Rd BP Ex	M.G.R. to Immingham NCB Termn	07 29 LD from Shirebrook L.I.P.
		TIMING LOAD		D	D	D	D	D	D	D	D	D	D	D	D	D	D	D	D	D
				MX AIR ■	TFO ■	MX AIR ■ Y	MX AIR ■	MSX Y	MFX AIR ■	MTX ■	SX AIR ■	MX AIR ■	SX AIR ■	THO ■ Y	MSX	SX	TWFO ■	THO ■ Y	SX AIR ■	SX Y
0.00		Deepcar F.D.	1								Ø-		Ø-							
		Nunnery Main Line Jn	2						03 44	04 03	04 15 MO		06 06 MO							
			3								Shirebrook		Shirebrook							
8.76	0.00	Woodburn Jn	4						03 47	04 07	R.S.		R.S.							
	0.28	Attercliffe Jn	5						MFX											
		Broughton Lane B.O.C.	6						UNTIL											
		Broughton Lane Jn	7						26 NOV											
		Shepcote Lane Jn	8						AND											
	3.27	TINSLEY N.Y. arr	9						FROM					01L 10	23 52		01L 10	01L 10		
			10						20 MAR					EF	EF		EF	EF		
	0.00	TINSLEY N.Y. dep	11						TWSO					05 55	06 10		07L*01	07L*01		
		Shepcote Lane Jn	12						29 NOV					06 00	06 16	06 54	07 06	07 06		
		Broughton Lane Jn	13						TO					06 03	06 19	06 56	07 09	07 09		
	2.78	Attercliffe Jn	14						17 MAR					06 07	06 23	06 59	07 12	07 12		
9.51	3.48	Darnall	15						03 49	04 09				06 12	06 26	07 01	07 15	07 15		
			16																	
11.57		Orgreave	17																	
		Woodhouse Jn arr	18		00RR09		01RR45													
13.19	0.00	Woodhouse Jn dep	19		00RR29		02RR11		03 57	04 16				06 19	06 33	07 08	07 20	07 20		
		Beighton Depot	20													07‖13				
	1.34	Beighton Jn	21		00 36															
17.37		Kiveton Park Colly	22				02 22		04 09	04 26				06 30	06 43	To work	07 27	07 27		
	0.00	KIRK SANDALL JN	23													the 07 43				
	5.38	St.Catherines Jn.	24													to				
	9.25	Firbeck Jn.A.	25													Mtsorrel				
	10.79	Maltby Colliery Nth. S.B.	26													Sdg				
	11.22	Maltby Colliery Sth. S.B.	27			③-														
	17.26	Dinnington Colliery Jn	28			Retford										Tinsley				
20.21	20.54	Brancliffe East Jn	29			Thrumpton										T.M.D.				
21.35		Shireoaks	30			S.B. and								06 38	06 50	dep 06‖44				
22.28		Shireoaks East Jn	31			ClrbroJ		03X10		04X35	04 45		06 36							07X54
22.55		WORKSOP S.S. arr	32					03‖14		04 39										07‖58
		WORKSOP S.S. dep	33	00 22		01 46													07 53	
23.11		Worksop West S.B. arr	34					To work												To work
		Worksop West S.B. dep	35	00X26		01X50	02 37	the 03 39	04 18		04 47		06 38				07 35	07 35	07X57	the 08 15
25.28		Manton Wood N.C.B.	36					to Garston	⑥		②		②							to Toton
31.04		Retford Thrumpton S.B.	37	00 37		02 01	02 48	Speke Sdgs	04 35		05 00		06 51				07 46	07 46	08 08	New Bank
35.00		Clarborough Jn	38	00 44		02 11	02 55		04 43		05 07		06 58				07 52	07 52	08 15	
		Cottam C.E.G.B. arr	39				⑤		④											
		West Burton C.E.G.B.	40									06 32								
39.70		GAINSBOROUGH TRENT JNS	41	00 51		02 18	03 07		04 55		05 14	06 40	07 05				07 59	07 59	08 22	

Working timetable, 3rd October, 1983 to 13th May, 1984.

WEEKDAYS — TINSLEY AND SHEFFIELD TO GAINSBOROUGH TRENT JNS,AND BRANCHES — YJ58

UP

Down- Shepcote Lane Jn to Attercliffe Jn.Nunnery Main Line Jn to Nunnery Jn

Mileage M.C.	M.C.			7D45	8M33	7D55	7E43	0M27	6E94	7E89	7D72	6B64	7D74	7E47	7E56	0M63	7E47	7E47	7D53	0M04
				M.G.R. to Immingham NCB Termn	23 38 MTHO COY Worksop S.S. to Longport Jn	M.G.R. to Immingham NCB Termn	20 44 SX M.G.R. Avenue Sdgs to Immingham NCB Termn	02 45 LD from Shirebrook L.I.P.	02 57 COY Earles Sdgs to Kirton Lime Sdgs	00 35 from Garston Speke Sdgs	04 02 M.G.R. Thoresby N.C.B. Ø to Immingham NCB Termn	COY to Fletton C.E.G.B	05 53 M.G.R. Thoresby N.C.B. Ø to Immingham NCB Termn	18 00 WO COY Llandarcy to Tuxford C BP Devlpmt	20 57 FSX Garston Speke Sdgs to Mansfield S.S.	LD	18 00 MTTHO COY Llandarcy to Gainsboro L Rd BP Ex	18 00 WO COY Llandarcy to Gainsboro L Rd BP Ex	M.G.R. to Immingham NCB Termn	07 29 LD from Shirebrook L.I.P.
		TIMING LOAD		D	D	D	D	D	D	D	D	D	D	D	D	D	D	D	D	D
				MX AIR ■	TFO ■	MX AIR ■ Y	MX AIR ■	MSX Y	MFX AIR ■	MTX ■	SX AIR ■	MX AIR ■	SX AIR ■	THO ■ Y	MSX	SX	TWFO ■	THO ■ Y	SX AIR ■	SX Y
0.00		Deepcar F.D.	1								Ø-		Ø-							
		Nunnery Main Line Jn	2						03 44	04 03	04 15 MO		06 06 MO							
			3								Shirebrook		Shirebrook							
8.76	0.00	Woodburn Jn	4						03 47	04 07	R.S.		R.S.							
	0.28	Attercliffe Jn	5						MFX											
		Broughton Lane B.O.C.	6						UNTIL											
		Broughton Lane Jn	7						26 NOV											
		Shepcote Lane Jn	8						AND											
	3.27	TINSLEY N.Y. arr	9						FROM					01L 10	23 52		01L 10	01L 10		
			10						20 MAR					EF	EF		EF	EF		
	0.00	TINSLEY N.Y. dep	11						TWSO					05 55	06 10		07L*01	07L*01		
		Shepcote Lane Jn	12						29 NOV					06 00	06 16	06 54	07 06	07 06		
		Broughton Lane Jn	13						TO					06 03	06 19	06 56	07 09	07 09		
	2.78	Attercliffe Jn	14						17 MAR					06 07	06 23	06 59	07 12	07 12		
9.51	3.48	Darnall	15						03 49	04 09				06 12	06 26	07 01	07 15	07 15		
			16																	
11.57		Orgreave	17																	
		Woodhouse Jn arr	18		00RR09		01RR45													
13.19	0.00	Woodhouse Jn dep	19		00RR29		02RR11		03 57	04 16				06 19	06 33	07 08	07 20	07 20		
		Beighton Depot	20													07‖13				
	1.34	Beighton Jn	21		00 36															
17.37		Kiveton Park Colly	22				02 22		04 09	04 26				06 30	06 43	To work	07 27	07 27		
	0.00	KIRK SANDALL JN	23													the 07 43				
	5.38	St.Catherines Jn.	24													to				
	9.25	Firbeck Jn.A.	25													Mtsorrel				
	10.79	Maltby Colliery Nth. S.B.	26													Sdg				
	11.22	Maltby Colliery Sth. S.B.	27			③-														
	17.26	Dinnington Colliery Jn	28			Retford										Tinsley				
20.21	20.54	Brancliffe East Jn	29			Thrumpton										T.M.D.				
21.35		Shireoaks	30			S.B. and								06 38	06 50	dep 06‖44				
22.28		Shireoaks East Jn	31			ClrbroJ		03X10		04X35	04 45		06 36							07X54
22.55		WORKSOP S.S. arr	32					03‖14		04 39										07‖58
		WORKSOP S.S. dep	33	00 22		01 46													07 53	
23.11		Worksop West S.B. arr	34					To work												To work
		Worksop West S.B. dep	35	00X26		01X50	02 37	the 03 39	04 18		04 47		06 38				07 35	07 35	07X57	the 08 15
25.28		Manton Wood N.C.B.	36					to Garston	⑥		②		②							to Toton
31.04		Retford Thrumpton S.B.	37	00 37		02 01	02 48	Speke Sdgs	04 35		05 00		06 51				07 46	07 46	08 08	New Bank
35.00		Clarborough Jn	38	00 44		02 11	02 55		04 43		05 07		06 58				07 52	07 52	08 15	
		Cottam C.E.G.B. arr	39				⑤		④											
		West Burton C.E.G.B.	40									06 32								
39.70		GAINSBOROUGH TRENT JNS	41	00 51		02 18	03 07		04 55		05 14	06 40	07 05				07 59	07 59	08 22	

WEEKDAYS TINSLEY AND SHEFFIELD TO GAINSBOROUGH TRENT JNS, AND BRANCHES YJ58

UP SEE SPECIAL NOTES		7E56	7D43	6D41	0L92	6D61	9J91	7D52	6S63	0M29	6D38	7E34	7D73	6E44	7E34	8J15	7D60	6V56	6D80
		11 00 M.G.R. Avenue Sdgs to Immingham NCB Termnl	M.G.R. to Immingham NCB Termnl	11 29 M.G.R. Immingham NCB Termnl to Doncaster Down Decoy	11 45 LD from Healey Mills N.Y.	13 00 COY Cottam C.E.G.B. to Lindsey Oil Refinery	12 06 from Crofton Depot	M.G.R. to Immingham NCB Termnl	13 40 ABS Scunthorpe West T.C. to Craignches Yard	13 58 LD from Shirebrook L.I.P.	13 05 M.G.R. Immingham NCB Termnl to Doncaster Down Decoy	10 17 Garston Speke Sdgs to Mansfield S.S.	15 02 M.G.R. Thoresby N.C.B. Ø to Immingham NCB Termnl	08 50 ABS Cardiff Tidal Sdgs to Scunthorpe Trent T.C.	11 12 Garston Speke Sdgs to Mansfield S.S.	15 25 Healey Mills N.Y. to Mansfield S.S.	M.G.R. to Immingham NCB Termnl	COY to Westbury Up T.C.	16 50 M.G.R. from ScntCHP
TIMING LOAD		D	D	D	D	D	D	D	D	D	D	D	D	D	D	D	D	D	D
		SX AIR ■	SX AIR ■	SX AIR ■	TO	MTTHO AIR ■ Y	THO	SX AIR ■ Y	SX AIR ■	SX	SX AIR ■ Y	MSX	SX AIR ■ Y	SX AIR ■	MO ■	SX	SX AIR ■	MWFO AIR ■	SX AIR ■
Deepcar F.D.	1						CCE a/c						Ø- 14 57 Ollerton N.C.B.						
Nunnery Main Line Jn	2																		
	3						Timed to a max. speed of 25 mph.												
Woodburn Jn	4																		
Attercliffe Jn	5																		
Broughton Lane B.O.C.	6																		
Broughton Lane Jn	7																		
Shepcote Lane Jn	8																		
TINSLEY N.Y. arr	9											13RR41			14RR39	16 50			
	10											EF			EF	EF			
TINSLEY N.Y. dep	11											14RR14			15RR00	17 14			
Shepcote Lane Jn	12											14 19			15 05	17 19			
Broughton Lane Jn	13				12 42		13 32					14 21			15 07	17 22			
Attercliffe Jn	14				12 45		13 36					14 24			15 10	17 26			
Darnall	15				12 47		13X40					14 27			15 13	17 30			
	16						GL												
Orgreave	17						④												
Woodhouse Jn arr	18	11RR52																	
Woodhouse Jn dep	19	12RR12			12 57		13 56					14 33			15 19	17 38			
Beighton Depot	20				13‖01		14 01												
Beighton Jn	21													15 08					
Kiveton Park Colly	22	12 23			To work the 13 52 to Crofton Depot							14 43			15 29	17 50			
KIRK SANDALL JN	23			12 46					14 20		14X32			15 54					17 26
St.Catherines Jn.	24			13RR24					14RR56		15RR21								17 42
Firbeck Jn.A.	25																		17 52
Maltby Colliery Nth. S.B.	26			St.Cathrns Jn arr 13RR04					St.Cathrns Jn arr 14RR38		St.Cathrns Jn arr 15RR01								17 57
Maltby Colliery Sth. S.B.	27																		17 59
Dinnington Colliery Jn	28																	18 03	18 17
Brancliffe East Jn	29																	18 23	
Shireoaks	30											14 50			15 36	17 59		18 26	
Shireoaks East Jn	31									14X23			15 49						
WORKSOP S.S. arr	32					13RR24				14‖26									
WORKSOP S.S. dep	33		12 52			13RR44		14 25									18 15		
Worksop West S.B. arr	34									To work the 14 51 to Toton New Bank									
Worksop West S.B. dep	35	12 36	12X56			13X48		14X29					15 51				18X19		
Manton Wood N.C.B.	36																		
Retford Thrumpton S.B.	37	12 47	13 07			13 58		14 42					16 03				18 30		
Clarborough Jn	38	12 54	13 14			14 04		14 49					16 10				18 37		
Cottam C.E.G.B. arr	39																		
West Burton C.E.G.B.	40																		
GAINSBOROUGH TRENT JNS	41	13 01	13 21			14 11		14 56					16 20				18 44		

Working timetable, 3rd October, 1983 to 13th May, 1984.

WEEKDAYS TINSLEY AND SHEFFIELD TO GAINSBOROUGH TRENT JNS, AND BRANCHES SUNDAYS

UP SEE SPECIAL NOTES		0M79	6M56	0J14	0D02	0J14	7D54	9P40	8D74	7D76	6B67	6E85	8E36	9E57	0E00	7E42
		LD	15 05 M.G.R. Immingham NCB Termnl to Avenue Sdgs	18 17 LD from Shirebrook L.I.P.	LD	18 46 LD from Shirebrook – L.I.P.	M.G.R. to Immingham NCB Termnl	To Snailwell Sdgs Snailwell Sdgs.		18 33 M.G.R. Ollerton N.C.B. Ø to Immingham NCB Termnl	COY to Fletton C.E.G.B	16 42 ABS Widnes West Deviation to Whitemoor Up Side	18 10 COY from Longport Jn	20 47 from Toton North Yard	21 07 LD Toton Old Bank to Worksop	19 00 COY COY Garston Docks to Mansfield C.S. y
TIMING LOAD		D	D	D	D	D	D	D	D	D	D	D	D	D	D	D
		MSX	SX AIR ■	FO	SX	FSX	SX AIR ■ Y	THO	SX	SX AIR ■ Y	SX AIR ■	SX AIR ■	MTHO	SX	MWFO	SX AIR ■ Y
Deepcar F.D.	1							CM&EE a/c		Ø- 18 20 Thoresby N.C.B.						y- Shirebrook R.S.
Nunnery Main Line Jn	2											21 03				
	3															
Woodburn Jn	4											21 06				
Attercliffe Jn	5															
Broughton Lane B.O.C.	6															
Broughton Lane Jn	7															
Shepcote Lane Jn	8															
TINSLEY N.Y. arr	9															22RR35
	10							ML	MY							EF
TINSLEY N.Y. dep	11							19 55	20 00							23RR32
Shepcote Lane Jn	12	18 06						20 02	20 07							23 37
Broughton Lane Jn	13	18 08						20 05	20 10							23 39
Attercliffe Jn	14	18 11						20 08	20 14						After working 18 03 from Dinning-ton Colly Jn	23 42
Darnall	15	18 13						20 12	20X19			21 07				23 44
	16								GL							
Orgreave	17															
Woodhouse Jn arr	18		18RR00										21RR15			
Woodhouse Jn dep	19	18 19	18RR20					20 19	20X29			21 13	21RR35			23 50
Beighton Depot	20								ML							
Beighton Jn	21		18 27													
Kiveton Park Colly	22	18 25						20 29	20 41			21 24	21 50			23 59
KIRK SANDALL JN	23				After working 16 50 from ScntCHP											
St.Catherines Jn.	24	Tinsley T.M.D. dep 17‖56						Timed to a maximum speed of 60 m.p.h. Condemned Coaching Stock								
Firbeck Jn.A.	25															
Maltby Colliery Nth. S.B.	26															
Maltby Colliery Sth. S.B.	27															
Dinnington Colliery Jn	28				18‖35											
Brancliffe East Jn	29				18 47											
Shireoaks	30															00 06
Shireoaks East Jn	31	18X31		18X42	18X50	19X11			20X53	21 00		21X30	22X04	22X22	22X29	
WORKSOP S.S. arr	32	18‖35		18‖46	18‖53	19‖15			20 57			21 33	22 08	22 26	22 32	
WORKSOP S.S. dep	33						20 11					21 53				
Worksop West S.B. arr	34	To work the 18 55 to Garston Speke Sdgs		To work the 19 08 to Tinsley N.Y.		To work the 19 27 to Tinsley N.Y.										
Worksop West S.B. dep	35						20X15	20 37		21 02		21X57				
Manton Wood N.C.B.	36											ML				
Retford Thrumpton S.B.	37						20 26			21 13						
Clarborough Jn	38						20 33	Retford 20/48		21 20						
Cottam C.E.G.B. arr	39															
West Burton C.E.G.B.	40										21 22					
GAINSBOROUGH TRENT JNS	41						20 40			21 27	21 30					

Right: Cottam Power station in 1994. In the foreground the railway into the plant can be seen. The original route of the railway is in the line of trees.
Chris Booth

Below: The SYJR is occasionally utilised by railtours. Here English Electric class '40' No. D200 (40122) is seen at Dinnington with a Train Tours Travel Club special in 1983.
Chris Booth

Yorkshire pickets sought also to close down the Aire and Trent generating stations. Drax had three m t of coal in stock, but none was coming in and about two-thirds of its 1,000 workers refused to cross the miners' picket lines. The remainder worked 12 hour shifts. The 'B' complex was not yet commissioned, but in 'A', unit one (660 MW) was run flat out, whilst output from units 2 and 3 were run at 'stand-by'. Throughout Britain, there were many coal-fired stations of which the 12 largest, apart from those on the Aire and Trent, were on the Thames and Blyth 'A' and 'B' in Northumbria.

With oil supplying only 40 pc of demand and Yorkshire virtually 'closed down', the stations on the Trent and the Thames became crucial. Had the strike been total throughout the UK, all generating stations' stocks would have been used within six months, as winter approached. Throughout the UK, coal-fired stations had a total of 23.4 m t in stock in March 1984, enough for 22 weeks, but this fell to 15.5 m t by September and 12 m t by the end of the strike in March 1985. A similar amount was in colliery yards and remained at 20 m t for rest of strike.

By contrast, from North Nottinghamshire in the first five weeks of the strike, working collieries sent 0.9 m t into market, or 75 pc of their usual amount. By various means, about 0.5 m t pw was moved into generating stations during the summer of 1984, rising to 0.6 m t pw by the autumn. Nevertheless the strike was reducing the county's production. By September at Harworth, which normally sent an average of 54,000 t pcm, or 75 pc of its production, to CEGB stations, mostly by SYJR m-g-r, output was 17 pc lower, compared with nearly 31 pc less for the whole county.

The striking miners were neither paralysing the country nor halting all coal production. To close down the generating stations, they needed the support of the rail workers, haulage drivers and electrical power workers. The executives of the NUR, ASLEF and the TGWU all supported the miners, but not all their members did; neither generally did the TUC nor other unions. Thus coal continued to move by rail, road and water, whilst the electricians (one third at Drax) continued to operate their stations partially as long as they had the coal.

However, m-g-r (ASLEF) drivers were stopping trains at token pickets, even those on bridges above the lines. All major coal depots were picketed and ASLEF spent more than a quarter of a million pounds making up the wages of its members who were sent home for refusing to drive coal trains, especially Doncaster men. BR management took no formal disciplinary action against them.

The SYJR closed

Although some remote working signal boxes were attacked, most signalmen in the Doncaster, Rotherham and Worksop areas supported the miners strongly, if quietly, particularly as many lived in the same villages or streets as the latter. They refused direct requests from BR managers to pass through SYJR coal trains, but still received their basic pay. The signal boxes were patrolled by BT police and opened only during the day shift of 6.00 am-1.00 pm. Only trains to Harworth Glass Bulbs were allowed to travel along the SYJR. Meanwhile, BR took the opportunity to relay the track between Brancliffe Junction and Dinnington with continuously welded rail.

At best therefore, helped by a increased pay offer to the unions, BR was able to run only about 40 of its usual 300 daily coal trains on the network. It lost £70 m during the strike and some customers permanently.

Relations also became very tense between miners and the steel workers, who required a minimum of coke to keep the furnaces alight or they would be destroyed. The miners supported by other unions had been able to prevent initial imports of iron ore to integrated steelworks at Scunthorpe through the Trent's Flixborough wharf. By June imports were flowing through, including coal from Poland which totalled 10 m t, thus more than replacing normal SYJR shipments. Inevitably steel production was cut and agreements made amongst the unions collapsed as the need for coke grew and road movements of coke increased.

Battle of Orgreave

At the end of May, the NUM chose the tactically-flawed site of the Sheffield coking plant at Orgreave, 8 km west of the SYJR, as the place to bring British industry to a standstill by halting the coke trucks. On 29th May, 1984, with 5,000 struggling pickets present, 82 were arrested and 28 required medical treatment, as did 104 policemen. However the coke trucks were not stopped nor on the second day when 3,000 pickets were present.

On 18th June, the final explosive day, 10,000 pickets and thousands of police including mounted units assembled, engaging in a violent confrontation, with 93 arrests and 72 police and 51 pickets injured. Overall, picketing at Orgreave involved a total of 32,500 miners and supporters, including many men from SYJR collieries such as Maltby and Dinnington. There were 273 arrests, including Arthur Scargill. Lacking enough men to set up 24 hr pickets everywhere, the NUM was poorly coordinated and the 'battle of Orgreave' took some pressure off working collieries such as Harworth and the generating stations.

PSUs in action

Thereafter Nottinghamshire collieries were able to keep the generators heavily supplied mainly by road and assisted by the great majority of the PSUs. Simultaneously relations greatly deteriorated between the South Yorkshire miners, including those along the paralysed SYJR, and police units, notably from London and Manchester. There were violent clashes leading to 60 arrests in Maltby on 7th-8th and 14th-17th June, including an attack on the police station, an act condemned by the local NUM secretary. About 100 Manchester officers were brought in. Maltby miners were very vigorous in enforcing the strike, as were those from Markham Main, Dinnington and Thurcroft, all threatened operations. In late June, Coal House in Doncaster was picketed and at Rossington colliery managers were briefly 'taken hostage' by militant strikers.

Tipper men (coal haulage) drivers were mostly non-union, unlike the long-distance men, and their industry was in trouble. Between 1981 and 1984 the cost of moving a tonne of coal by truck from Harworth to West Burton had fallen by 14 pc. It rose again by 11 pc - to £1.50 - during the strike, the only means by which Harworth coal could be moved, with the SYJR closed. By the summer of 1984, the equivalent of 100 train loads of coal was being delivered each week to generating stations by tipper trucks. West Burton and Cottam, for example, received around 500 daily truck loads compared with 180 normally before the strike.

Talks between the NCB and NUM in June and in July failed and 180,000 miners remained on strike, whilst 12 UK collieries (none on the SYJR) had closed for ever. Through most of July and August, all was quiet, but on 20th August the return of one miner at Silverwood led to violence, particularly around SYJR collieries.

The following day at Armthorpe, a PSU entered the village and was stoned. Police vans escorting working miners out of Markham Main were attacked. By 6.30 am the following morning 1,000 pickets had assembled and erected barricades. The arrival of a PSU, 400 officers from Manchester, led to more violence and the hot pursuit of pickets through houses, including some NCB ones rented by non-miners. There were 24 arrests, including eight local miners, and accusations against the police of wanton damage.

The return of some workers at Yorkshire Main meant more 'outside' police (London Met), greatly disliked by the locals, in Edlington. In September, violent confrontations outside Maltby colliery spilled over into the town, where catapults and (even an air rifle) were allegedly used. Such incidents led to accusations of police 'occupying' communities. Particularly resented also was the police tactic of advancing in wedges and beating shields with truncheons, a big change from the old 'push and shove' tactics.

By early November (week 35) mass picketing had virtually ceased, to be replaced by isolated violent incidents in SYJR communities such as in Dinnington, where the police station and town centre shops were attacked by 40 people.

Return to work

The major struggle between the NUM and the NCB centred on persuading or not men to return to work. To men deeply in debt, the NCB offered financial incentives to those who returned before 19th November. In Yorkshire only a few score miners had gone back to work by early November. Elsewhere the drift back was unstoppable. Five thousand returned in one week in mid-November and 15,500 in the month according to the NCB, which it said, brought the total to 62,000 men working in 146 UK collieries. Twenty-eight others remained fully closed.

Overall, according to the NCB, the percentage of returnees increased from 25 to 37 by December, but often intimidated and under heavy police protection. On 20th December the Nottinghamshire miners voted to leave the NUM and on 2nd August, 1985, 30,000 men established the Union of Democratic Mineworkers (UDM).

Early in January 1985, the CEGB experiencing a record demand, called in Drax, which normally burnt 100,000 t pw, to supply full power. The Energy Secretary announced that no power cuts would be necessary that year. By then, 71,000 UK miners were at work, including 3,500 in Yorkshire with 100 at Dinnington. All 53

Yorkshire collieries were open, according to the NCB, of which four were producing. By reason of this, the failure to close down Drax, the return to work by 10,000 more UK miners in January and the acceptance of pay awards by both NACODS and managers - who could have closed down and destroyed every colliery - the defeat of the NUM had become simply a matter of time.

On 25th February more than 3,800 men returned in one day, bringing the total to more than 95,000 at the end of the month - a figure denied by the NUM. Those returning along the SYJR included only 96 at militant Maltby, but 353 at Thurcroft and 472 at Dinnington. At the last, severe flooding had put a question mark over its future and indeed during the strike a total of 56 of the UK's 490 coal faces were lost permanently through flooding.

Finally on 1st March NUM delegates voted by 98-91 to call off the strike from 9th March, with Yorkshire voting *no*. By the 7th even the militant 1,500-strong workforce at Markham Main, the last Yorkshire mine on strike, voted to return and soon afterwards the SYJR's coal trains started to run again. The NCB announced a total loss of 32 m t of Yorkshire production, worth £1.4 bn of which the South Yorkshire area's share was £232 m.

The failure of the NUM to bring the country to a standstill by power cuts is shown by the statistics of generation below.

UK Electricity Generated (gigawatts/hours)

	1982	*1983*	*1984*	*1985*
	256,000	261,000	266,000	280,000
of which				
Steam nuclear	40 k	45.7 k	49.5 k	56.3 k
Steam other	210	209	209	216
Gas turbines and oil	0.58 k	0.4 k	2.0 k	1.1 k
Coal used m t	80	81	53	74
Oil used m t	6.2	4.7	21.3	13

A class '56' is seen on a train of empty m-g-r wagons at Worksop. *P. Stanyard*

Chapter Thirteen

The SYJR and the Disappearing Coalfield, 1986-1993

More closures

For 1984-1985, the NCB announced a record UK loss of £2.2 bn of which 75 pc was accounted for by deep mines, whilst BR lost 'only' £278 m.

In October 1985, with lowered production causing losses of £83 p t, Yorkshire Main closed, the first purely economic closure after the strike, but agreed by a large majority vote of the miners, who received redundancy payments of £1,000 per year of service, plus pensions for over-55s. Nevertheless, Yorkshire Main was the second closure amongst the original eight accessing the SYJR and a serious loss of business for BR.

However, 1985 also represented a new start for the coal industry in many ways. With the NUM disabled, the NCB renamed British Coal (henceforth, BC) in 1987 was able to begin closing down rapidly loss-making collieries. These closures included Cadeby one the pioneers of the deep coalfield in the 1890s and the other main user of the DVR which was closed on 21st October, 1985 between St Catherine's Jn and Yorkshire Main and eventually dismantled.

To secure these closures locally and amicably the government was prepared to make heavy redundancy payments. In 1985-1986, a total of £546 m was paid to departing UK miners, whilst a further £900,000 was paid in industry support, resulting in BC making a small operating profit. By 1990 the global closure costs had risen to £4 bn at a cost (in 1999 prices) of more than £60,000 per job. In 1986-1987 these payments peaked at £1.14 bn. The average age of departing miners was 41 who, excluding pensions, each received an average of £18,000. Overall between 1985 and 1990 the number of UK collieries fell from 169 to 96 and the work force from 171,000 to 65,000. Meanwhile, opmy rose by 89 pc to 1,100 t during the same period.

During this contraction Arthur Scargill was, by a 54 pc vote in 1987, re-elected president of the NUM, now a much impoverished union after losing more than £7 m during the strike. Two years later, the NUM had only 60,000 members.

The Coalfield, 1989

In 1985 the NCB had re-merged the three 1967 local areas into one South Yorkshire area administration. It also announced that the latter's output was set to be raised by almost 13 pc by 1990 and, with a new area record oms for all employees of 3.13 t, was on the way to this. More worryingly, at Dinnington, where half its Haigh Moor production was sold as coke to BSC, the annual output of 'only' 450,000 t was creating a loss of one million pounds. BC offered redundancy to 350 out of its 800 men and £10 m investment programme, to improve productivity and reduce losses.

The latter was a small part of the total investment of £250 m approved for South Yorkshire during 1985-1989. Of this £66 m was spent in the first year and

St Catherine's curve at Black Carr to the ex-GN/GE Joint line and East Coast main line on 6th September, 2001. *Author*

Class '56' No. 56108 departs from Markham Main colliery with the 7H19 to Drax on 7th March, 1994. *Chris Booth*

£89 m in year four, with 43 pc of the latter going into the huge Parkgate project at Maltby. There the weekly production record rose from 25,000 t in March 1987 to 27,000 in October and 28,000 a year later. Developments at Maltby seemed certain not only to ensure its survival but, by reason also of the excellent long-term prospects at Harworth, the survival of the SYJR also. Indeed with increasing productivity after the strike, all the remaining collieries in South Yorkshire seemed safe, whilst Margaret Thatcher was keen to reward the 1984-1985 loyalty of UDM members, mostly south of Yorkshire.

By 1988-1989 there were only 18 collieries remaining in the new South Yorkshire area (94 in the UK). They employed less than 18,000 miners (89,000 in the UK), compared with 38,750 (181,000 in the UK) before the strike. The effect on Doncaster was that the percentage of males employed in coal, which had been 32 pc in the mid-1950s, fell between 1984-1989 from 16 pc to less than seven, helping to create a 20 pc (male) unemployment rate. Admittedly BC Enterprise also spent £69 m across the UK coalfields by March 1990 creating 71,000 new jobs.

The total South Yorkshire area production of 12.65 m t in 1989 was 15 pc of the UK deep-mined total. It cost £35.57 pt to produce but sold for £40.77, which resulted in a total area profit of almost £70 m. Of this 12.65 m t output, 10.75 or 85 pc went to generating stations and 0.8 m t to British Steel.

The 1987 figures for the 'burn' at the Aire, Ouse and Trent generating stations illustrate the dependency upon these sales which the local coal industry, including the SYJR collieries, had developed. Drax used 9.1 m t, whilst Ferrybridge, West Burton, Cottam and Eggborough took respectively 5.8, 5.35, 5.35 and 5.1 m t. High Marnham took 2.3 and Thorpe Marsh 1.8, a grand total of 34.8 m t. West Burton and Cottam together used 90,000 t pw from South Yorkshire collieries, mostly arriving on SYJR and Rossington m-g-r trains.

In addition to Harworth, by 1989 only four of the 18 South Yorkshire collieries then had a direct access onto the SYJR. The workforce at the former was reduced to 772 and during the 1987-1988 construction of a new coal preparation plant, Harworth had sent 380,000 t by road to the generating stations reducing SYJR revenues. In January, Rossington with low operating costs and a workforce of 873 produced a face oms of 30 t compounding decades of coal freight lost to the SYJR. Fortunately the long decline of traffic on the SYJR would hopefully soon be compensated for by Maltby's expansion and enhanced rail shipments.

Modernisation at Maltby

By early 1987, Maltby's £170 m Parkgate project was well on the way to completion after six years' work, with the coal being extracted from the 1.6 m high seam running along the 275 m, fluorescent-lit S 24 face. Each team of 18 miners, who travelled 2.5 km by locomotive to the face, worked under a moving steel canopy, which cost £3 m and was capable of supporting 300 t. Using a coal-cutting machine which could sense and follow the gamma radiation from the seam, it extracted 14,000 t pw, almost tripling oms. This example of a 'heavy-duty' face illustrates the principal trend in technology and capital investment in coal extraction in the 1980s. Between 1982-1988 the number of such faces in the UK increased from 32 (6 pc of the total) to 117 (48 pc).

By October 1988, Maltby coal was being raised from a depth of 991 m up the new 8 m diameter No. 3 shaft, sunk at a cost of £26 m. The four 22 t capacity skips, powered by a 4,000 hp winding engine, and offering an annual maximum capacity of 2.6 m t, could lift 1,200 t per hour. A new £23 million coal preparation plant, was also part of the large and ambitious project. The plan was to double Maltby's production from 1 m t pa to 2 or even 2.5 m t pa, with obvious very beneficial results for SYJR/BR revenues.

Already the 1,000 strong workforce had reached the 1 m t output in the 1989 year several weeks earlier than during the previous 1973 record, and had achieved a face oms as high as 26 t. Both Rossington and Maltby, with low costs had produced 1989 operating profits of more than £11.5 m, despite the latter being troubled by four underground fires that year. In June 1989, to mark the success of Maltby's £170 m investment programme, a powerful new locomotive was named *Maltby Colliery* at a ceremony there. About 90 pc of Maltby's output was then being dispatched along the SYJR to generating stations on m-g-r trains hauled by such locomotives. Each train carried an 1,100 t load. Harworth meanwhile produced 1.4 m t in 1990, of which at least one m t was hauled away on the SYJR. Between them Maltby and Harworth alone seemed set to challenge the 1929 record figures for originating tonnage on the SYJR.

Threats to Coal

Despite this apparently optimistic scenario, the long-term prospects for coal and thus the SYJR were still gloomy. Despite considerable sales to the CEGB, BC's other sales fell by an annual total of 8 m t between 1985-1990. Mining jobs were disappearing and the NUM was disabled and impotent. So also was OPEC in 1986 when oil prices fell by 50 pc, but this affected coal also, so that BC was forced to reduce its prices to the CEGB. Colliery revenues declined by 25 pc between 1985-1990. The Conservative Government re-elected for a second time in 1987 was planning to privatise the electricity industry. There was no long-term guarantee it would continue to buy British coal and the Government was quite happy to see cheaper imports increasing.

Privatisation came about in 1990. The CEGB was broken into the National Grid, National Power and Power Gen, whilst the 12 Regional Electricity Companies were sold in December for £5.2 bn. After difficult negotiations with BC, the new power generators agreed to buy 71, 70 and 65 m t over the next three years. This kept the SYJR busy, but after 1993 BC was on its own.

The swathe of colliery closures which continued for a decade following the end of the strike included in 1990-1993 the large Doncaster collieries of Askern, Bentley, Brodsworth, Frickley and Hatfield This was to prepare the coal industry also for privatisation, which as far back as 1981 (Lord) Nigel Lawson, the then Energy Secretary, had suggested to the Chancellor (Lord) Geoffrey Howe in a memo. Publicly it was (Lord) Cecil Parkinson, the Energy Secretary, who first spoke of it, at the 1988 Conservative Party conference. In preparation for privatisation, the 1989 Coal Industry Bill wrote off the industry's debts, totalling £6.6 bn in 1990, and provided another £1.5 bn for miners' redundancy payments.

A decade later even these huge sums were being equalled by the costs of ex-miners' health problems. In addition to pneumoconiosis, another serious problem was vibration whitefinger, a permanent numbness in the hands, caused by prolonged use of machinery. By 2002, following a successful court action, more than 300,000 former miners had made compensation claims for these conditions. The Government had to meet these claims which by then had reached £750 m and could reach £6 bn, according to *The Economist*.

By 1990, the Government was discussing also the privatisation of the railways, naturally including the SYJR, which served mostly one sector of BR's large freight business, Train Load Freight (TLF) Coal. In July 1992 TLF (Coal) operated 220 main line locomotives, 42 shunters, and more than 10,000 wagons. However by then its revenue and profits were being devastated by the colliery closures.

Challenge from gas

A question mark over the need for large quantities of coal first appeared with the dramatic fall in oil prices back in 1986, when North Sea production had peaked at 127 m t. This brought into focus also the future of the SYJR and its remaining collieries. However, coal prices were falling also, partly negotiated and partly through production increases overseas. Through stepped price reductions, BC successfully maintained sales to the CEGB at 76-80 m t pa until 1990.

The real damage to coal came, however, from booming natural gas production in the North Sea and abroad. Following the privatisation of the electricity industry at the end of 1990, the Government approved the construction of 20 Combined Cycle Gas Turbine (CCGT) power stations. Between 1993-1998, the share of electricity generation from these new efficient operations rose from 7 to 28 pc, fuelled largely from the North Sea. Between 1989-1993 some 36 new North Sea fields were contracted to 19 UK different companies - but only 25 pc of the fields went to British Gas. Another blow to the coal industry came with the approval for Sizewell 'B' nuclear station, following a public inquiry which straddled the strike. After approval, construction began in March 1987 and it was commissioned in 1995, the last nuclear station of the 20th century.

More Yorkshire closures

Surrounded by threats from nuclear, gas, and imported coal, BC fought back. Between 1990 and 1992, it reduced the number of collieries and its workforce by a third and average colliery operating costs fell by 26 pc. Meanwhile opmy had risen from 504 t in 1982 to a creditable 1,357 t pa a decade later. Plans were made to cut deep-mined production from 75-50 m t pa by the mid-1990s.

WEEKDAYS BRANCLIFFE EAST JN TO GAINSBOROUGH TRENT JNS AND BRANCHES — SUNDAYS — YJ41

Mileage M.C.	Mileage M.C.	UP		6D67	6P50	6P50	6D12	0D09	0D11	0D10	6D67	SUNDAYS 6D67
				21 45 Sun. CON from P'bro Westwood Sdgs	CON to Little Barford Monier	CON to Little Barford Monier	Dept'mtl to Healey Mills S.S.	LD	20 10 LD from Doncaster Up Decoy	LD	21 35 CON from P'bro Westwood Sdgs	21 40 CON P'bro Westwood Sdgs to W.Burton Flyash Sdgs
		TIMING LOAD		D	D	D	D	D	D	D	D	D
				MO	MX	MO	SX	SX	SX	SX	SX	
							Y					
		Beighton Depot	1		Timed to a max speed of 55 mph	Timed to a max speed of 55 mph	11 18				Timed to a max speed of 55 mph	
		Beighton Jn.	2				11RR46					
		Kiveton Park B.C.	3									
	0.00	KIRK SANDALL JN.	4									
		Markham Main B.C. dep	5	Timed to a max speed of 55 mph			Beighton Jn arr 11RR26					Timed to a max speed of 55 mph
		Doncaster L.I.P. dep	6							22‖45		
		Doncaster Down Decoy dep	7									
	5.38	St.Catherines Jn. arr	8									
		St.Catherines Jn. dep	9				RCE a/c		20 15	22 50		
		Harworth Glass Bulbs	10									
	9.25	Firbeck Jn.	11						20 25	23 00		
		Maltby B.C.	12									
	11.22	Maltby Colliery S B. arr	13									
		Maltby Colliery S B. dep	14						20 32	23 07		
	17.26	Dinnington Colliery Jn.	15						20 48	23 23		
0.00	20.54	Brancliffe East Jn.	16						20 57	23 32		
1.14		Shireoaks	17									
2.08		Shireoaks East Jn.	18						21 00	23 35		
2.35		WORKSOP S.S. arr	19						21‖03	23‖38	23RR16	23RR35
		WORKSOP S.S. dep	20					12‖30			23RR36	23RR55
2.71		Worksop West S.B. arr	21									
		Worksop West S.B. dep	22								23 41	00 01
5.08		Manton Wood B.C.	23	←								
10.64		Retford Thrumpton S.B.	24	00 12				12 40			23 52	00 12
		Whisker Hill Jn.	25									→
		Retford arr	26					12‖45				
12.62		Clarborough Jn.	27	00 19							23 59	
		W.Burton Flyash Sdgs.	28	00 26	02 37	02 54					00 07	
17.52		GAINSBOROUGH TRENT JNS.	29		02 45	03 02						

Working timetable, 14th May, 1990 to 30th September, 1990.

WEEKDAYS GAINSBOROUGH TRENT JNS TO BRANCLIFFE EAST JN AND BRANCHES — SUNDAYS — YJ40

Mileage M.C.	Mileage M.C.	DOWN		6D09	0D22	6D10	6D67	SUNDAYS 6D67
				CON	LD	CON to Belmont Up Yard	21 35 CON P'bro Westwood Sdgs to W.Burton Flyash Sdgs	21 45 CON P'bro Westwood Sdgs to W.Burton Flyash Sdgs
		TIMING LOAD		D	D	D	D	D
				SX	SX	SX	SX	
			1				Timed to a max speed of 55 mph	
0.00		GAINSBOROUGH TRENT JNS.	2					
		W.Burton Flyash Sdgs.	3					
4.70		Clarborough Jn.	4					
		Retford dep	5	13 40			23S00	23S16
		Whisker Hill Jn.	6					
8.56		Retford Thrumpton S.B.	7	13 45				
		Manton Wood B.C. dep	8					
16.49		Worksop West S.B. arr	9					
		Worksop West S.B. dep	10				23 12	23 31
17.05		WORKSOP S.S. arr	11	14 00			23RR16	23RR35
		WORKSOP S.S. dep	12		14‖15	21 23	23RR36	23RR55
17.32		Shireoaks East Jn.	13		14 18	21 27		
18.35		Shireoaks	14					
19.45	0.00	Brancliffe East Jn.	15		14 21	21 30		Timed to a max. speed of 55 mph
	3.28	Dinnington Colliery Jn.	16		14 33	21 42		
	9.32	Maltby Colliery S B. arr	17					
		Maltby Colliery S B. dep	18		14 48	21 56		
		Maltby B.C.	19					
	11.19	Firbeck Jn.	20		14 54	22 00		
		Harworth Glass Bulbs	21					
	15.16	St.Catherines Jn. arr	22					
		St.Catherines Jn. dep	23		15 03	22 07		
		Markham Main B.C. arr	24					
	20.54	KIRK SANDALL JN.	25					
		Doncaster Down Decoy arr	26		15‖08			
		Doncaster Up Decoy arr	27			22 17		

WEEKDAYS — GAINSBOROUGH TRENT JNS TO TINSLEY AND SHEFFIELD,AND BRANCHES — YJ42

DOWN
UP Nunnery Jn to Nunnery Main Line Jn

Mileage M.C.	Mileage M.C.		No.	6D64	6D64	6D65	6M25	6M25	0M63	6D74	7D66	6D41	6D82	6D35	7D80
				23 35 SUN COY from Peterboro West Yd	23 15 SX COY from Fletton C.E.G.B	M.G.R.	07 31 COY Kirton Lime Sdgs to Earles Sdgs	07 55 COY Kirton Lime Sdgs to Earles Sdgs	10 23 LD from Tinsley T.M.D.	10 06 SCN from Doncaster Down Decoy	10 09 M.G.R. Thurcroft B.C. to Scunthorpe BSC C.H.P.	10 19 SLK from Belmont Up Yard	M.G.R.	12 00 SLK from Harworth Glass Bulbs	12 34 M.G.R. Thurcroft B.C. to Scunthorpe BSC C.H.P.
		TIMING LOAD		D	D	D	D	D	D	D	D	D	D	D	D
				MO	MX	SX	THO	SO	MTHO	SX	SX	SX	SX	SX	SX
							Ⓖ	Ⓖ				Y		Y	
			1												
0.00		**GAINSBOROUGH TRENT JNS.**	2	01 26	01 36		07 58	08 22							
		W.Burton Flyash Sdgs. arr	3	**01 31**	**01 41**										
4.70		Clarborough Jn.	4				08 04	08 27							
8.56		Retford Thrumpton S.B.	5	Timed to a max. speed of 55 m.p.h.	Timed to a max. speed of 55 m.p.h.		08 10	08 34							
		Manton Wood B.C. dep	6												
16.49		Worksop West S.B. arr	7												
		Worksop West S.B. dep	8				08 18	08 45							
17.05		**WORKSOP S.S.** arr	9												
		WORKSOP S.S. dep	10			**07 45**							**10 24**		
17.32		Shireoaks East Jn.	11			07 49							10 28		
18.35		Shireoaks.	12												
19.45	0.00	Brancliffe East Jn.	13			07 52							10 31		
	3.28	Dinnington Colliery Jn. arr	14								**10RR19**				**12RR44**
		Dinnington Colliery Jn. dep	15			08 04					**10RR39**		10 43		**13RR04**
		Thurcroft B.C. arr	16			**08 14**							**10 53**		
	9.32	Maltby Colliery S B. arr	17									**10RR45**		**12RR28**	
		Maltby Colliery S B. dep	18								10 55	**11RR05**		**12RR48**	13 20
		Maltby B.C.	19												
	11.19	Firbeck Jn.	20								11 02	11 14		12 57	13 27
		Harworth Glass Bulbs.	21					⑤- Woodburn Jn and Nunnery Main Line Jn				**11 30**			
	15.16	St.Catherines Jn. arr	22							**10RR12**					
		St.Catherines Jn. dep	23							**10RR32**	11 12			13 07	13 37
		Markham Main B.C. arr	24							**10 57**					④
	20.54	**KIRK SANDALL JN.**	25								11 26				**14*y32**
		Doncaster Down Decoy. arr	26												
		Belmont Down Yard. arr	27											**13 14**	
22.33		Kiveton Park B.C.	28				08 24	08 55							Y- arr 13*55
	0.00	Beighton Jn.	29						**10cRM40**						
		Beighton Depot.	30						**10‖45**						
26.51	0.79	Woodhouse Jn.	31				08 30	09 01							
30.19		Darnall.	32				08 35	09 09							
		TINSLEY N.Y. arr	33												
			34					⑤- Woodhouse Jn and Darnall							
	0.00	**TINSLEY N.Y.** dep	35												
		Shepcote Lane Jn.	36												
		Broughton Lane Jn.	37												
	2.78	Attercliffe Jn.	38												
30.74	3.27	Woodburn Jn.	39				08 37	09 16							
		Nunnery Main Line Jn.	40				08 40	09 26							

Working timetable, 14th May, 1990 to 30th September, 1990.

WEEKDAYS — GAINSBOROUGH TRENT JNS TO TINSLEY AND SHEFFIELD,AND BRANCHES — SUNDAYS — YJ43

DOWN
SEE SPECIAL NOTES

	No.	6D66	6D09	8E77	7D48	6D80	6D10	6M38	6M38	6D48	6D67	SUNDAYS 6D67
		13 25 M.G.R. from Scunthorpe BSC C.H.P.	14 40 COY from Belmont Down Yard	15 02 Dept'mtl from Mtsorrel Sdg	17 16 M.G.R. Thurcroft B.C. to Scunthorpe BSC C.H.P.	16 06 M.G.R. from Scunthorpe BSC C.H.P.	COY to Doncaster Up Decoy	19 00 COY Whitwell Quarry to Toton Old Bank	19 30 COY Whitwell Quarry to Toton Old Bank	20 43 M.G.R. from Scunthorpe BSC C.H.P.	19 03 COY from Little Barford Monier Ø	20 12 COY from Peterboro West Yd
TIMING LOAD		D	D	D	D	D	D	D	D	D	D	D
		SX	SX	MTHO VB	SX	SX	SX	TTHO	FO	SX	SX	
	1			RCE a/c								
GAINSBOROUGH TRENT JNS.	2										22 51	22 13
W.Burton Flyash Sdgs. arr	3										**22 56**	**22 18**
Clarborough Jn.	4											
Retford Thrumpton S.B.	5										Ø- 20 51 THO Peterboro West Yd	Timed to a max. speed of 55 m.p.h.
Manton Wood B.C. dep	6											
Worksop West S.B. arr	7		**15 42**			**17 49**				**22 26**		
Worksop West S.B. dep	8		**15PR44**			**17PR51**				**22PR28**		
WORKSOP S.S. arr	9		**15PR49**			**17PR56**		**19RR22**	**19RR52**	**22PR33**		
WORKSOP S.S. dep	10						**19 00**	**19RR45**	**20RR12**		Timed to a max. speed of 55 m.p.h.	
Shireoaks East Jn.	11						19 04	19 48	20 15			
Shireoaks.	12											
Brancliffe East Jn.	13						19 07					
Dinnington Colliery Jn. arr	14	**14RR49**			**17RR26**							
Dinnington Colliery Jn. dep	15	**15RR09**			**17RR46**		19 19					
Thurcroft B.C. arr	16	**15 19**										
Maltby Colliery S B. arr	17											
Maltby Colliery S B. dep	18				18 02		19 35					
Maltby B.C.	19											
Firbeck Jn.	20				18 09		19 42					
Harworth Glass Bulbs.	21											
St.Catherines Jn. arr	22											
St.Catherines Jn. dep	23				18 19		19 52					
Markham Main B.C. arr	24											
KIRK SANDALL JN.	25				**18*y50**							
Doncaster Down Decoy. arr	26				SGL							
Belmont Down Yard. arr	27				②							
Kiveton Park B.C.	28											
Beighton Jn.	29			16 39	Y-							
Beighton Depot.	30			**16 45**	arr 18*33							
Woodhouse Jn.	31											
Darnall.	32											
TINSLEY N.Y. arr	33											
	34											
TINSLEY N.Y. dep	35											
Shepcote Lane Jn.	36											
Broughton Lane Jn.	37											
Attercliffe Jn.	38											
Woodburn Jn.	39											
Nunnery Main Line Jn.	40											

A pair of class '20s' form the last train out of Thurcroft colliery, the 7F47 to Cottam power station on 31st January, 1992. *John H.M. Millar*

Class '58' No. 58034 *Bassetlaw* loads its train, the 6F88 for Cottam power station, at Silverwood colliery on 15th December, 1993. *Chris Booth*

Thus inevitably, more collieries along the SYJR closed. Whilst Maltby and Harworth continued to produce heavily and efficiently, the three other SYJR collieries all still had ongoing technical difficulties in 1989. The 409 miners at Dinnington produced 330,000 t pa of which 70 pc went to generating stations and 30 pc to Scunthorpe steelworks. Unfortunately output there was 16 pc below the break-even figure but as noted, BC was attempting to increase this by a one million pound investment in the Swallow Wood seam. Despite severe ongoing geological problems, Thurcroft's 576 men were raising 9,000 t pw from two faces, with steel as the major customer. At Markham Main a new record face oms of 25 t was posted in February 1989 and in 1991 its 770 miners produced a massive 830,000 t, but it was troubled by problems with gas, overheating and water ingress. By 1992 it had accumulated a £30 m loss in five years.

Within the next three years, 100 more UK collieries would close and 150,000 miners would have taken redundancy since the end of the strike, including those at Dinnington and Thurcroft. At the former, high costs and geology had resulted in the previous year's loss of £4 m cumulating to £38 m over the decade. In a 91 pc turnout in October 1991, 80 pc of miners voted for closure. This brought to an end the first SYJR colliery, an operation lasting almost exactly 90 years, which had cost 74 lives and in memory of whom a £15,000 memorial was dedicated in 1994. The last SYJR train ran from Dinnington colliery on 13th February, 1992. A major employment initiative costing two million pounds involved the creation of 28 workshops and 19 larger units on the colliery site.

Two months after Dinnington's vote, Thurcroft miners also voted for closure and the last train from there ran to Cottam on 31st January, 1992. According to BC, the reason for closure was that Thurcroft was losing £300,000 p w and was 'the most dangerous colliery in the UK'. Over 300 men were kept on for salvage work or offered employment in other coal mines with a £4,000 transfer payment, but a workers' buy-out failed. The rail line between these two closed collieries was itself closed on the last day of 1992, but the signal box at Dinnington Colliery Jn survived until a major re-signalling project November 1997.

Privatisation legislation

After the 1992 general election, the Queen's Speech reaffirmed the Conservative Government's intention to privatise both the coal and rail industries and a White Paper on the latter was published in July. The Railways Act to bring this about was passed in November 1993, establishing Railtrack to own and manage the railway track, land and infrastructure, including naturally the SYJR, which would come under London North East Zone (York).

Meanwhile in October 1992, the Board of Trade announced the closure by April 1993 of 27 of the remaining 51 deep mines, with a further four to be kept on care and maintenance. This would make redundant 62 pc of the remaining 48,000 miners, to add to the 150,000 gone since 1985. There would be further job losses on the railways, by reason that 80 pc of UK coal went to generating stations mostly by m-g-r. This all led to huge protests and demonstrations.

In December 1992, the TUC General Council held its monthly meeting in Doncaster to show support for the coal industry. A number of union leaders including the TUC general secretary, Norman Willis, visited Markham Main where only 140 miners remained of the 1991 'record breakers' and mothballing was soon to follow. This left only Harworth, Maltby and Rossington open amongst the original SYJR-accessing collieries.

Reducing the workforce

Meanwhile, the High Court ruled that the Government's mine closure programme was unlawful, forcing it to freeze it. A White Paper, *Prospects for Coal,* allowed to remain open for two years 12 of the 31 scheduled to close. Six more were mothballed and 10 would close, two immediately and be put up for sale. With the sale of UK coal to generating stations scheduled to fall from 40 m t in 1993-1994 and to 30 m t thereafter, a subsidy of £500 m was offered to enable BC to find new markets. This was a most difficult task and only £1.7 m was ever paid out. Redundancy terms to miners were extended to the end of 1993, with 8,000 in the pipeline and a further 30,000 expected to follow. For miners with lung disease and 20 years or more of service, a disablement benefit was available.

This further threat to coal prompted a one day strike on 2nd April, 1993 for which the NUM had voted 60-40. All Yorkshire's remaining collieries struck and only one m-g-r train ran in the county that day, but the 13 'UDM' mines worked normally and there was no TUC support.

A few days later, BC stopped production at 16 out of the 31 collieries slated for closure, including, Hatfield/Thorne - the first being saved by a management buy-out - and despite their expensive modernisation programmes and having vast reserves - both Maltby and Rossington, which were 'mothballed'. This precipitated a second one day strike on 16th April, but only half the 40 deep mines struck, without NUR (now RMT) support.

A further blow to the industry came on 26th May, 1993 when the High Court ruled that BC had now acted lawfully in negotiating the closures. During the summer 20 more collieries ceased production and 20,000 more miners took redundancy, leaving a total of only 30 deep mines employing 30,000 men. Of these survivors, 25 were in the East Midlands coalfield, where two including Maltby were 'under development' and there were 13 open-cast operations.

By 1993, production of deep-mined coal in the UK had declined to 50 m t and a further 17 m t was produced on open-cast sites. More than 18 m t was imported, giving a total supply of almost 85 m t. Generating stations which had used 81 m t in 1992 dropped to 66 m t and then to 62.4 m t in 1994. Coke ovens used 8.5 m t in 1993 and industry and domestic users consumed about 10 m t combined. The number of BC employees fell dramatically from 58,000 to 13,000 over these three years. This decline was reflected in BR's coal-freight movements which had totalled 77 m t in 1987, but dropped to 68 by 1993 and 49 m t in 1994. With only Harworth then seemingly with a certain future of the original eight SYJR-accessing collieries, a large question mark appeared over the future of the line.

The Coal Authority

Such then was the reduced state of the UK coal industry which the Government quickly began to privatise, a policy which it believed would end the various heavy subsidies poured into coal since 1947. The sale of BC's remaining land-holdings - some 100,000 ha, of which 90 pc was sold in three years - brought large funds to the Treasury. The Coal Industry Act, 1994 established a Coal Authority to replace BC, undertaking many of its duties, but primarily to own the reserves and issue licences to private mining companies.

One such company RJB Mining plc (named after its founder Richard Budge and renamed UK Coal plc in 2001), made a successful bid of £815 m to take over all 20 deep mines in England, including the SYJR-served collieries of Harworth, where 528 men had just produced 2 m t of coal and the modernised Maltby, which as noted, had been 'mothballed' in March 1993. Rossington, whose 500 miners had produced 700,000 tons in 1993, was also part of this deal and taken 'out of mothballs' in December 1994. RJB Mining also bought 24 open-cast coal sites.

Meanwhile, the closed Hatfield colliery was the successful subject of a management buy-out. Markham Main did not survive, although it was bought by Coal Investments in June 1994 and began supplying Eggborough in March 1995. Technical (overheating) and group financial problems led to its final closure in 1996, bringing to an end an operation of more than 70 years, during which 87 miners had been killed.

On 23rd December, 1994 another casualty - 94 years after its first sinking and despite having produced a mammoth 1.4 m t in 1992 - was the neighbouring Silverwood colliery, connected to the SYJR by the ex-GCR-MR Jt line. Here almost 14 months later, thieves stole 1.5 km of rail lines and 1,400 sleepers. Railtrack spent £112,000 to replace the track so that the last of the colliery stock-pile could be finally removed on 7th June, 1996.

Memorial to Markham Main miners, 6th September, 2001. *Author*

Class '56' No. 56089 is seen under the loading bunker at Maltby colliery, while loading the 7H33 for Drax on 7th June, 1995. *Chris Booth*

Class '58' No. 58029 *Rugeley Power Station* leaves Cottam with the 6F04 to Worksop on 2nd June, 1994. *Chris Booth*

Chapter Fourteen

Privatisation - Into the New Century, 1994-2001

SYJR operations privatised

On 1st April, 1994 the ownership of BR's operational track - about 16,500 km (10,312 miles), and which naturally included the SYJR - and land and stations was vested in Railtrack. This was a government company which was floated on the stock exchange in 1996, but seemingly renationalised after financial difficulties in 2001.

BR's bulk trainload freight business was divided into three companies, of which one Loadhaul, based on Trainload Freight (TLF) North East, absorbed the SYJR's coal trains. On 2nd February, 1996, these three companies were sold for £225 m to the American Wisconsin Central Railroad company which also bought Railfreight Distribution for an undisclosed sum. The whole operation was renamed English, Welsh and Scottish Railways (EWS), an operation employing 6,000 workers and whose 650 main-line locomotives moved 100 m t of freight pa in 1,100 daily trains. On 30th December, 1994, RJB Mining, with contracts to supply 29 m t pa to the generating companies until March 1998, took over the deep-mined coal industry in England. The company's 20 deep mines and 24 opencast produced 53 m t in 1995. Two million shares in the company were given to the miners with £890,000 to buy them, giving employees a 7 pc stake in the company.

Thus as the 20th century drew to a close, SYJR operations was once again after nearly 50 years privately owned - by the shareholders of Railtrack and of RJB Mining. The coal produced was purchased very largely (87 pc in 1998) by the privatised power companies and to which it was delivered mostly by the privately-owned m-g-r trains of EWS or by privately-owned road hauliers. In the summer of 1997, yet another symbol of the nationalised coal industry was sold for £375,000 - Coal House, the former HQ of NCB/BC in Doncaster since 1966.

Fierce competition

Unfortunately this new scenario of privatised activity did not bring to an end the diverse human and economic problems which had been besetting both the rail, and particularly the coal industries for much of the 20th century. The basic problem facing the SYJR and the remaining UK collieries was the almost unrestricted competition in the electricity supply industry, to which they had long been sending so much of their output. Furthermore, National Power (NP), the largest generating company (with 35 pc of total output in 1995-1996), had already announced that it was planning to close 10 of its 18 coal-fired stations by 2000. Doncaster's Thorpe Marsh station had closed in March 1994. Although NP signed a contract with RJB Mining in May 1997 to buy 6 m t, thus providing the latter with total contract sales of 18 m t, nevertheless, by the end of that year, falling UK demand and coal prices saw cuts planned at Maltby, from 1.9 m t to 1.2 m t pa. This threatened 300-400

Maltby colliery from the north-east in March 2002, its future is under threat once more. This view was taken from Stainton Church tower. *Chris Booth*

Class '58' No. 58019 *Shirebrook Colliery* at Rossington colliery with a train for West Burton power station on 7th February, 1995. *Chris Booth*

Class '66' No. 66514 prepares to leave Harworth with a train for Drax on 4th April, 2001.
Chris Booth

Class '66' No. 66130 emerges from the discharging bay at Drax electricity generating station, 28th September, 2001.
Author

A class '66' heads a train towards Maltby *en route* to West Burton on 8th March, 2002 (also taken from Stainton Church tower). *Chris Booth*

redundancies there, although by 1999 the number employed had fallen by fewer than one-third that number. Also in decline were RJB Mining's profits which had fallen heavily from almost £166 m in 1995 to £12.5 m in 1999.

A growing awareness of the environmental damage caused by acid rain and global warming and to which coal-fired stations made large contributions, was another problem for the industry. Under the Environmental Protection Act of 1990, the UK was pledged to reduce SO^2 emissions in 2005 by 85 pc compared with 1991 levels. To achieve this nuclear and gas-fired generation increased throughout the 1990s, and more and cheaper opencast (and less sulphurous) coal was imported (21 m t in total in 1998) from Colombia, the USA, Poland and elsewhere, much of it subsidised. Simultaneously, the total output of UK deep-mined coal declined remorselessly from almost 73 m t in 1990 to 35 m t in 1995 and to 25 m t in 1998.

Labour in power

The landslide election of a 'New' Labour Government in May 1997, with its face set against reversing the Thatcher-Major privatisation revolution, brought little comfort to the coal industry. Indeed, in October approval was granted for three new CCGT generators, but two months later the Government brought in a moratorium on such, whilst encouraging coal-fired generators to have a least one station fitted with flue-gas desulphurisation equipment (FGD) to reduce SO^2 emissions.

Labour also established the Coalfields Task-force to seek to revitalise the coalfields economically and later the Coalfields Regeneration Trust with £55 m for community-led initiatives. This did not guarantee coal any long-term future.

Meanwhile, RJB Mining's five year 'inherited' concessionary contracts, signed between BC and the three main coal generating companies came to an end in 1998. One of the principal generating companies, the Eastern Group then agreed to buy an extra 21 m t of coal between 2003-2009 for West Burton, which brought its total purchases to 50 m t (£1.4 bn). Powergen agreed to buy £35 m t worth £1 bn in 1999-2003 and National Power had agreed to buy 18 m t for 1998-2001, bringing RJB's sales up to 2003 to 81 m t. Also in April 1999, RJB Mining and National Power agreed a sale of 28 m t for Drax, Eggborough and Didcot stations and a year later AES Drax Power Ltd, the new American owners, agreed with RJB to buy up to 25.5 m t, worth £700 m.

Whilst it seemed that the collapse of coal had been averted, Parker thought that the generating companies were more persuaded to support the UK coal industry by the Government's approval for intra-industry acquisitions such as Power Gen's take-over of East Midlands Gas.

Colliery outputs

To help to meet its new and existing contracts, RJB Mining's saleable output in 1998-2001, from the former SYJR area was as follows:

		Million tonnes			
		1998	*1999*	*2000*	*2001*
Harworth	Deep soft seam	0.9	1.58	0.92	1.07
Maltby	Parkgate seam	1.4	1.26	0.87	1.54
Rossington	Barnsley seam	0.8	0.90	0.68	0.44

Rossington's decline in output in 2001 was the result of industrial action which lasted from 19th July to 3rd November. The three collieries above produced only part of the group's output. In 1999 for example its 14 deep mines produced 17.5 m t with a further 5 m t coming from open-cast operations and coal recovery schemes.

Fewer miners

By 1997 the number of miners in Yorkshire (5,000) had declined to one-thirteenth the number of 1979, at the start of 18 years of Conservative Government. Whilst to raise its 1999 local tonnage, which was about 68 pc of the combined total for the eight collieries accessing the SYJR 40 years previously, RJB Mining employed only one-tenth the number of men. These figures indicated huge gains in productivity since the 1947 nationalisation of coal. There were 1,524 miners in the three collieries in 1999 distributed as follows, and whose opmy was, given differing conditions, roughly equal across the three:

	Surface	*Underground*	*Total*	*OPMY*
Harworth	118	505	623	2,546 t
Maltby	157	375	532	2,372 t
Rossington	85	284	369	2,441 t

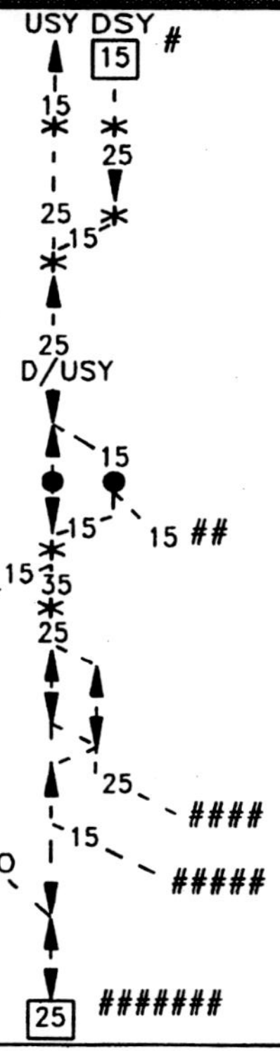

Location	Mileage	Running Lines & Speed Restrictions	Signalling & Remarks
		BRANCLIFFE EAST JN TO KIRK SANDALL JN	
Brancliffe East Jn	0 00	USY DSY 15 #	AWS not provided # see page 4 16 Controlled by Worksop (WP) Signal box DSY = Down South Yorkshire USY = Up South Yorkshire
	0 03*	15 25	CW Down at 00 06
	3 14*	25 15	Controlled by Worksop (WP) Signal box
Dinnington Jn	3 17*		TB Worksop (Dinnington Jn) to Maltby Colliery
		25 D/USY	D/USY = Down/Up South Yorkshire
Maltby Colliery	9 31	15	D/U Colliery Line = 76
	11 17*	15 15 ##	## To/From Maltby Colliery
Firbeck Jn	11 20	15 35	Controlled by Maltby Colliery (M) Signal box
	14 20*	### 25	### To/From Harworth Colliery
	14 62		see page 4.33
St Catherines Jn	15 17		St Catherines Jn to Kirk Sandall Jn Controlled by Doncaster (D) Signal box
Low Ellers Curve Jn	15 55	25 ####	#### To/From Decoy South Jn see page 4 33
		15 #####	##### To/From Potteric Carr Jn see page 4 34
Markham Main Colliery G.F.	17 69	10 ######	###### To/From Markham Main Colliery
Kirk Sandall Jn	20 49	25 #######	####### see page 4 30

Sectional Appendix Table A Section 4 Page 32 Dated 4th April 1998

Railtrack plan of SYJR running speeds (mph), 1998.

The numbers employed at the three collieries above showed no major changes in 2000 and 2001 with their combined totals in 2001 being 10 more than in 1999. However whilst opmy in 2001 rose to 2,697 t at Maltby, the dispute at Rossington drove it down to 1,156 t there.

RJB Mining's three Selby coalfield deep collieries in North Yorkshire employed 1,830 miners in 1998 and produced a total of 7.1 m t, most of being burnt at Drax, Eggborough and Ferrybridge. By 2001 Selby's output had fallen to 4.5 m t with closure probable. In 1999 RJB's dozen or so open-cast sites employed an almost identical size workforce to Selby, producing almost 7 m t. In total in 1999, RJB Mining employed 6,424 miners and 1,009 other workers.

RJB miners worked one of three daily shifts of 7.25 hrs each on a five days per week basis, but the company was unwilling to divulge their 1999 average earnings. However the NUM newspaper, *The Miner* of April 1999, reported that the RJB Mining had an reached agreement with the union, following a 57 pc vote in favour of threatened strike action, to consolidate the existing 40 pc incentive and bonus, plus a further 10 pc into miners' basic pay. This created an basic wage of either £15,074 or £17,375 pa for underground workers and for those on the surface either £12,149 or £12,893, i.e. overall between £233-£334 pw.

However, in 1992 average earnings in the UK coal industry had already reached £350 pw and by 1999 this latter figure was also the average weekly earnings of *all* workers in South Yorkshire. With basic mining wages long equalling half of all earnings, it is reasonable to assume that the best paid RJB miners in 1999 were earning around £35,000 or double the figures quoted in *The Miner*.

SYJR operations, 1995-2001

Following privatisation, the SYJR was open 24 hours per day, six days a week, with engineering work sometimes on Sundays. Coal traffic has declined by almost 24 pc, although unevenly. The line had 422 pathways available, more than in 1970, of which only 25 pc (Short Term Planning paths) were utilised.

SYJR Rail operations (m t of coal traffic, originating from)

	Harworth	*Maltby*	*Total SYJR*	*(Rossington)*
1995	1.148	1.793	2.941	0.584
1996	1.182	1.407	2.589	0.793
1997	1.742	0.967	2.709	0.621
1998	0.789	0.829	1.618	0.661
1999	1.133	0.759	1.892	0.779
2000	1.464	0.833	2.297	0.544
2001	0.998	1.255	2.253	0.355

Remarkably however, when comparing the above totals with the 1929-1938 output of the eight collieries and with minimal road-haulage competition at that time, only in the relative 'boom' year of 1929 did there originate a rail-hauled tonnage (2.948 m t) slightly greater than that from the two SYJR 'survivors' in 1995. Furthermore in 1995, six per cent of all UK coal traffic, including imports,

Class '58' No. 58031 hauls the 7A15 Harworth to Ratcliffe m-g-r train became the last working to leave the SYJR at Brancliffe East Junction under semaphore signalling on 29th November, 1997.
Chris Booth

The new signalling at Brancliffe East Junction in 1998, with the now disused signal box.
Chris Booth

originated on the SYJR, compared with less than 0.5 pc in 1913 and less than 2 pc between 1929-1970. In 1997, when UK rail-hauled coal tonnage had revived to 51 m t (from 49 m t three years previously), rail sales via the SYJR still produced a larger tonnage than throughout 1931-1938, whilst 1996 tonnage also exceeded 1931-1935, admittedly the worst depression years. Even in 2000, when almost 658,000 t was moved out by road from Harworth and Maltby, SYJR rail shipments almost exceeded those of 1932, 1933 and 1935. Had that 658,000 t also been shipped out on the SYJR, then the total for 2000 would have been at the equivalent of 2.908 m long tons, only 40 k t short of the 1929 all-time record for tonnage originating on the SYJR. Once again these figures confirm the remarkable productivity increases since 1947 and the large capital investment required to achieve it.

The SYJR drivers who delivered these large tonnages used mostly class '58', but sometimes also '56' and by the turn of the century class '60' and '66' were used ever more frequently. These can handle 36 wagon sets or even 42, up to a total maximum weight of 1,650 t, of which 1,100 t is coal. For this work (UK) locomotive drivers' earnings in 1999 averaged £506 p w.

In addition to SYJR-originating traffic, the line also provides pathways for trains on longer journeys, bringing coal from Scottish open-cast sites, imports from Hunterston, Redcar and Immingham and more local coal from the Selby field. These are mostly m-g-r trains for the Trent stations, such as Cottam and West Burton, High Marnham and Rugeley (Staffs). In 1998 m-g-r trains from the surviving Nottinghamshire collieries were also supplying the Aire stations using the SYJR and a thrice-weekly sand train ran to a Doncaster glass factory.

SYJR maintenance and signalling

In 2000, the SYJR was maintained under two infrastructure maintenance contracts, for which Railtrack was unwilling to provide any financial details. The line from Kirk Sandall Junction to a point just north of the former Tickhill and Wadworth station, where the line crosses the A1 (M), was included in the ECML South contract awarded to East Coast ISU (now Balfour Beatty Rail Maintenance) on a seven year contract which was re-tendered in 1999. The remainder of the line to Brancliffe East is part of the Doncaster contract, awarded originally in 1994 and again in 2000 for five years to North East ISU (now part of Jarvis Facilities Limited's Rail Division). However, by 2002 Balfour was earning almost £700 m from rail work whilst Jarvis earned more than £200 m.

Most of the SYJR is controlled by colour light signalling with track circuit block, except around the one remaining signal box at Maltby South, which is semaphore and opens only eight hours daily. The section to Firbeck, which Maltby controls, was re-signalled in 1990, when the North box at the latter was closed. From Maltby to Dinnington, the line is still worked under tokenless block regulations and the line from about 1.5 km south of Maltby to Brancliffe East was re-signalled in 1997, as part of the Eros project and is now controlled by the new Worksop box. The signal boxes at Dinnington Colliery Jn (renamed Dinnington Jn) and Brancliffe East Jn were therefore closed at the end of November 1997 and key token exchanges ceased.

Two views of Harworth colliery on 16th February, 2002 - but under threat. *(Both) Author*

As part of the Doncaster re-signalling in 1978-1981, the line from Kirk Sandall came under the control of the Doncaster Powerbox. The SYJR would be of a suitable standard for passenger trains if fitted with an automatic warning system throughout.

RJB Mining's future

During the first six months alone of 1997, RJB Mining's coal output of 16.5 m t contributed largely to a group turnover of more than £565 m and healthy pre-tax profits of more than £87 m (£172 m for the year). Profits then fell to £50 m for the whole of 1998, but by 1999, with the full year's coal sales declining to 22.5 m t, and group turnover down to £699 m, profits were only £11 m. However, when some extraordinary items of £141 m were added, such as the cost of depreciation and mine closures, this translated into a loss of £130 m. RJB Mining's share price which had stood at 600p in 1996 fell to less than one-sixteenth that figure, by autumn 2000. In 2001 operating losses reached £47 m on its 13 deep mines.

The first reason for RJB Mining's declining situation (and thus also for the revenue earned by the SYJR's originating traffic) is, as noted above, the fierce competition in electricity generation from other sources, particularly gas and nuclear power. Second was the increasing imports of coal - 21 m t, totalling £687 m in 1998, of which Poland provided one m t at prices as low as US $ 8.00 pt. This was estimated to be only 25 pc of the total production costs and highlighted starkly the main financial problem facing British coal producers, namely the unique lack in Europe of a subsidy for their industry. At the end of 1999, when the international price of coal had fallen by 50 pc, the combined coal subsidy in France, Germany and Spain in 1998 for 63 m t of output totalled £3.2 bn. Italy's mines were also heavily subsidised.

To win contracts, RJB Mining had to face competition, from subsidised European producers and low-cost open-cast operators in Australia, the USA or Columbia. Imported coal additionally was much less sulphurous and, being 30 pc cheaper, was according to RJB Mining at a 25 year low. Thus the price that RJB Mining could obtain for SYJR coal from generating stations, whose owners include Americans at Drax, Ferrybridge and Fiddler's Ferry has also fallen well below the prices pertaining 20 years earlier.

Furthermore, as noted, the Government agreed at the end of the century to cut the high sulphur emissions (of UK coal) from generating stations, commenting that the 1997 ban on new gas-fired stations would also cause carbon emissions to rise by 4 m tonnes. The alternatives were to use cleaner imported coal or to fit FGD as at Drax, but this added 10 pc to costs.

RJB Mining's customers

The SYJR's originating coal traffic declined to well below 2 m t in 1998 and 1999, reflecting the decline on the national network which, by 1999-2000 had fallen to 44 m t. In one week, at the end of February 2000, Harworth sent 13 train loads to

The entrance to Maltby colliery in 6th September, 2001. *Author*

A train discharging its coal at Drax power station in 28th September, 2001. *Author*

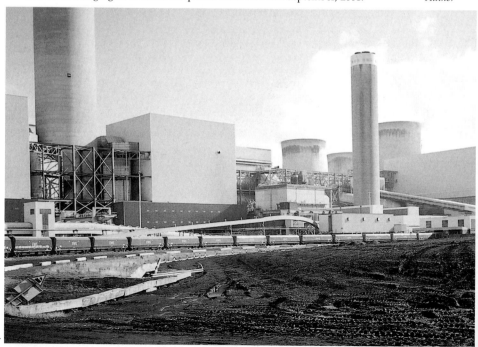

Cottam and a total of 24 to four other generating stations, Fiddlers Ferry (7), West Burton (7), Didcot (6) and Ferrybridge (4), a grand total of about 40,000 t.

Maltby also supplied Drax and West Burton very heavily, but in addition had contracts with Monkton Coal and Chemical works, Blue Circle, Buxton Lime and Coalite. In June 2000, Maltby secured a 300,000 t contract with Castle Cement in Clitheroe, to be supplied along the SYJR. In one week in February 2000, it sent 11 loads to Cottam, eight to Eggborough, and one to its cement customers, a grand total of 30,000 t, whilst Rossington sent 12 train loads to Drax, 19,000 t. Rossington also supplied West Burton generating station, and YPO, Coalite, the domestic market and several industrial customers.

Overall therefore, generating stations such as the giant Drax remained immensely important to the remaining deep-mine industry and to the SYJR in 2000 as shown by its annual operational statistics. During that year, Drax burnt 8.495 m t of coal, at a cost of more than £263.45m, more than 16 pc cheaper at £31 pt than the NCB price of £37 pt charged to the CEGB in 1981. With this coal Drax produced more than 23,048 gigawatt/hrs, representing *19 pc of all UK coal-fired electricity production* and six pc of total production from all sources. To deliver this coal mountain, 7,680 m-g-r trains were required, an average of 21 pd year-round, but the maximum on any one day was 39 or one train discharging every 37 minutes. Of these 7,680 m-g-r trains, 474 carrying 520,961 t, originated at Maltby. This represented about 40 pc of the latter's annual output, whilst Harworth sent a further 76 trains of 83,553 t with Rossington's 49 trains delivering 54,137 t. Thus these three surviving 'SYJR' collieries provided 7.75 pc of Drax's total fuel requirements in 2000. In effect these three provided the fuel for almost 1.5 pc of the UK's annual electricity consumption through Drax and even more via other generators.

Behind these movements, however, lay the story of a continued decline in coal sales. Between 1998 and 1999 UK coal consumption declined by 17 pc to 45 m t. Of the latter, 86 pc or 39 m t went to generating stations, with the contribution of RJB Mining being more than 19 m t. Compared with 80 pc in 1983 and 37.5 pc in 1998, coal produced only 33 pc of all UK electricity in 2002. CCGT (gas) production rose from 7 pc in 1993 to 28 in 1998 and to 37 pc of the total in 2002. Indeed, by early 1999 some 22 CCGT were actually in operation, with several in the East Midlands and along the Lincolnshire coast where gas comes ashore. But nuclear generation at 22 pc in 2002 was well behind the CCGTs. Nevertheless within a decade the dominance of coal had evaporated.

UK subsidy

This combination of adverse factors in the industry, at the end of 1999, resulted in the collapse of capital investment in UK deep-mined coal. RJB Mining predicted the demise of the industry (a scenario also threatening the SYJR's future). It asked the Government for a three year subsidy of £73 m. There was no objection from the European Commission, which was already committed (July 1999) to providing a £700 m Objective One Status grant to the officially impoverished South Yorkshire, a sum to be matched by an equal UK government grant.

Wagons discharging their coal through bottom doors into hoppers at Drax on 28th September, 2001. *Author*

Class '66' No. 66527 *Don Raider* discharges the 6G21 Immingham to West Burton at West Burton power station on 20th September, 2001. *Chris Booth*

In April 2000, the Government agreed to pay a £100 m subsidy to UK coal producers, whilst simultaneously lifting the restrictions on building more CCGTs. However, by mid-2000 coal prices were rising again, as were gas and oil. According to the journal *Coal UK*, RJB Mining's pre-sold contracts stretching to 2005, its substantial land-holdings worth many tens of millions, the Government's binding agreement in November 2000 to pay up to £110 m subsidy (RJB Mining to receive about two-thirds) and its small operating profitability, made it reasonably attractive for a take-over. However, six new CCGTs was the price of this coal subsidy and, although dependent upon the future price of oil and gas, these posed a threat to much of the future of the remaining coal industry and indirectly to the SYJR.

Americans in charge?

Following the absorption of TLF Coal into the American-owned EWS Railways and the sale of generating stations to US companies, it was perhaps no surprise that by the summer of 2000, RJB Mining was also being considered for a take-over. Three suitors were named by the media, but each disappeared, possibly aware that US coal mines were three times more productive than UK ones. Then, following the departure of Richard Budge from the company, RJB Mining was renamed UK Coal plc and remained nominally British in 2001. By 2002 it was called UK Coal Mining Ltd.

Epilogue: Nottingham and Doncaster in 2000

In February 2000, the Government announced that more than 50,000 unemployed over-25s who had been without work for more than a year would be given pagers and sums up to £5,000 each as part of a £112 million programme to tackle the 15 worst pockets of UK unemployment. Eight months later the Government pledged £800 m through the Neighbourhood Renewal Fund (NRF) to fight poverty and exclusion in 88 of some of most deprived English areas. Unsurprisingly Glasgow, South Wales, Liverpool, and London's East End were amongst the 15 areas with high unemployment, as were the last two, Bradford, Hull, Manchester and Newcastle amongst the '88'.

Appearing in these lists also were both Nottingham, erstwhile 'capital' of the once hugely productive and profitable East Midlands coalfield and Doncaster, whose £17.580 m share of the NRF was the eleventh largest overall, more than Leeds' and almost as large as Sheffield's, despite their greater populations.

Such then was the fate of Doncaster, a town once with an unemployment rate of only one per cent, during the coal and railway booms of 1923. Not only did Doncaster then have to recruit miners from many areas to work in its expanding collieries, whilst becoming the 'capital' of the South Yorkshire coalfield, but it was also both a main centre for the LNER locomotive and wagon building and the headquarters of arguably the UK's most profitable mineral line of the 20th century, the South Yorkshire Joint Railway.

Appendix One

SYJR Capital and Revenue Accounts

SYJR Capital Account

Half year	*Amount invested (£)*	*Dividend as percentage of capital invested (£)*
31.12.1904	17,500	Nil
30.06.1905	27,500	Nil
31.12.1905	51,149	Nil
30.06.1906	187,500	Nil
31.12.1906	239,671	Nil
30.06.1907	287,500	Nil
31.12.1907	357,500	1.07
30.06.1908	381,154	-
31.12.1908	410,871	0.80
30.06.1909	437,500	0.56
31.12.1929	710,679	6.16 (1922)

SYJR Revenue Account, 1929

Receipts	£	*Expenditure*	£
Passengers	226	Maintenance, track	19,549
Mail	62	Maintenance, locomotives	1,540
Minerals	119,610	Traffic expenses	10,092
Parcels/freight/livestock	8,178	Running powers	14,412
Miscellaneous	10	Miscellaneous	2,383
		Net receipts	80,110
	£128,086		£128,086

Appendix Two

Population Growth

	1901	*1911*	*1921*	*1931*	*1951*	*1961*	*1971*	*1981*	*1991*
Anston (N&S)	1,394	2,184	2,152	2,293	2,651	3,487	7,065	10,468	10,459
Armthorpe	314	381	625	6,135*	6,321	7,631	10,135	12,257	12,256
Dinnington	258	4,897*	5,874	7,426	7,053	7,514	7,747	7,074	7,781
Doncaster	28,932	30,516	54,064	64,708	82,054	86,322	82,505	†	†
Edlington	158	580	5,298*	7,440	6,781	8,557	9,686	9,223	8,309
Harworth	554	939	1,156	6,027*	7,621	8,289	9,259	7,949	7,813
Maltby	716	1,700	7,531*	10,010	12,488	13,693	14,050	16,771	17,111
Rossington	342	371	3,029*	9,547	8,214	10,190	11,085	12,602	12,472
Rotherham	54,349	62,483	68,022	75,223	82,341	85,478	84,646	†	†
Tickhill	1,565	1,806	2,107	2,297	2,546	2,582	3,257	4,956	5,421
Worksop	16,219	20,387	23,206	26,285	31,034	34,311	36,034	36,382	38,222

* Colliery opened in previous decade

† Doncaster and Rotherham became Metropolitan boroughs in 1974, with differently computed (and greatly enhanced) areas and populations.

Bibliography and Sources

Archives
Public Record Office, Kew
Coal 48 and 84 - SYJR collieries (post-1947 reports)
Rail 390, 410, 417, 783, 641 (1-27) SYJL Committees etc. 1903-1939
Rail 417 (6 &13) LMS - LNER Jt lines Committee
Rail 1110 (432), 1116, 1117 SYJL Reports and Annual Accounts
ZSPC 11/740 Railway Clearing House Map, South Yorkshire, 1912
Sheffield City Archive holds a large local NCB collection.

Periodicals and newspapers

Coal Magazine, Coal News, Doncaster Gazette, Doncaster Star, Economist, The Engineer and Engineering, LNER Magazine, The Guardian, Morning Telegraph (Sheffield), *Railway Gazette, Railway Magazine, Rotherham Advertiser, Rotherham Star, Sheffield Independent, South Yorkshire Guardian, South Yorkshire Times, The Times, Worksop Guardian.*

The Local History rooms of Doncaster, Rotherham and Sheffield Central Public Libraries have *inter alia* relevant newspaper cuttings collections, whilst the National Railway Museum at York, Reading Room, has large holdings of railway magazines.

Books etc.

The South Yorkshire Coalfield (and Coal in the UK generally)

Aberconway, Lord, *Basic Industries of Great Britain*, Benn (1927)
Annual Abstract of Statistics, *passim*, HMSO
Arnot, R.P., *The Miners in Crisis and in War*, Allen & Unwin (1961)
Ashworth, W., *A History of the British Coal Industry Vol. 5, 1946-1982*, Oxford University Press
Auckland, C., *Growth of a Township* (1989)
Benson J. & Neville R.G., *Studies in the Yorkshire Coal Industry*, Manchester University Press (1976)
Britain - An Official Handbook HMSO (1946-)
Clark, N., *Unofficial Strikes in the South Yorkshire Coalfield in the Second World War* (University of Warwick MA Thesis, 1976)
Coates B.E. & Lewis G.M., *British Landscape through Maps: No. 8 The Doncaster Area* (Geographical Association, 1966)
Colliery Yearbook and Coal Trades Directory (annual 1923-1964)
Court, W.H.B., *Coal*, Longman/HMSO (HSWW, 1951)
Ellis, N., *South Yorkshire Collieries*, Reflections of a Bygone Age (1995)
Glyn, A., *Colliery Closures and the Decline of the UK Coal Industry*, London School of Economics (1996)
Gray, G.D.B., *The South Yorkshire Coalfield* (Geography 1947)
Griffin, A.R., *The Nottinghamshire Coalfield*, 1881-1981, Moorland
Heap, C., *Mines and Miners of Doncaster* (1977)
Hill, A., *The South Yorkshire Coalfield: History and Development*, Tempus (2001)
Jenkins, D., *Sheepbridge* (1995)
Kirby, M.W., *The British Coal Mining Industry 1870-1946*, MacMillan (1972)
Lloyd, D.W. & Swallow F.C., *The North Country & Yorkshire Coal Annual* for 1921
McCormick, B., *Strikes in the Yorkshire Coalfield, 1947-1963* (Economic Studies 1969)
Maltby Main Colliery, Golden Jubilee 1911-1961 (1961)
Morgan W.J. & Coates K., *The Nottinghamshire Coalfield & the British Miners' Strike, 1984-1985*, University of Nottingham (1992)

NCB leaflets:
Coal in Doncaster Area (1969)
Coal in North Nottinghamshire (1970)
Coal in South Yorkshire (1970)
NCB Yorkshire, Annual Review, 1983-1984
NCB/BC Annual Reports & Accounts 1946-1994
Newham H.E.C., *Hull as a Coal Port* etc. (1915)
ed. Page, W.A., *History of Yorkshire, Vol. 2,* Victoria County History (1912)
Parker, M.J., *Thatcherism and the Fall of Coal,* Oxford University Press (2000)
Peace, K., *Some Changes in the Coalmining Industry of Southern Yorkshire, 1951-1971* (Geography, 1973)
Rayner, D.H. & Hemmingway J.E., *The Geology and Mineral Resources of Yorkshire,* Yorkshire Geological Society (1974)
RJB Mining PLC, Annual report and Accounts 1995-1999
Robens, Lord, *Ten Year Stint,* Cassell (1972)
Simpson, E.S., *Coal and Power Industries of Post-War Britain,* Longman (1966)
Slater, L., & Wandless, A.M., *The Yorkshire Coalfield* (1948)
Slaughter, C., *The Strike of Yorkshire Miners,* May 1955 (Sociological Review, 1958)
Supple, B., *A History of the British Coal Industry, Vol. 4 1913-1946,* Oxford University Press (1987)
Ward, R.L., *Old King Coal, On the mining District of South Yorkshire,* (1941)
Winterton, J. & R., *Coal, Crisis and Conflict: The 1984-1985 Miners' Strike in South Yorkshire,* Manchester University Press (1989)

Books etc: Railways in South Yorkshire (and in the UK generally)

Abell, P., *Transport and Industry in South Yorkshire* (1977)
Aldcroft, D., *British Railways in Transition* (1968)
Allen, G.F., *British Railfreight Today and Tomorrow* (1984)
Appleton, J.H., *The Railway Network of South Yorkshire* (Transactions and Papers of the Institute of British Geographers, 1956)
Bagwell, P.S., Doncaster, *Town of Train Makers, 1853-1990,* Doncaster Books (1991)
Barnett, A.L., *Railways of the South Yorkshire Coalfield,* Railway Correspondence & Travel Society (1984)
Bell, R., *The History of British Railways during the War, 1939-1945* (1946)
Bonavia, M.A., *History of the LNER, 3 Vols,* Allen & Unwin (1982-1983)
Bradshaw's Monthly Railway Guide, *passim*
British Railways Board, *The Reshaping of British Railways,* HMSO (Beeching Report, 1963)
Crump, N., *By Rail to Victory* (1947) (LNER)
Dow, G., *The Great Central Railway,* Vol. 3, Ian Allan (1966)
Ellis, C.H., *The Midland Railway* (1953)
Ellis, N., *South Yorkshire Railway Stations,* Reflections of a Bygone Age (photographs - 1995)
Goode, C.T., *The Dearne Valley Railway* (1986)
Goode, C.T., *Railways in South Yorkshire* (1990)
Gourvish, T.R., *British Railways 1948-1973,* Cambridge University Press (1986)
Hughes, G., *Economic History of the LNER* (Unpublished PhD thesis, University of London, 1990)
Joy, S., *The Train that Ran Away* (1973)
Kitchen, Fred, *Brother to the Ox,* Dent, (1940)
Mason, E., *The Lancashire and Yorkshire Railway in the Twentieth Century,* Ian Allan (1954)
Munns, R.T., *Milk Churns to Merry-Go-Round, A Century of Train Operations,* David & Charles (1986)
Pratt, E.A., *British Railways and the Great War,* 2 vols (1921) (Selwyn & Blount)
Simmons, J., and Biddle, G., *The Oxford Companion to British Railway History,* Oxford University Press (1997)
Wrottesley, J., *The Great Northern Railway,* Vol. 3, Batsford (1981)

Index